GOVERNING SEXUALITY

Governing Sexuality explores issues of sexual citizenship and law reform in the United Kingdom and continental Europe today. Across Western and Eastern Europe, lesbians and gay men are increasingly making claims for equal status, grounded in the language of rights and citizenship, and using the language of international human rights and European law. This book uses same sex sexualities as a prism through which to explore broader questions of legal and political theory concerning democratic legitimacy; rights discourse; national sovereignty and identity; citizenship; transnationalism; and globalisation. Case studies are widely drawn: from New Labour's sexual politics in the United Kingdom to the decriminalisation of same sex sexualities under pressure from the EU in Romania; to new civil solidarity laws in France.

Governing Sexuality

The Changing Politics of Citizenship and Law Reform

CARL F STYCHIN

Professor of Law and Social Theory, and Head of the School of Law, The University of Reading

• HART •
PUBLISHING

OXFORD AND PORTLAND, OREGON

2003

Hart Publishing
Oxford and Portland, Oregon

Published in North America (US and Canada) by
Hart Publishing c/o
International Specialized Book Services
5804 NE Hassalo Street
Portland, Oregon
97213-3644
USA

Hart Publishing is a specialist legal publisher based in Oxford, England.
To order further copies of this book or to request a list of other publications please write to:

Hart Publishing, Salter's Boatyard, Folly Bridge,
Abingdon Road, Oxford OX1 4LB
Telephone: +44 (0)1865 245533 or Fax: +44 (0)1865 794882
e-mail: mail@hartpub.co.uk
WEBSITE: http//www.hartpub.co.uk

British Library Cataloguing in Publication Data
Data Available
ISBN 1–84113–267–5 (hardback)

Typeset by Hope Services (Abingdon) Ltd.
Printed and bound in Great Britain on acid-free paper by
Biddles Ltd., www.biddles.co.uk

To Ian, in friendship
and
to Adrian, a cosmopolitan citizen

Contents

Acknowledgments

This book is the product of several years of labour, and my intellectual and other debts in producing it are too varied to list fully here. I would like to acknowledge, first, those friends and colleagues who have read draft chapters (often very 'drafty') and have responded with critical but constructive comments. In particular, I thank Nico Beger, Richard Bellamy, Jon Binnie, Jon Goldberg-Hiller, Morris Kaplan, Cecile Laborde, Susan Millns, Jo Shaw, Anna Marie Smith, and Alex Warleigh. Thanks to Dennis van der Veur and Martijn Quinn for generously giving their time to be interviewed in connection with chapter 6, and special thanks to Adrian Coman for making that chapter possible. I am also indebted to Carla Baker for her superb research and translation assistance with respect to chapter 3.

Throughout my career in the United Kingdom, I have been enormously fortunate to have had the enduring intellectual support, as well as friendship, of my two 'pretend' sisters, Davina Cooper and Didi Herman, and I again want to acknowledge my gratitude to them both (for everything!). This book has also been enhanced by the friendship of Martha-Marie Kleinhans, Linda Mulcahy, and Sally Wheeler, as well as by the support of Bill Flanagan, who has provided wise counsel on many matters over the life of this manuscript. I also have benefited from the intellectual camaraderie of my colleagues on the editorial board of *Social & Legal Studies: An International Journal*, and I thank them for that. I also thank my colleagues at the University of Reading for their support. As always, I thank my mother, Grace Baranyk, for her unquestioning support and encouragement, even when (obviously) sceptical of some of the ideas raised in this book.

I also have financial debts to acknowledge. I am grateful for the financial support of the Economic and Social Research Council, which provided generous support to an ESRC project, 'Strategies of Civic Inclusion in Pan-European Civil Society', within the 'One Europe or Several?' research programme, with which I was associated, and which funded the research and writing of chapter 5. I am grateful to the project coordinators, Richard Bellamy, Dario Castiglione and Jo Shaw, for inviting me to be involved in this project. I acknowledge the financial support of the British Academy, which awarded me a personal research grant, which funded the research on which chapter 6 is based. I also want to acknowledge the financial support of my home institution, the University of Reading and its Research Endowment Trust Fund.

Particular thanks are owed to my publisher, Richard Hart, for his support of this project when it was little more than a sketch of an idea, and for proving (yet again) to be a publisher willing to support non-traditional, politically committed legal scholarship.

This book has benefited hugely from the comments of audience members at numerous academic gatherings over the past few years: Socio Legal Studies Association Conferences (Loughborough University, 1999; Queen's University Belfast, 2000; University of Wales at Aberystwyth, 2002); Law and Society Association Conferences (Chicago, 1999; Miami, 2000; Budapest, 2001); the 'Rights, Identities and Communities of the European Union' workshop, sponsored by the University Association of Contemporary European Studies (University of Leeds, 1999); the 'Rethinking Citizenship' Conference (University of Leeds, 1999); the Conference of the International Association for the Study of Sexuality, Culture and Society (Manchester Metropolitan University, 1999); the EU Citizenship Workshop 'Citizenship and Governance in the EU', sponsored by the Leverhulme Foundation (University of Reading, 1999); the workshop on European Citizenship and Social and Political Integration of the European Union, funded by the European Commission (University of Sassari, Italy, 2000); the American Political Science Association Conference (Washington, DC, 2000); invited papers presented in the School of Law and to the Department of Government (Cornell University, 2001); the 'Same-Sex Partnerships: Wedding Rights to Marriage in Europe' Conference (Kalamazoo College, Michigan, 2002); the 'Gender, Sexuality and Law II' Conference (Keele University, 2002); and, finally, numerous law school research seminar series (Queen's University Belfast, 1999; Keele University, 1999; University of Nottingham, 2000; University of Newcastle-upon-Tyne, 2000; University of Aberdeen, 2001; University of Bristol, 2001; University of Hull, 2001).

Finally, I acknowledge permission to reproduce previously published, earlier versions of portions of this book: 'Sexual Citizenship in the European Union', (2001) 5 *Citizenship Studies* (http://www.tandf.co.uk) (chapter 1); 'Civil Solidarity or Fragmented Identities? The Politics of Sexuality and Citizenship in France', (2001) 10 *Social & Legal Studies* (reprinted by permission of Sage Publications Ltd © Sage Publications Ltd, 2001) (chapter 3); '*Grant*-ing Rights: the Politics of Rights, Sexuality and European Union', (2000) 51 *Northern Ireland Legal Quarterly* (chapter 4); and ' "A Stranger to its Laws": Sovereign Bodies, Global Sexualities, and Transnational Citizens', (2000) 27 *Journal of Law and Society* (chapter 5).

Introduction

IN WHAT WAYS are the politics of same sex sexualities changing, particularly in the United Kingdom, but more widely, in the context of an integrating European Union? What are the implications of law reform strategies around 'homosexuality,' in an era in which those strategies seem to be increasingly destined for success? And once law reform is achieved, what remains of a politics of sexuality? At that point, should we be content with how our sexualities are governed through law and, if not, what directions should activism take?

These are the questions which provoked me to embark upon *Governing Sexuality*. To illustrate why I believe it is appropriate to speak of a changing politics of sexuality, I begin with three 'moments' which stand out in my mind as illustrative of the dynamic character of sexuality politics today.

FIRST MOMENT

In July 2000, gay 'World Pride' is staged in Rome with hundreds of thousands making a pilgrimage to the cradle of European 'civilisation' to march in the streets. The event is predictably denounced by the Pope, but Italians are fascinated by the unprecedented scale of the march, and media coverage is largely sympathetic. The idea of a worldwide event raises for consideration the extent to which lesbian and gay identities *are* 'worldwide,' cosmopolitan and universal phenomena and, indeed, whether they are even shared *European* identities. But the contrast to the commercialised slickness of American pride parades is also apparent, which may itself indicate something of the uniqueness of European sexuality politics.

SECOND MOMENT

In May 2002, a right-wing, openly gay politician in the Netherlands, Pim Fortuyn, is shot dead by an environmental campaigner in the middle of an election campaign. Fortuyn was best known for his anti-immigration, anti-Islamic platform which appeared to be increasingly appealing to Dutch voters. His death turns him (at least momentarily) into a martyr, defending freedom of speech. His party is swept into second place in the elections and obtains four cabinet seats in a centre-right coalition government. He justified his hostile views on Islamic immigrants in part on the basis of his perception that Islam is opposed to homosexuality and the equality of women. His sexuality thereby justifies his anti-immigrant sentiments, and it appears to be no hindrance to his popularity.

THIRD MOMENT

In July 2002, Alan Duncan MP becomes the first Conservative Member of the British Parliament to declare openly his gay sexuality. The frontbench spokesman makes a statement in a newspaper interview, and receives the uneqivocal support of his leader, Iain Duncan-Smith. The Conservative Party now is supposedly 'gay friendly' and socially inclusive, and there is talk that Duncan could be the first openly gay (and Conservative) prime minister in the years to come.

What do these snapshots at the beginning of the twenty-first century reveal? Although, like photographs, they capture nothing more than particular historical moments, I believe that they do suggest something of significance about the changing political climate and culture within the United Kingdom and European Union today, in which old 'certainties' about gay politics no longer always hold true. Gays march to popular support on the doorstep of the Catholic Church. Tories are coming out of the closet. A far-right Dutch gay politician achieves considerable popular support in the Netherlands. The politics of sexuality, I argue in this book, is indeed changing in some (but not all) respects.

What is also changing, again in some moments and in some respects, is the role of law. Most studies of the legal regulation of same sex sexual practices and identities in the past have focused on 'anti-gay' laws in various forms (particularly in a UK context), or the failure of progressive reforms due to 'backlash' and conservative responses (especially in the context of central-local government relations). The focus of this book, by contrast, is on 'liberal', 'progressive' law reform in the context of the United Kingdom and European Union (including the Central and Eastern European countries who seek to join the European Union), and the ways in which sexuality is *governed* within such a climate of liberalisation.

Furthermore, much academic analysis of 'law and same sex sexualities' in the past has focused on North America, either as a laboratory in which progressive legal developments were occurring (particularly in Canada), or as underscoring the most extreme versions of anti-gay legislative and judicial thinking (as in parts of the United States). It is now clear, however, that in a widening and deepening European integration project, the European Union is a rich source of material for any study of the role of law in the regulation of sexualities. Moreover, an analysis of UK sexuality law and politics within the European Union provides an additional dimension. My own view is that sexuality politics (like much other politics) in the United Kingdom has an interesting position, in that it is influenced by American gay politics, but also increasingly we are part of a European gay 'community' and, moreover, the United Kingdom has its own unique historical trajectory and experience.

In addition, *Governing Sexuality* is informed by the context, not only of the transnationalism of EU political and legal integration, but also more generally, by a recognition of the importance of the forces of neoliberal economic and cultural globalisation, which also deeply affect legal and political developments. Globalisation also influences sexual identity categories, arguably making *some* lesbians and gays into more cosmopolitan citizens who more easily transcend the constraints of community and nation. It also facilitates the practice of citizenship as consumer consumption across borders, allowing for the adoption by some gays of the identity of the globalised gay consumer. In this moment, homosexuality becomes simply a *lifestyle* choice, or 'ways of life and forms of culture (cor)responding to the modern conditions of life' (Bech, 1997: 196). As one recent book describes it, all of these developments together suggest that we are currently living 'in a queer place' (Chedgzoy, Francis and Pratt, 2002). It is the role of law in this place, at this historical moment, that interests me here.

At this point, I should make clear my premises and prejudices in this work. The first is a theoretical claim. In writing *Governing Sexuality*, I remain deeply influenced by the view that law operates not only in repressive (or, indeed, progressive) ways, but also as a means to regulate and manage individual behaviours (and identities), particularly by encouraging us to manage ourselves, and to live our lives in particular ways. Consequently, this work can be located within a body of theoretical legal scholarship which has applied and developed insights gleaned from Foucault's (1972; 1977; 1980; 1981) conception of power, as both juridical and disciplinary (as well as power as sovereignty). Although there has been much interesting academic commentary on precisely what role Foucault imagined that legal discourse might play in the operations of power, that is well beyond the scope of *Governing Sexuality* (see especially Smart, 1989; Lacey, 1998). Rather, my premise is that law can operate both in an explicitly juridical way through repression and social control (the enforcement of anti-gay sex laws exemplifies this), but also that legal discourse can operate in a more subtle, disciplinary mode, by encouraging, in an infinite variety of ways, individuals to conform to how the law constructs proper—even civilised—behaviour. I will also argue that the way such behaviour is constructed by law is informed by a wider neoliberal economic hegemony that emphasises the privatisation of responsibility for others, and the withdrawal of the state from many aspects of care. This foreshadows how law acts as a force for the *discipline* of the self, and it is this concept of *normalisation* which runs throughout this book.

In this way, *Governing Sexuality* differs from some other books on law and same sex sexualities. My theoretical premise demands that the tone of this book is cautious and, at times, critical, of the value of liberal law reform as it is often formulated, and moreover, of activist strategies which increasingly place law at the centre of political struggles. In other words, I do not subscribe wholeheartedly to the idea or ideal of liberal legal 'progress.' At the same time, I will readily agree that with disciplinary power inevitably comes resistance by individual subjects, which often takes unpredictable forms, which can circumvent and undermine the disciplinary function of law. Furthermore, I also (happily) concede that law can operate in enabling as well as restrictive ways, and this provides the indeterminacy at the heart of Foucauldian inspired analyses of the power of legal discourse. In *Governing Sexuality*, my focus is primarily on the disciplinary function of law, rather than on its enabling potential. This choice is strategic and corrective on my part. Other commentators demonstrate an enormous faith in law, and I leave it to them ably to put law's 'case' (see eg Wintemute, 2000). In sounding a cautionary note, however, I recognise that I may seem a bit of a 'spoiler' at a party to celebrate progress, but I accept that this may be my role in intellectual life.

In this regard, I also need to 'come out' on a more explicitly political issue. In considering the disciplinary function of law, my focus is often on the legal recognition of same sex relationships, which is rapidly occurring across the Member States of the EU at national level (with 'gay marriage' as the ultimate issue on the horizon). Readers may well detect a critical view on my part in this regard, and on this they will be right. I remain fairly sceptical of an activist agenda which places partnership entitlements in certain forms at centre stage. This is not because I am opposed in principle to such benefits, nor because I believe that 'traditional' same sex relationships are necessarily 'assimilationist' with respect to a heterosexual norm that I believe should be challenged (or transgressed) instead. Rather, the concern which runs throughout *Governing Sexuality* is that the disciplinary, normalising function of liberal law reform may constrain us, by acting to limit the variety of ways of living—of styles of life—which sexual dissidents historically have developed. That is, my fear is that legal recognition may limit our ability to recognise that we can construct our lives so as to defy the categories which law traditionally has sought to impose upon us.[1] Yet, at the same time, I readily concur with the view that law is not an 'all powerful' discourse operating on our lives. My hope is that this book, in some small way, might encourage readers to consider, by contrast, how law might be used to facilitate (or at least remain neutral towards) an endless variety of ways of living, less constrained by a heteronormative world order. In my view, that would be a progressive, radical, and even (dare I say) queer legal turn.[2]

It should now be apparent what *Governing Sexuality* is not. This is not a work on 'law and homosexuality' which systematically traces recent developments in British and European law, with an emphasis on human rights (see eg Walker 2001). Nor is it a book on the law of same sex partnerships (see

[1] On the ways in which law produces 'limitations on imaginations,' see especially Fineman (1995: 14–33).

[2] As a political matter, I also fully support the idea that all ways of living can and should be interrogated on the basis of their ethical premises and everyday practices, rather than celebrated unquestioningly simply on the basis of the value of pluralism and diversity. On the 'ethical dimension' of critical legal theory, see Lacey (1998: 157).

Wintemute and Andenaes, 2001). It is not an explication of a political theory of same sex sexualities either (see eg Phelan, 2001), nor is it a sociology of legal rights struggles around same sex sexualities (see eg Herman, 1994a; 1997). Rather, what I have tried to write is a theoretically informed study of several *vignettes* of law reform and legal struggle in a British and European legal context, in which I attempt to analyse them as examples of struggle over the realisation of *sexual citizenship*, a concept which is central to my analysis. The potential and limitations of citizenship—a key political concept more generally at this historical juncture—unite the various examples which I present here.

In chapter 1, I elaborate upon the concept of sexual citizenship and foreshadow its use in the case studies which follow in subsequent chapters. This chapter outlines my theoretical framework and sets the scene for the struggles around citizenship which I then go on to explore. In this opening chapter, I also consider an emerging concept of the 'European citizen' and how this might intersect with the 'sexual citizen' at the heart of *Governing Sexuality*.

In chapter 2, I attempt to ground the sexual citizen in the particular context of current UK sexuality politics and, in particular, New Labour's Third Way ideology. Within the Third Way, citizenship (and appropriate citizenship behaviour) is central, and New Labour sees itself as pluralistic in terms of its sexuality politics. In this chapter, I interrogate New Labour discourses around sexuality law reform—specifically, on section 28 of the Local Government Act 1988 and the equalisation of the age of consent—to investigate what happens to sexual 'dissidents' as they come to be socially *included* as citizens of a *New* Britain.

In chapter 3, I present a contrast to current developments in the United Kingdom by turning to law reform and social change in France and, in particular, I examine the debates surrounding the enactment of a new civilian French legal status: the *pacte civil de solidarité* (PACS). My turn to France is an attempt to demonstrate the sharply divergent ways in which citizenship and sexuality are understood within the European Union which, in turn, raises interesting questions regarding European legal harmonisation in the face of cultural and political divergence. Republican ideology is central to the French debates, and republicanism is constituted through its opposition to an 'Anglo-Saxon' politics of identity, of which the United Kingdom is seen in France as emblematic.

The departure point for chapter 4 is the judicial politics of the European Court of Justice in *Grant v South West Trains* (249/96) [1998] ECR I–621, the decision which held that a refusal by an employer to grant travel concessions to a person of the same sex with whom a worker has a 'stable relationship' does not constitute discrimination based directly on the sex of the worker, as prohibited by European law. This chapter seeks to analyse this legal struggle in terms of the political economy of rights, sexuality and citizenship, and it asks whether lesbians and gays should be cautious in signing up to the construct of the European 'market citizen' as a pathway to equality.

Chapter 5 shifts from the right not to be discriminated against, to freedom of movement. In this chapter, I examine the centrality of mobility for lesbians and gay men, and the ways in which movement across national borders historically has produced anxieties within the nation state which have been highly sexualised. I then interrogate recent moves towards the legal recognition of same sex relationships which cross national borders to determine what these developments suggest about citizenship, community, and cosmopolitanism, in the context of a globalising economic and political world order.

In chapter 6, these themes continue to be the focus of my attention, but the context shifts markedly to one of the accession countries of Central and Eastern Europe: Romania. This chapter interrogates the impact of sexual identity politics on the likely expansion of the European Union, focusing on how European politics allowed social movement actors in Romania to struggle successfully for reform of the draconian laws against same sex sexual practices and identities. In this chapter, sexuality proves a central site of struggle through which broader issues around identity, westernisation, international human rights, globalisation and transnationalism are all articulated in a variety of ways.

Finally, I conclude *Governing Sexuality* by reflecting on the key themes of the book, and I raise some questions for further inquiry.

1

The Sexual Citizen

INTRODUCTION

WITHIN WESTERN CAPITALIST societies, it is now widely argued that 'citizenship' has assumed a new priority in political theory and practice. Whether through a neoliberal discourse of individual responsibility in relation to the common good; through the appeal to voluntarism as a corrective to the self-interest of the capitalist ethos of the 1980s; or with reference to active participation of the socially excluded as a corrective to the bureaucratised welfare state, citizenship is now invoked with an increased frequency and a self-evident character which 20 years ago would not have been imagined. Not surprisingly, then, citizenship is a central theme running throughout *Governing Sexuality*, and, in this first chapter, I focus on two different—but, I argue, reconcilable—uses of the language of citizenship: in the contexts of the 'sexual citizen' emerging from sexual identity politics, and the transnational 'European citizen' of the European Union. Both uses of citizenship discourse are central to my analysis, and this chapter aims to provide the foundations for my deployment of the term in the studies which follow. Citizenship is frequently grounded in a normative discourse of 'civic inclusion', and citizenship provides the framework within which to make many legal claims. I argue in this chapter that, historically, citizenship has been constitutively built on a series of exclusions made possible through a number of theoretical, binary divisions. Through their deployment, individual subjects not only could be included as citizens within the broader polity, but also excluded as 'non-citizens.' I then go on to show how citizenship remains an appealing concept in the domain of sexual identity politics, and it has been invoked widely, especially given its close connection to the language of rights and entitlement. It is at this point that the potential of European integration—and its focus on rights discourse—starts to become apparent. I also consider how citizenship may prove a limiting, disciplining, and regulatory concept, particularly in the domain of sexuality. The 'flipside' of rights discourse is the language of duties and responsibilities of citizenship, and the ways in which these are constituted proves important. Moreover, the language of rights can be seen, not as grounded in entitlement, but as part of a reciprocal arrangement involving individual responsibility.

But the potential of citizenship discourse, not unlike rights themselves, may be in its ability to *exceed* this disciplinary and regulatory aspect, precisely because of its indeterminacy as a concept, creating the possibility of active, democratic, and politically empowering forms of citizenship, a tradition which has had little historical resonance in EU politics. In the final section of the chapter, however, I suggest that sexual citizenship claims, as they are emerging in the European Union, may *potentially* illustrate this aspect of citizenship, despite the paucity of formal democratic structures in the EU political arena. It is thus both the potential and the limitations of sexual citizenship in the European Union which is the central claim, not only of this chapter, but of this study as a whole. This chapter thus aims to examine and outline the key theoretical claims which will then be tested through the series of case studies which follow in the remainder of *Governing Sexuality*.

THE BINARY LOGIC OF CITIZENSHIP

It has been frequently commented upon that the modern invention of citizenship has relied upon the deployment of the public/private dichotomy. Bryan Turner (1990: 206), for example, describes the public/private distinction as one of the two central axes upon which citizenship has been constituted. The other is the active/passive dichotomy, and these two axes are closely related. Roberto Alejandro (1993: 11) argues that it was the invention of the sovereign individual in modernist thought which differentiates ancient and modern conceptions of the citizen, because individuality facilitates the prioritisation of a private realm in which the individual can choose how to live a good life.

However, it also has been argued that the public/private distinction has deeply gendered implications and that it has never lived up to its liberal promise (Lister, 1997). To the extent that citizenship has been constituted in terms of participation in the public sphere, it has been, and continues to be, highly gendered. Women have been required to leave the home (the quintessential space of the private), in order to participate as citizens, but the realities of lack of money and time have often precluded full participation (Walby, 1994: 386). Many Black and working class white women in Western societies, by contrast, have been forced by necessity to work (and sometimes live) in a private sphere belonging to others. Citizenship discourse devalued the private sphere and did nothing to facilitate women's access to the public. Rather, paid employment has become increasingly key to citizenship, yet unequal pay has not been widely seen as a citizenship issue (Lister, 1997: 139). At the same time, the public/private distinction has masked how the private sphere can be a central site for surveillance and regulation, particularly for Black and working class families (Cooper, 1993: 164). Thus, the private is not necessarily shielded from the glare of the state, and the public is far from universally inclusive.

The gendered implications of the public/private dimension of citizenship can be seen through a closely related dichotomy: rights and needs. Wendy Brown

(1995: 161) argues that the public sphere is characterised within citizenship discourse as the realm of rights, in which the pursuit, not of the common good, but of self-interest, is the central focus. The private realm of household and family becomes the sphere for the satisfaction of human needs, of relationships, and of the 'selflessness' of family. The liberal male subject historically has moved freely between the two realms—between the rights of civil society (the public) and the prerogatives of home (the private)—while women have been associated with the selflessness of the latter, and frequently have been condemned as selfish when they have sought actively to participate in the public sphere.

Moreover, the public/private dichotomy informs another central binary: active and passive forms of citizenship (Turner, 1990: 206; Riesenberg, 1992: xxii). With the invention of the modern citizen, citizenship lost the centrality it possessed (for those few men granted its privileges) in the classical era. For the ancients, the centrality of participation in politics was the key to the good life. For moderns, by contrast, citizenship came to be constituted in terms of rights and entitlements obtained (by some men) in the public sphere (along with prerogatives located in the private). The active, civic dimension of citizenship withered, creating, some would argue, a dependency culture in which rights have been separated from notions of community and responsibility (a theme which I pursue further in the context of New Labour politics in Britain in chapter 2). In that sense, citizenship is a 'contested concept'—involving 'a status to which rights attach or a practice involving civic virtue and participation in the polis' (Lister, 1997: 3). Rights, as one side of this equation, are sometimes associated with a *private* domain of consumption (Dietz, 1992), while participation is part of the active sphere of the polis, which further demonstrates how the public/private divide is highly malleable. This distinction is sometimes described as the difference between the status and practice of citizenship (Arendt, 1958; Lister, 1997; Shklar, 1991).

It is hardly surprising that 'active' citizenship as a normative, political concept has experienced a revival in recent years, particularly through its focus on voluntarism, families, communities, and neighborhoods (Bellamy and Greenaway, 1995). There may well be *potential* in this citizenship discourse for correcting the historical limitations and constitutive exclusions of liberal citizenship, through the problematising of the distinctions between public and private, and rights and needs. It might facilitate the reconciliation of the individual and the broader social context within which individual autonomy and rights are constituted. However, active citizenship has come to be primarily appropriated by the 'civic republican' tradition of citizenship discourse, in opposition to the liberal citizenship model (Habermas, 1996: 22).[1] This distinction between liberal and communitarian versions creates highly indeterminate political implications, in

[1] The civic republican vision of citizenship should not be confused with the French republican citizenship ideal, which is related but distinct. I explore the implications of French republicanism for sexual identity politics in chapter 3.

terms of the constitutive exclusions of citizenship (ie, who is a citizen of *this* community? who is a *responsible* citizen deserving of the rights of members?). While liberalism has its well documented exclusions—such as gender—the civic republican ideal is not necessarily any more inclusive (Benhabib, 1992; Young, 1995). Indeed, it has been argued that both liberal and civic republican traditions have been built on the exclusion of women (Moynagh, 1997). The inclusions and exclusions of communitarianism, liberalism, and citizenship generally, centrally inform all of my case studies.

In this regard, Ruth Lister (1997: 25) has shown how civic republicanism's narrow definitions of the political and of the citizen have been exclusionary, reproducing the more obvious and blatant exclusions of its classical predecessor. In particular, the privileging of formal political processes as the central dynamic of citizenship has erased the informal political networks to which women have been historically attracted. Moreover, civic republicanism privileges a single 'common good' as the citizenship ideal, which necessarily devalues political participation designed to further individual or group interests. Furthermore, the active/passive citizenship dichotomy has been historically deployed to construct women's duties to the polis passively; centred on the home and procreation of the 'national' family, thereby foreclosing active (male) 'political' involvement.

Thus, Nancy Fraser (1997b: 86) has criticised the emphasis of civic republicanism on the production of a single 'we' of citizens, which inevitably produces exclusions and relations of dominance, and which precludes genuine dialogue between differently located subjects. Civic republicans have failed to recognise that there never has been only one public sphere. Rather, in response to an exclusionary civil society, there emerged numerous 'subaltern counterpublics' of the excluded. These spheres provided important political spaces, both for withdrawal (and shelter) from official civil society, and also for engagement with it in order to achieve broader social inclusion. Fraser supports the continuation of this multiplicity of public spheres, even if the exclusions of civil society could be eradicated. At the same time, she advocates at least one comprehensive arena for the bringing together of the multiplicity of spheres in dialogue. Fraser's analysis here is similar to Alan Sinfield's (1996) elaboration of sexual identity politics as requiring both separate spaces for the development of a shared subculture and an ongoing focus on the integration of groups into broader social forms. This provides a useful way of 'troubling' the dichotomy between social assimilation and separatism (or, for that matter, between normalisation and transgression). Neither side of the dichotomy can be renounced, for both become 'moments' which are of ongoing importance for the possibility of genuine social inclusion. The politics of assimilation, separatism, normalisation and transgression—which have been historically central to both the theory and politics of sexuality—will recur in a number of different contexts in the case studies. It has become increasingly clear to me that this is a highly indeterminate politics, in which neither social assimilation nor separatism (and neither normalisation nor transgression) alone can be politically viable or desirable. In other words, *both* gay subculture *and* mainstream political acceptance must be seen as important practices of citizenship in which, in fact, each may be a moment which is dependent upon the other for its viability.[2]

The focus of civic republicanism on politics narrowly conceived has clear implications for sexual identity politics. For civic republicans, 'political life is superior to the merely private pleasures' (Kymlicka and Norman, 1995: 293), and the construction of non-heterosexually identified people as centred on (or obsessed with) pleasure and the body easily allows for claims grounded in sexual identity to be trivialised. These claims are *merely* about the body and pleasure, rather than the common good of civic republican politics. This also relates to the relationship between rights and responsibilities, and the construction of the 'responsible' citizen. Maurice Roche (1992: 240) articulates this most clearly in his claim that duties to family and community should be seen as prior to the claiming of rights. The emphasis here is not only on the perceived selflessness of the familial realm with its focus on relationships, but on self-control and 'what is necessary for a society to claim to be civilized' (241) (a point which arises in many of my case studies).

Thus, if the body politic represents the movement from a state of nature to 'rational' society—the triumph of reason over desire—then 'gays are not capable of being domesticated' because of a lack of bodily (and social) discipline (Goldberg-Hiller, 1998: 532). In Christian Right discourse, for example, this lack of discipline is comprehensively constructed to include not only sexual acts, but also as manifesting itself through narcissism, avariciousness and anarchic tendencies. Such *inherent* qualities *justify* citizenship disenfranchisement. As Didi Herman (1997) suggests, the construction of the unsuitability of homosexuals for citizenship is not simply based upon sexual indiscipline (central as that is), but is grounded in homosexuals' overconcern with the self more generally; a kind of 'hyperindividualism' which runs counter to social and familial responsibility (the other side of the rights coin). If responsible citizenship is based on self-restraint and 'relies on responsible personal life-style decisions' (Kymlicka and Norman, 1995: 291), non-heterosexuals can be constitutively disqualified. As Jonathan Goldberg-Hiller (2000) argues, this has been a central discourse in the American debates over same sex marriage rights, in which the status and rights of marriage (a debate which largely has been framed within the language of citizenship), are grounded in the particular and unique contribution

[2] Some readers may see this statement as a shift in my own political leanings, particularly compared to some claims made in my first book (Stychin, 1995b). I leave that to others to consider, but I do think that in a liberal legal culture such as ours, voices which emphasise the importance of transgressive moments, and which caution against disciplinary and normalising liberal legal developments, are particularly valuable. For that reason, despite my belief that citizenship and rights discourses are both disciplining and politically enabling, I will concentrate primarily on the disciplinary side of the coin in the case studies. I trust that others—more enamored by liberalism and rights—will ably highlight the empowering dimension of liberal progress.

of heterosexual couples to the common good. In this way, rights and duties connect, and the promotion of the common good is located in the heteronormative private sphere of the nuclear family. This enclave must then be privileged through the granting of 'special rights,' precisely because it is where the values of good citizenship are produced. Thus, rights are dependent upon evidence of the common good. They follow from responsible behaviour. Homosexual acts are not what 'good' citizens do. The family, by contrast, is a realm of self-discipline and selflessness opposed to the hyperindividualism characteristic of late modern societies. This is another central theme of this book: the rights of sexual citizenship seem only to flow to responsible citizens who contribute to the common good.

APPROPRIATING CITIZENSHIP

Given the exclusionary history of citizenship, it is perhaps surprising how it has come to be embraced within lesbian, gay and queer political theory (see eg Bell, 1995; Evans, 1993; Kaplan, 1997; Phelan, 1995; 2001; Plummer, 1995; Watney, 1990; Weeks, 1995).[3] This appropriation speaks to the power of citizenship, and to the lack of alternative languages which express both a desire for rights and participation. As Davina Cooper (1993: 168) notes, citizenship contains 'different traces of meaning', including both duty and empowerment, and always has the *potential* to be rearticulated, depending 'upon the precise historical circumstances' at issue.

Simon Watney's (1990) early advocacy of citizenship is perhaps the most wholehearted of this genre of writing. For Watney, the claiming of citizenship as *entitlement*, as well as the embrace of the nexus of rights and responsibilities, amounts to one of the 'practices of freedom' available to non-heterosexually identified people. Of course, this discourse is an increasingly tenuous basis for any claim in the West in the twenty-first century, with the widespread repudiation of public entitlement, in light of the material withdrawal of the state from many arenas. Nevertheless, citizenship rights, and rights discourse more generally, particularly in the British context, are undoubtedly appealing as an alternative to claims for 'concessions' from dominant society (Sinfield, 1996: 274), and this may prove to be particularly true in the era of the Human Rights Act 1998.

Nevertheless, the optimistic accounts of citizenship's potential in relation to sexual identity claims—described, for example, by Morris Kaplan (1997: 238) as 'manifest in erotic self-making and a variety of institutions of intimate association'—are but one side of the citizenship equation. That is, citizenship can be conceived through yet another binary: the distinction between the citizen as self-

[3] A most thorough and balanced analysis of sexual citizenship can be found in Bell and Binnie (2000).

created and as existing prior to the granting of the status of citizenship; and, by contrast, citizenship as 'a creation of techniques of social discipline' (Burchell, 1995: 543). If rights and responsibilities are the two sides of the citizenship coin, then the historical construction of the 'responsible' citizen cannot simply be 'transcended.' Rather, this provides a central 'semantic legacy' which citizenship carries (Cooper, 1993: 168). This disciplined, responsible citizen will prove to be a central figure reappearing throughout *Governing Sexuality*. It is the way in which responsibility (both to self and to society) is *conceived* which is of particular interest to me in the case studies, in the context of the ways in which lesbians and gays may be 'granted' (at a price and from on high) social inclusion through citizenship.

This disciplinary function of citizenship is an often cited, but equally often, highly ambiguous, Foucauldian-influenced claim, which possesses almost as many valences as citizenship itself. For example, Wendy Brown (1995: 65) argues that disciplinary power is inevitably produced when identities become politicised (such as when 'lesbian' and 'gay' became *politically* charged terms). Recognition of identity thus inevitably 'disciplines' it in the very recognition, a point reiterated by Jeffrey Weeks (1995: 111) (and many others) in the context of sexual identity. That is, there become recognised *ways* of being, and ways that one (of your *kind*) should not behave. Put very crudely, that is my understanding of disciplinary power. The claim here is that something valuable ('freedom') is 'lost' in these inevitable processes of disciplinarity, which comes with the recognition of an identity within liberal, rights-based societies. This inchoate 'something' is often referred to as the status of political 'outlaw' (Jones, KB, 1997: 3; Escoffier, 1998: 226). In this moment, discipline is synonymous with 'normalisation,' particularly a sexual normalisation which forces sexual identities into a model which, at best, replicates heterosexual monogamy but in a far more privatised form. Thus, the 'desire' for the recognition of same sex partnerships in law—often framed in the language of citizenship entitlement—could be interpreted as the ultimate desire to be 'unfree.' I will explore this point in a number of different legal, political and cultural contexts.

This conception of the disciplined citizen has always struck me as intuitively persuasive, particularly for those who are sceptical of the focus of some activist strategies on same sex marriage rights and military service as emblematic of citizenship status. But the citizenship debate in this form raises the question whether politics (and lives) are ever *wholly* disciplined, or whether, alternatively, rights and citizenship (and people living their lives) retain an unruly and unpredictable political and social edge (through *resistance* to discipline). The claim of irresistable (in both senses) discipline is theoretically troubling because it reproduces the type of 'grand theory' now widely eschewed in social theory more generally. Moreover, it demands a rather extraordinary false consciousness on the part of rights and citizenship advocates. A more balanced appraisal of the indeterminacy of citizenship and rights is to recognise that 'their capacity to generate critical leverage and escape co-optation is entirely relative to their situation' (Fraser, 1989: 63). As Jeffrey Escoffier (1998: 226) neatly summarises:

> every institutionalized form of political rights (a passive achievement) also enables disciplinary and normalizing forms of domination (not necessarily good things). Yet, only the active exercise of democratic rights allows a group to resist, modify, or restructure the forms of domination operating through discipline and normalization.

Thus, the interesting questions in relation to sexual citizenship turn not on whether citizenship disciplines, or whether it can serve as a means of resistance or empowerment, for undoubtedly the language of citizenship and rights can do both simultaneously. Rather, of interest is *how* citizenship discourse might be deployed, a quintessentially *political* question going to issues of strategy and the role of legal discourse. As a way of entering into these debates, I turn to the political space of the European Union, as an example of the role of rights and citizenship generally, as well as in particular relationship to claims made through the prism of sexual identities.

CITIZENSHIP UNBOUND

In this section, I sketch out the ways in which the idea of European citizenship has been analysed in academic discourse, and I then go on to connect that to the construction of sexual citizenship. I interrogate the relationship between European and sexual citizenship, examining the ways in which theoretical work in these two areas interestingly relate, and how they might usefully inform each other. Such connections are appropriate to make, given the development of sexual identity politics in the arena of the European Union, which is often articulated to the language of citizenship (a point which I develop further in subsequent chapters). The challenging of boundaries is central to this analysis, both in terms of national (and transnational) citizenship, membership, and 'belonging,' as well as to the ways in which the categories of sexual identity are conceived. There is an underlying tension between the need for boundaries, grounded in an inside/out dichotomy, and the potentiality of European (and sexual) citizenship for contesting those boundaries.

As a starting point, the history of citizenship discourse within the EU inverts Marshall's (1950) influential analysis of citizenship as involving an historical movement from civil to political to social rights. Although the idea of citizenship grounded in membership of the European Union has been overwhelmingly rights based, with little official conception of duty, the rights articulated have been primarily socio-economic market rights. Indeed, because of the often cited 'democratic deficit' within EU institutions, the political processes themselves are widely viewed as extremely distanced from individual citizens, and it is claimed that they do little to inculcate an 'active' form of citizenship (Armstrong, 1998a; de Lange, 1995). There appear to have been few opportunities for active, democratic practices of citizenship, given the democratic deficit, the historically narrow focus of rights discourse, and the lack of citizen identification with European institutions. Citizenship in the context of the European Union historically has been a legalistic, market-centred concept (Shaw, 1998). Perhaps as a consequence, rights discourse—because it is now an entrenched feature of EU law and politics—is considered a most productive site for the construction of an 'active' European citizen (de Búrca, 1995). Rights might be instrumental in creating a sense of European belonging. Another inversion of 'traditional' citizenship discourse thereby becomes apparent. Political processes are associated with passivity, distance, elitism and corruption. Rights, by contrast, may come to be associated with the active and involved citizen, relating to and making claims through the institutions of the European Union, as well as within national institutions through the language of European law. European citizenship, as it emerges through these discourses, thus underscores how a simple active/passive dichotomy cannot unproblematically be deployed as a way of analysing rights and citizenship. As well, the claim that rights discourse can be located on the 'private' side of the public/private dichotomy also becomes problematic. While the enjoyment of rights may be centred in a private, depoliticised sphere, the *pursuit* of rights—the campaign, rather than the judicial result—sometimes can be an active, public, and potentially democratic endeavour (although that is not *necessarily* the case). It now occurs, not only on the national stage, but in the transnational sphere.

However, the language of rights in the European Union has been historically tied to a particular conception of the good, namely, the promotion of the economic integration of the Union, and the creation of a 'transnational capitalist society' (Ball, 1996). Rights thus were constructed as a tool towards the achievement of an economically grounded, integrationist aim (de Lange, 1995). For example, the original justification for sex equality rights—fundamental to European rights discourse—was not a broad-based concern with participation by women on equal terms in the public sphere, but a desire to ensure a level playing field in the cost of factors of production between the Member States of the European Economic Community. In the EU context, republican notions of individual and collective responsibility thus were linked to the discipline of the market.

But the potential unruliness of rights discourse also may be apparent here, as rights now exceed narrow, economic integrationist conceptions of the good. In fact, the original economic impetus for equal rights has broadened out to include a political, normative rationale grounded in 'equality' as a fundamental tenet of EU citizenship in its own right. This potentiality of rights to grow roots deeper than the purely economic integrationist dimension of the Union has prompted some to claim that it could provide a counterbalance to the primarily economic focus of the European Union; serving to ground a more explicitly 'political' citizenship (a point which I have considered elsewhere; see Stychin, 1998: 115–30). Thus, while republican/civic virtue citizenship forms might be linked to the market and its discipline, liberal rights citizenship discourse is associated with litigation and ultimately with the European Court of Justice (the 'supreme court' of the European Union). I will consider the role of the European Court of Justice in chapter 4.

Moreover, European citizenship inhabits a tension between the economic goal of 'free movement' between Member States, which provides the original grounding for many EU rights, and a universalistic notion of *human* rights. The latter trajectory is demonstrated by the fact that the European Convention on Human Rights is one of the sources of law now recognised within the EU legal order.[4] Thus, although citizenship of the Union is a concept still closely associated with the rights of rational, self-interested, economic actors, able to move factors of production freely across the national boundaries of EU Member States (provided they possess nationality of a Member State and are gainfully employed), the claim is that citizenship has the potential to mean something *more*, and it is this excess which potentially might be exploitable in the cause of active, democratic citizenship. The potential of human rights discourse is particularly stark with respect to the requirements being imposed on the accession countries of Central and Eastern Europe seeking to join the European Union, an example of which I explore in chapter 6. At the same time, the European Union certainly underscores how, in late capitalist societies, the paradigm of active citizenship increasingly is defined in terms of employment, rather than military service. It is the citizen employed in the transnational marketplace who now claims a right to cross borders freely. This problematising of national, sovereign boundaries through mobility may provide one of the keys to the invigoration of European citizenship, and I consider the relationship between mobility and sexuality in chapter 5.

The point here is that rights in the EU context may usefully problematise the active/passive binary, and they may also trouble the liberal/republican dichotomy in the process. Rights may be central to active participation in this transnational polity, and also are key to the cultivation of an active, meaningful European identity. But rights discourse by itself may provide insufficient 'glue' to bind (or cobble) together such an identity, based around citizenship of the Union (Warleigh, 1998). In this way, the active/passive dichotomy re-emerges, as the claim is made that in order to be meaningful, citizenship demands not only supranational rights, but also active participation which goes *beyond* the claiming of rights in the name of citizenship, through *membership* in a transnational polity.

Rights discourse around sexual and gender identities is being invoked with increased frequency. Claims to rights which emanate from the United Kingdom have been made before the European Court of Justice and thereby have entered the transnational legal and political arena. In terms of strict legal outcomes, the results have been mixed. Litigants have argued that the guarantee of sexual

[4] The Convention has an increasingly interesting role to play in sexuality politics and rights discourse, but that is beyond the scope of this chapter.

equality in employment protects transgendered people from dismissal (*P v S and Cornwall County Council* (C13/94) [1996] ECR I–2143) and, in another case, that it demands equal employment benefits be paid to same sex couples as are paid to non-married heterosexual couples, when partnership benefits are an element of pay (*Grant v South West Trains* (C249/96) [1998] ECR I–621).[5] The transgendered claim was successful, but the partnership benefits case was not. However, both claims involve employment and, in the case of partnership benefits, it might seem removed from the domain of active, political citizenship. Indeed, arguments for sexual equality are often normatively grounded in part in the importance of rights as a means to 'perfect' competition in the labour market, and I consider this issue in detail in chapter 4.

But the cases both assumed considerable political significance amongst interested constituencies in the United Kingdom and transnationally in the European Union, serving to some degree to energise and politicise communities. Defeat before the European Court of Justice in *Grant* (1998) itself might be important to transnational mobilisation, particularly since the Court sent a clear message to the governments of the Member States that concerted action on their part in the form of new European legislation was advisable.

The possibility of such legislation was facilitated by the Treaty of Amsterdam (a constitutional agreement of the European Union). The Treaty *empowers* member states to enact European legislation to combat discrimination on the basis of sex, racial or ethnic origin, religion or belief, disability, age or sexual orientation. The inclusion of sexual orientation can be attributed to pressure from lobbyists in several Member States, as well as active support from some governmental officials (Bell and Waddington, 1996: 333). The Treaty is seen as a means of enriching European citizenship more broadly. More recently, the provision has enabled the adoption by the Council of the European Union of a general framework directive on equal treatment in employment, which includes 'sexual orientation' amongst the prohibited grounds. As a consequence, all rights conferred must be implemented in the national laws of Member States (by 2 December 2003). Thus, with respect to sexuality, claims which might originally appear to be passive, private and even disciplined, may be coming to possess an active, public, political and even democratic component as they emerge in the political space of the European Union. Yet, on the other side, the EU political processes, through which the framework directive was produced, remain largely closed and highly elitist in many respects, hardly resembling an active, inclusionary and democratic form of politics.

In sum, sexual citizenship articulates sexuality in the public sphere through claims for rights and participation, while also cultivating (and claiming a right to) separate spaces for subcultural life. These spaces sit uneasily on the public/private

[5] See also *D v Council* [1999] ECR–SCHI, for a further example of struggles over benefits for same sex couples, this time in the context of EU civil servants recognised under Swedish 'registered partnership' law.

divide, but historically have been subject to close surveillance by the state. At the level of the private sphere 'proper,' sexual citizenship highlights the *relevancy* of sexuality in the private sphere to public claims, while simultaneously creating the conditions for normalisation by bringing sexuality into the public sphere through the claim to citizenship. Finally, the mobility dimension of European citizenship—free movement—has impacted directly upon lesbian and gay Europeans, as it has facilitated their ability to move between and among public and private spheres throughout the European Union, to create connections between them, and to reimagine their relationship to national space (Binnie, 1997). Moreover, I would argue that technology—specifically, the Internet—is facilitating a reimagination of space and belonging. It has the potential to assist in the development of what Gerard Delanty (2000: 5) has called a 'cosmopolitan public sphere', giving rise to a civic cosmopolitanism based on sexual identification that transcends the national and the local.

With respect to European citizenship, this is all highly relevant, because historically 'the Community has refrained from intervening in what are seen as controversial matters of sexuality and gender relations, often associated with national identity and specificity' (Kofman, 1995: 132). As transnational institutions slowly come to recognise sexuality issues, and as citizens see themselves as transnational and cosmopolitan, these dynamics become increasingly salient. This more fluid, less fixed notion of space and belonging also might provide one strategy for challenging the normalising power of rights and politicised identities which has been identified by Wendy Brown (1995) and others, in that it suggests a movement away from fixed notions of who 'we' are, towards a 'wider solidarity' and alliances with those who appear to be 'different' from 'our' selves (Weeks, 1995: 122). As Morris Kaplan (1997: 68) has argued, drawing on the work of Hannah Arendt, citizenship needs to 'avoid the homogenizing assumptions implicit in unitary and exclusive conceptions of identity'. Public, as well as subcultural spheres potentially can be sites of contest and education both over European and sexual identities, in which the term—be it 'European' or 'homosexual'—'cannot fully or exhaustively perform its referent' (Butler, 1997: 108). Put more simply, what it means to be 'European,' or what it means to be 'gay,' or (and this for me is the question at the heart of this book), what it means to be a 'gay European,' become highly contestable issues in which there can be no single right, final answer, for there can be no final boundary around the identities in issue.

The implications of this more open and less fixed politics (broadly conceived) have been fairly widely considered in the context of sexual identities. Shane Phelan (1995: 345), for example, in her analysis of lesbian and gay politics, suggests that a recognition of the diversity of people who identify as non-heterosexual demands a rejection of an overarching and ultimately fictitious unitary 'lesbian and gay' identity, to be replaced by the imagining of politics as grounded in more loose 'affinities' and coalitions between people who are 'different.'[6] The shift from identity to coalition underscores the importance of the *activity* of politics. After all, a coalition must be continually reconstituted in order to survive, much more so than a fixed identity. Its precariousness and provisionality are explicitly acknowledged, as is its likelihood of shifting shape in the future. The creation of spaces for deliberation is emphasised by Phelan; deliberation amongst people who may form an affinity because they have something in common, but who may not consider themselves as sharing an identity, because they do not have *that much* in common. This politics of affinity as a grounding for citizenship could inform European politics and citizenship discourse because, as with lesbians and gay men, the group who have 'Europeanness' in common inevitably will be a disparate collection in which differences far exceed commonalities and in which loose political coalitions around specific issues may be preferable to a fixed (politically problematic and even dangerous) essential notion of what it means to be European.

An emerging European politics of sexuality may be facilitating an affinity which crosses national boundaries of the European Union. Rights also have facilitated mobilisation at the *national* level of the Member State (as in *Grant*), and the EU context highlights the ways in which engagement at national and transnational levels can intersect. That is, social movement politics locally and nationally feed into the transnational sphere through rights struggles and political alliances. However, these processes also may result in a kind of colonisation of sexuality by legal discourse. Being gay becomes a question of law—determined by lawyers and judges—rather than one of politics or other means. The expansion of the European Union will make this of some importance in the future, as it raises the possibility of a movement towards a European-wide consensus around the *meaning* of sexuality, not only as warranting anti-discrimination protection, but also more fundamentally as an identity. This dynamic might also produce a conservative, anti-cosmopolitan, communitarian reaction in some nation states, 'asserting the normative authority of the local and the national over the global and international' (Turner, 1990: 212) (a point I consider further in chapter 6). Equally important, European integration raises the role of identity politics across the European Union, as it may well come to be superimposed on national contexts in which it has little by way of 'tradition'. For example, the construction of citizenship claims around sexuality based on 'difference' rather than 'universality'—similar to those emerging from other identity-based social movements—may well sit uneasily with republican conceptions of *le citoyen* in France, which I consider in chapter 3.

It is partly for these reasons that a citizenship model founded on a more fluid basis than a fixed identity is important in terms of how both European and sexual citizenship are conceived. As for sexual citizenship, the transnational

[6] The idea of affinity as a way of understanding this politics emerged from Phelan's (1995) observation and experience of lesbians working politically with gay men, where the fictitious character of a 'lesbian and gay' political identity was often all too apparent. Yet, a common struggle remained shared in the face of political differences.

context underscores why a construction of fixed identities is problematic. The issues raised by rights discourse lend themselves to the imagining of a coalition-based model. It is through active, democratic political strategies that coalitions will continually emerge, change, and evolve, as individuals identify (or not) with particular aspects of rights struggles. Issues of sexuality in Europe seem particularly suited to Phelan's (1995) model of coalition and affinity, rather than identity. Same sex sexuality undoubtedly is a bond which may bring peoples together, but the differences between them seem far too great to establish anything like a fixed and stable identity. Indeed, to attempt to construct one is to engage in disciplinarity of the highest order. An example of coalition might be common endeavours and mutual support around rights struggles between transgendered people and lesbians, gays, and bisexuals, which have been facilitated by the character of EU anti-discrimination law with its focus on 'sex' discrimination. While dialogue across differences here may prove valuable, any attempt to construct a fixed identity would not adequately acknowledge difference (and would create the potential for conflict as well as coalition).

But the *problems* of dialogue across difference also need to be considered, and the transnational context may well exacerbate them. While civic republican forms of citizenship herald active participation in a dialogue over the common good, Nancy Fraser (1997b: 78) quite rightly points out in response that politics and deliberation can become 'infected' by 'social inequalities.' Thus, she argues that a politics of social and cultural *recognition* cannot be divorced from a politics of economic *redistribution* in order to foster the conditions of social equality and an egalitarian dialogue across difference. This is extremely apt in the EU context, both in terms of European politics generally, and sexuality politics specifically. Economic inequalities inevitably undermine the possibility of egalitarian political alliances. The relationship between claims for recognition and those of redistribution recurs throughout my case studies. The enormous economic and class differences between those who may identify as gay makes the possibility of genuine egalitarianism in political dialogue (as in friendship and relationships) extremely difficult and precarious. I would argue, however, that it remains a struggle worth pursuing.

For example, the dangers of dominance by Western, Northern, likely male, economically affluent, politicised (around identity) activists, located in cultures in which a strong support structure for litigation is present, must surely be a cause for concern. The extent to which economics is in large measure *constitutive* of sexual identities deserves consideration, for it suggests that East/West, North/South divisions may well be central—for economic reasons—to the way in which sexuality is constructed within Europe, especially given the historical focus of sexual citizenship on consumer consumption.

This point also underscores the limitations of a cosmopolitan citizenship form, that transcends notions of local and national community (see generally Hutchings and Dannreuther, 1999). As Delanty (2000: 2) pointedly notes, 'it is capitalism, not citizenship, that is truly cosmopolitan today.' The presence of economic inequality thus should be an issue within transnational (and national) sexual identity politics, and more generally in the construction of EU (and national) citizenship. It highlights the importance of attempts at economic redistribution as a necessary corollary to cultural recognition. It also exemplifies how the focus of rights struggles within the European Union on same sex economic benefits privileges the interests of those for whom such benefits are a realistic possibility.

Thus, my argument is largely a normative one, concerning how sexuality politics within the European Union should mirror the claims currently being developed around EU politics more broadly. Namely, it should aspire to be a site of exchange across differences, rather than becoming an arena for the colonisation of difference through the privileging of particular experiences (Bańkowski and Christodoulidis, 1999). The focus shifts from fixed identities to more fluid conceptions of space and belonging. The language of networks, movements and flows is no less apt for lesbian and gay politics as it is for European politics generally (Walker, 1999). But, at the same time, sexual citizenship might inform the ways in which European citizenship is itself imagined. A politics of affinity and coalition—in which the possibility of a singular and homogeneous identity is eschewed—may provide a useful antidote to attempts at forging a European identity, along with the exclusions wrought in the construction of such a bounded and fixed concept. The central tension between bounded space and more fluid conceptions of belonging is one which runs throughout *Governing Sexuality*, but I want now to consider on a micro level how these tensions play out in the context of citizenship struggles around sexuality in the European Union.[7]

FINDING A PLACE IN A EUROPEAN CIVIL SOCIETY

I now look briefly at a particular example of transnational politics in the European Union, through a consideration of the role of ILGA Europe (the European division of the International Lesbian and Gay Association). The reasons why I have chosen ILGA Europe are straightforward. It is a European regional association within an overarching international NGO; it has been quite successful in being accepted at an official level within the institutions of the European Union; it has received funding from the European Commission to produce reports; it has carried out lobbying functions with the various institutions of the European Union, including the European Parliament; and, most importantly for my immediate purposes, it has produced major reports, such as *Equality for Lesbians and Gay Men: A Relevant Issue in the Civil and Social Dialogue* (1998), which illuminate many of the tensions around both European and sexual citizenship which I have examined. This report was part of a broader

[7] For further background reading, and a nuanced analysis of these issues, see Beger (2001).

project supported by a grant from the European Commission (see generally Bell and Waddington, 1996; Bell, 1998).[8]

The title of the Report foreshadows its central theme of 'mainstreaming' issues concerning sexual identity politics in the debates around European integration. More generally, ILGA Europe articulates its claims within a discourse of civil society popular in European citizenship debates. It provides an umbrella for the bringing together of national and local organisations across a range of issues which increasingly traverse the national boundaries of the European Union. The Report, for example, focuses on youth, aging, families, housing, poverty, disability, and racism. It underscores the possibilities for the synthesis of rights discourse and citizenship participation. The importance of rights as *status* is emphasised, but so too is the crucial role of social inclusion of non-heterosexuals in all activities and programmes of the European Union (so as to ensure their equal participation in society).

The Report recognises that sexuality does not amount to an uncontested identity in the sense of a clearly defined 'group' across the European Union. Rather, the importance of equality discourse around rights and participation stems from the interrelationship of the 'social, political, and economical environment' (International Lesbian and Gay Association Europe, 1998: 15). But the Report also asserts the meaningfulness of sexual identity categories, particularly in the context of the Treaty of Amsterdam provision which recognises sexual orientation. ILGA Europe demanded that steps be taken transnationally to implement the empowering Treaty Article (and on this it has proven successful).

Thus, ILGA Europe is forced as a matter of practical politics to assert a coherent identity which traverses Europe and, simultaneously, it necessarily claims a certain 'naturalness' to the identity 'European' from which claims to citizenship flow. In this way, the construction of rights appears to be founded on a belief in groups—'lesbians and gays'; 'Europeans'—and the assumption is that an agenda for politics can be constructed for groups despite multiple differences of nation, gender, age, race, etc. But the Report also recognises the potential of the language of coalition, including coalitions with other movements focused on related issues in the European Union. Thus, ILGA Europe advocates something resembling the politics of affinity that I have explored in this chapter.

There is a certain irony at work here, in that the institutions of the European Union appear to be *facilitating* a fairly active form of citizenship around sexuality, while European citizenship has been predominantly perceived as a passive construct focused on status. This underscores how actors within civil society can always, through the language of rights *and* participation, breathe active life into what may appear to be static citizenship constructs. Furthermore, it is ironic that this form of active citizenship has been achieved largely through the financial support of the European Commission, an institution of the European

[8] ILGA Europe's role in the accession countries of Central and Eastern Europe will be considered separately in chapter 6.

Union widely thought to be distanced from its citizens. The focus of ILGA Europe on both the achievement of legal rights, as well as 'mainstreaming' towards full participation in civil society, thus demonstrates the claim that a synthetic relationship between rights and participation in citizenship is possible.

However, the role of ILGA Europe also can be seen as underscoring the limitations of NGO politics in the European Union, to the extent that it facilitates participation by a relatively small group of professionalised activists, in a form of politics in which rights discourse (and, more generally, law) has come to predominate. Moreover, the 'insider' status achieved with respect to the institutions of the European Union itself deserves critical reflection, suggesting the possibility of distance between grass roots mobilisation and high level insider lobbying; and, thus, between active participation and the institutional claiming of rights. In this way, both the potential, as well as the limitations, of European sexuality politics are apparent.

CONCLUSIONS

In this chapter, I have argued that the politics of sexuality in the European Union provides a useful microcosm for analysing citizenship in the Union more generally. The tension between universality and difference runs throughout the politics of sexuality and the politics of European citizenship, and it underscores how an acknowledgement of difference and multiplicity—increasingly central as a normative matter to the articulation of European citizenship—still demands some final point of reference, some commonality, through which to make sense of difference. As Roberto Alejandro (1993) suggests, while we might aspire to a citizenship grounded in 'competing traditions and competing languages' (206), we also need 'a common vocabulary to deliberate about a shared life' (225).

I have suggested in this chapter that the politics of sexuality provides a laboratory for EU citizenship discourse, underscoring the potential and limitations of a transnational public sphere. It highlights the problematics of citizenship, while also sometimes reproducing them. Like sexual citizenship, European citizenship more generally is shaped by a tension between the need to construct meaningful categories of belonging and the need to 'live with' the differences which challenge and undermine the fixity of boundaries which contain the categorisation. More fundamentally, this analysis raises the question whether citizenship and belonging need inevitably to be bounded in order to be coherent and meaningful.

Alternatively, can we apply the language of coalition and affinity as a means of moving away *from* identity *towards* something less fixed? Affinity suggests a commonality—elements of a history that in some sense might be shared across difference—but in which ebbs and flows across and between spheres of politics occur, depending upon the issue at stake. Public (and not so public) spheres intersect and interact without merging, and a common public sphere of

European citizenship remains a permanent site of contest over its meaning and future. This model can be described in terms of recognising communities characterised by rights and participation, but in which the boundaries of communities are always open to dispute; sites of community in which discipline is resisted (despite its inevitable occurrence), and in which democratic politics is recognised as vital. However, the 'political' is itself a site of contest, challenging the historical construction of public and private, which has been so central to citizenship discourse. Just as the relation of public and private is problematised, so too is the distinction between active and passive citizenship, and the way in which rights have been constructed as a site of passivity. The possibilities of European citizenship lie in the potential to synthesise rights and belonging, in the creation of opportunities for democratic contestation in the interstices between liberal rights, the disciplinarity of the free market, and across the differences between and within national identities. In the remainder of *Governing Sexuality*, I explore these possibilities, as well as the limitations, of sexual citizenship, through a series of legal case studies in which I will seek to ground these theoretical claims in particular political contexts. I will consider the extent to which liberal law reform around same sex sexuality issues lives up to the promise (or, indeed, the perils) of this analysis of citizenship discourse.

2

Queering the Third Way: Sexuality and Citizenship in 'New Britain'

INTRODUCTION

THIS CHAPTER EXPLORES the changing politics of sexual citizenship and law reform in the United Kingdom through a close analysis of 'progressive,' reform minded discourses around same sex sexualities that circulated in the various House of Commons debates on the age of consent and the repeal of section 28 of the Local Government Act 1988, which occurred during Labour's first term of office. I seek to locate the arguments for law reform in the context of the broader New Labour ideology, sometimes referred to as the Third Way. In so doing, the chapter gives an evaluation of what Third Way politics might mean for lesbians and gay men. I do not, however, aim to provide a scoresheet of law reforms (which include changes to adoption law, as well as proposed anti-discrimination legislation on the basis of 'sexual orientation'). Rather, this chapter seeks to engage with some foundational questions which are central to this book. What is the relationship between sexual dissidents and the emergence of important discourses which focus on social inclusion, community, equality, and the linking of rights and responsibilities? What *form* of sexual citizenship is on offer to lesbians and gay men and to whom exactly is it being offered? Is there a 'choice' not to be socially included or has inclusion become mandatory? In answering these questions, I will return to the themes discussed in chapter 1, particularly the idea of 'responsible' citizenship and the disciplinary role of citizenship discourse.

In examining these issues, this chapter does not provide a detailed analysis of conservative voices on sexuality, and the arguments that conservatives articulated during the Parliamentary debates.[1] Some commentators have claimed that, in the latest 'round' of debates on sexuality, conservatives have refined the positions taken in the 1980s, in that blatant homophobia has given way to more subtle arguments, couched in the language of moral (non)-equivalency (Moran,

[1] Nor do I focus on the House of Lords, and the predominantly conservative views that have emanated from the upper chamber.

2001: 77; see also Epstein, Johnson and Steinberg, 2000; Waites, 2000; Wise, 2000; McGhee, 2001: 147–61). That analysis lies beyond the scope of this chapter.[2] By contrast, my interest is in analysing what the reform-minded had to say. The importance of these voices derives, not only from the fact that this position is increasingly hegemonic, but also because the arguments raised during the sexuality debates reveal much about New Labour on key issues that go far beyond the immediate legislative reforms. In that sense, it seems time to turn the glare of analysis away from the conservatives and towards the reformers. As Melissa Benn (2000: 309) pointedly asks, is New Labour 'the party of tradition and marriage . . . or is it the party of personal postmodernity, promoting contingency and responsible pluralism in private life?'. Given that New Labour seeks to identify both with stengthening the family, as well as with supporting equality and social diversity, a searching inquiry into the 'emerging ambiguities of Blairism as a site of sexual politics', may be revealing (Epstein, Johnson and Steinberg, 2000: 7).

Parliamentary discourse continues to provide a rich source of primary research material on same sex sexualities, and the combination of the age of consent debates and the attempt to repeal section 28, together took up considerable debating time during Labour's first term. With respect to the attempt to equalise the age of consent as between gay male and heterosexual intercourse, there were three debates (in 1998, 1999, and 2000).[3] The issue was first raised by Ann Keen MP, on 22 June 1998, when she introduced an amendment to the Criminal Justice Bill designed to achieve equalisation. The House of Commons voted by a majority of 322 to 129 for the amendment, but the House of Lords overturned it. In January 1999, the second attempt at equalisation again failed due to the opposition of the Lords. In February 2000, pursuant to the Parliament Acts, the House of Commons voted in favour, and despite opposition from the Lords, equalisation of the age of consent at age 16 became law.

[2] This chapter is also limited in its scope in that its focus is on law reform within the Parliamentary sphere, rather than the claiming of rights through the courts pursuant to European or human rights law. I consider the use of rights discourse in more detail in Chapter 4. It is important to keep in mind, however, that the political developments documented in this chapter occurred in the context of the decision of the European Commission in *Sutherland v United Kingdom* (1998) 24 EHRLR 117, which held that an unequal age of consent is a violation of Article 8 of the European Convention on Human Rights (respect for private life), taken in conjunction with Article 14 (right to non-discrimination in the enjoyment of rights). Also in the background has been the coming into force of the Human Rights Act 1998, and possible legal challenges thereunder (such as with respect to s 28). For another example of the successful use of human rights discourse to challenge UK law, this time in the context of discharged armed services personnel, see *Lustig-Prean and Beckett v United Kingdom* (1999) 29 EHRLR 548 and *Smith and Grady v United Kingdom* (1999) 29 EHRLR 493.

[3] By way of background, when Labour took office, the age of consent for heterosexual intercourse was 16, and for gay male sex, 18 (and previously had been 21). Equalisation has been a major agenda item for many gay rights campaigners, and has had the active support of a significant number of Members of Parliament, for several years.

Repeal of section 28 of the Local Government Act 1988 also has occupied a considerable amount of Parliamentary time.[4] Unlike the age of consent, which was treated as a free vote on all sides of the House, repeal of section 28 was a Labour Party commitment and was subject to a 'whipped' vote by the Official Opposition. It was the basis of two Parliamentary debates, again due to the opposition of the House of Lords, where it was defeated for a second time in July 2000, by 270 to 228 votes. The repeal of section 28 is complicated by the devolution of powers, in that it was successfully repealed in Scotland in June 2000, after an acrimonious public debate.

For the purposes of this chapter, I draw on all of the House of Commons debates, as and when useful for illustrative purposes. Obviously, the age of consent and section 28 raise different issues, but sexuality is constructed and understood quite similarly by the Parliamentary speakers in both, in large measure because of the centrality of young people's sexuality in the two legislative contexts. Often, the actual issue of consent, or promotion of homosexuality, fades into the background in the speeches. As a consequence, I would argue that drawing on the debates interchangeably is methodologically justifiable.

Furthermore, it must be acknowledged that Parliamentary discourse does not represent the sum of official discourse by any means. However, political debates do encapsulate both state and civilian perspectives, and offer an important condensation of ideas. Particularly to the extent that hegemonic shifts in understandings of sexuality can be detected, Parliamentary debates may well provide interesting insights into wider social changes and continuities in attitudes and belief systems (see Herman and Cooper, 1997: 416).

LOCATING THE DEBATES: CITIZENSHIP AND THE THIRD WAY

Before analysing the debates themselves, it is useful first to locate them within the dominant ideology of New Labour and the Third Way. I use these terms interchangeably in this chapter, as they provide a useful shorthand for a cluster of ideological currents that characterise the current government, and which differentiate it both from traditional socialist as well as Conservative politics.[5]

[4] Section 28, a Thatcherite legislative innovation, states:

(1) A local authority shall not
  (a) intentionally promote homosexuality or publish material with the intention of promoting homosexuality;
  (b) promote the teaching in any maintained school of the acceptability of homosexuality as a pretended family relationship.

(2) Nothing in subsection (1) above shall be taken to prohibit the doing of anything for the purpose of treating or preventing the spread of disease.

Repeal of s 28 has been a Labour Party commitment. For the background politics of s 28 and its legal impact, see Stychin (1995b: ch 2).

[5] On New Labour's Third Way, see eg Rose (2000); Sevenhuijsen (2000); Powell (2000). Relatedly, on the Third Way and the corporation, see Wheeler (2002).

Thatcherite Conservative discourse around 'homosexuality' was subjected to close academic scrutiny, and this focused on the way in which lesbians and gays were constructed as outside the boundaries of the imagined community of the nation state, while also appearing as the enemy within (see eg Cooper and Herman, 1995; Smith, 1994). As Anna Marie Smith (1994: 18) argued, Conservatives also preached toleration of a figure which she describes as the 'good homosexual': 'a law-abiding, disease-free, self-closeting homosexual figure who knew her or his proper place on the secret fringes of mainstream society. They insisted that they fully accepted this imaginary figure as a wholly legitimate member of British society.' This homosexual (unlike the 'dangerous queer') controlled his predatory, seductive, and compulsive desires, which, if unchecked, threatened the nation itself. Within that discourse, there is no space for a politics of sexual citizenship, except perhaps through the workings of capitalism and the citizenship form of consumer consumption (which I considered in chapter 1)—the consumer as citizen—summed up by the (problematic) phrase the 'pink pound.'

Within New Labour ideology, by contrast, there are a number of key concepts, all of which were put into circulation during the sexuality debates. First is the centrality of the idea of social inclusion. Ruth Levitas (1998) has analysed the deployment of this discourse by New Labour, and she underscores the significance of inclusion, which has replaced the language of economic equality and redistribution in Labour ideology. But social inclusion is defined largely, if not exclusively, in terms of paid employment. Economic growth therefore is the key to inclusion and having a job is what constitutes it. In this way, structural economic inequalities are left uninterrogated, and social inclusion (again, meaning employment) becomes *the* individual moral duty, which will be facilitated by the state (and there are clear Christian overtones here) (114). If inclusion is defined as employment, then to be unemployed is to be socially excluded (and employment alone constitutes the movement of the individual across the binary) (see Powell, 2000: 46).

Secondly, the linking of rights and responsibilities: the enjoyment of rights as being conditioned upon the acceptance of responsibilities as citizens (Levitas, 1998: 122). This is closely related to the discourse of social inclusion, with its moral overtones. By focusing on inclusion rather than economic equality, the importance of duties, responsibilities and opportunities can supplement the language of rights (particularly with respect to employment or welfare rights). To the extent that rights discourse retains discursive power, it becomes increasingly a form of rights conditioned upon the taking of individual moral responsibility (and morality and employment are interwoven).

Third is the role of community as performing a key function of inculcating the values of citizenship, social inclusion, and the social control of deviant behaviour. Community, though, is a highly malleable concept, and there has been critical interrogation of the slippery use of communitarian discourse by New Labour (see eg Fairclough, 2000; Freeden, 1999; Driver and Martell, 1997).

Generally speaking, communitarianism as a political theory is understood as an ideal type in opposition to the dominance of liberalism. Whereas the latter (allegedly) aims to be normatively neutral (providing only a set of procedural rules), communitarianism focuses on shared values, cultural traditions, and the embededness of the individual in a (usually single) wider collectivity, generally the nation state. In recent years, communitarianism has been deployed as the claimed antidote to the perceived excesses of liberalism: individualism, rights, consumerism, etc (concepts which will recur in several of my case studies) (see generally Frazer and Lacey, 1993; Christodoulidis, 1998; Kukathas, 1996).

New Labour clearly has an attraction to aspects of communitarianism, and certainly to the language of community. Communitarianism as theory itself takes many forms, and elements of it can be appropriated all across the political spectrum. For New Labour, one of the attractions of 'community' is the way in which it seems to provide an alternative to the (perceived) Thatcherite focus on the atomistic individual and individual self-interest (and an alternative to Old Labour discourses of redistribution). The situatedness of the individual in community facilitates the deployment of the language of individual responsibility to that collective and, in this way, communitarianism is conditional upon the fulfilment of individual obligations. But the scale and scope of that community remains flexible and ill-defined. This allows New Labour's version of community in some moments to be quite pluralistic, yet in other ways, highly conformist. While pluralism may take the form of multiculturalism and social diversity, the conformist pressure can be seen in the emergence of a conservative moral agenda around the family, education, employment, and social in/exclusion (designed to lead to greater economic competitiveness in a global marketplace). On these subjects, there is little space for acceptable moral diversity or dissent from communal norms. These moral values are the basis, then, for social cohesion and inclusion, which is the key to strengthening and rebuilding community (or 'communities', depending on the scale invoked).

Fourthly, New Labour emphasises the role of family—very closely related to the emphasis on communitarianism—in producing responsible, active new citizens. The family is the community writ small, as well as being 'the basis of community' on a larger scale (Frazer, 1999: 157).[6] In ensuring that children are raised to become good, responsible citizens (which means law-abiding, educated, in work and not delinquents), the family is a central site because children are central to the community.[7] As well, the family—like the community—provides the counterbalance to Thatcherite individualism. Society is 'governed through the family' (Vaughan, 2000: 356) and 'the social good is accessed through the prism of the family' (McRobbie, 2000: 100). Not that the family challenges

[6] On the construciton of 'family' in an American context, see especially Fineman (1995).

[7] As Diane Richardson (2000: 80) persuasively argues, however, it is 'the traditional, middle-class nuclear family' that becomes the model of good citizenship, 'necessary for ensuring national security and a stable social order'—not *all* forms of heterosexuality per se.

neoliberalism, but it cushions the individual from the harshness of the marketplace, especially in the context of economic globalisation, which is presumed to be unstoppable (Bell and Binnie, 2000: 111).

Successful families are central to the rebuilding of strong communities, and provide the key defence against antisocial behaviour. They teach children the values of citizenship, and ensure that they learn responsibility and the importance of active citizenship participation (but, most crucially, the importance of paid employment). As former Home Secretary Jack Straw made explicit in his introduction to the Government's *Supporting Families* consultation paper, 'family life is the foundation on which our communities, our society and our country are built' (Home Office, 1998: 3). Although New Labour may recognise the existence of a diversity of family forms (and, in that sense, may be interpreted as 'pluralistic'), it also takes a highly conformist and singular view of the role of the family. Interestingly, the New Labour 'model' family now seems to feature two working parents, suggesting a changed view of 'motherhood' in cultural production, and there also appears to be a realisation that families can be dysfunctional and violent social units (Pascall, 1999: 261). Yet, at the same time, the family remains on a pedestal, and there is a role for the active state in ensuring that families meet their social responsibilities (Barlow and Duncan, 2000b: 133–34). In this regard, it has been argued that the focus on the family allows New Labour to individualise (or 'familialise') social problems, in that 'bad' families (or, more accurately, 'bad' parenting) is to blame (Pascall, 1999: 264). This serves to implicate, in particular, families who do not fit the 'ideal' form. However, a discourse of blame is largely avoided in favour of a focus on 'efficiency'; the two working parent family is the most efficient model since it most easily combines work and parenting (and that family form will be assisted by the state, which will encourage enterprise to adopt 'family friendly' workplace policies) (Pascall, 1999: 263; Barlow and Duncan, 2000a: 28). But the efficiency value of a two parent household—and even a 'democratic' family—easily slips into the advocacy of the institution of marriage, which, according to *Supporting Families,* remains 'the surest foundation for raising children' (Home Office, 1998: 4), and, most helpfully, 'sets out rights and responsibilities for all concerned' (thereby providing a useful microcosm of the social) (31). The centrality of the family raises, of course, the question 'what is a family?'—and 'what is a "good" family?'—questions which New Labour is quite willing to tackle, and which play a key role in the debates.

Fifthly, New Labour emphasises the importance of consensus within One Nation. It supports a multicultural society characterised by tolerance and acceptance of 'difference' (but with limits to difference); in which there are claimed to be no underlying, structural conflicts between diverse interests, and in which social cohesion prevails (Levitas, 1998: 113–15). Such a society is not only good in itself, but is crucial to economic competitiveness under global capitalism. In the Third Way, there is nothing fundamentally wrong with society that cannot be fixed by stronger communities, social inclusion (ie paid work), and strong families who know how to raise children; and the state can help facilitate those things, all of which lead to a consensual national space (Fairclough, 2000: 65).

Sixthly, and finally, there is a faith in managerialism and law. Social problems can be solved if we think about them carefully enough, and come up with strategies to manage them and to encourage the individual to manage herself (to act responsibly, aware of the risks of behaviour) (Bell and Binnie, 2000: 114). In this, there is a role for the state and for law, and law is assumed to be effective as a device for encouraging responsible behaviour (from criminal law to taxation), creating self-disciplined and self-governing citizens through the proper incentives and disincentives. For those who fail to govern themselves, more punitive legal measures may follow. There is obviously a built-in assumption here about individuals as rational choice decision-makers, and there is an apparent contradiction between a faith in communities (suggesting a devolution of power to the local, however it may be defined), and a belief in the managerial power of law as a centralising, juridical tool which promotes social control and discipline (see Barlow and Duncan, 2000b: 141; Driver and Martell, 1997: 43; Epstein, Johnson and Steinberg, 2000: 12).

What should be readily apparent is that these concepts are all highly mobile and manipulable and, while they may not, in all cases, seem immediately relevant to the sexuality debates, I argue that they all play a vital role. They all function both in 'progressive' ways, in widening and deepening an idea of sexual citizenship, but also, simultaneously, they operate in ways which shape and constrain it (or, to use terminology from chapter 1, to discipline and normalise). In this way, we can find both continuities with the 'old' conservative discourses around sexuality, but also clear breaks with the past; and both are significant.

The connection between these core concepts of New Labour's Third Way, and the politics of sexuality, is central to this chapter. It has been suggested that there is a fundamental tension within New Labour. On the one hand, there appears a genuine belief in social pluralism, evident in support for 'gay rights' claims and a rhetoric of inclusivity, as well as in the central role for equality discourse. On the other hand, the rhetoric of community, family, nation, morality, and the linking of rights to responsibilities, can easily be deployed in ways inimical to lesbian and gay politics (see generally Bell and Binnie, 2000). Furthermore, there is a strongly Christian underpinning to much of the Blairite ideology, evident in a recognition of an important role for religion in shaping and guiding community (see Wilkinson, 1999). This feature of the Third Way may give many lesbians and gays (and no doubt many others) cause for concern. As Alan Wilkinson (1999: 49) pointedly asks, summing up the tension between these two faces of New Labour: 'there is an unresolved tension between Blair's libertarianism about gay rights and gender and his rejection of it over the family. What happens when pluralism threatens the common good?' (see also Durham, 2001: 473). Of course, it all depends on how the common good is to be constituted; and this, I would suggest, is where an analysis of Parliamentary discourse can play a useful role.

Although the majoritarian consensus upon which communitarian discourse is founded *could* certainly be constituted in such a way as to be supportive of lesbian and gay politics (ie through a progressive, inclusive, voluntary form of communitarianism), history suggests that sexual dissidents should be wary of communitarian rhetoric. Communitarianism—with its frequent focus on family, morality, responsibility, and nationhood—has tended to either ignore or exclude (sometimes vociferously) lesbians and gays.[8] Yet, as Carlos Ball (2000) has argued, an ideological recognition of the important role of communities in forming individual identity certainly is compatible with many lesbian and gay experiences of coming out, and could usefully be deployed to validate that experience. It is also closely related to a lesbian feminist standpoint epistemology which envisions community as the locus of intelligibility, authority and authenticity. However, as Ball also notes, communitarianism tends to downplay communities of 'choice' in favour of communities of 'birth,' as choice comes to be associated with liberalism, autonomy, and voluntarism (the antithesis of the communitarian impulse) (474). Moreover, for those constituted as 'minorities,' liberalism and rights will seem appealing in the face of the communitarian emphasis on the common good, civic virtue and homogeneity (particularly when communitarianism becomes tied to conservative religions). Thus, while the core concepts of community, family, and nation may be highly mobile and manipulable, it is hardly surprising that many should remain sceptical, given that these concepts have not tended to be interpreted progressively on their behalf. For that reason as well, a close interrogation of the use of these discourses within Parliamentary debates around sexuality issues seems timely and appropriate.

Turning to the debates themselves, my focus is primarily upon the speeches of Labour MPs, especially those identified with New Labour, but also opposition MPs who supported reform (particularly to the extent that they may also appropriate elements of Third Way ideology).[9] Opponents of reform demonstrated discursive continuities with earlier debates during Conservative governments. But, at the same time, these conservative speakers also sought to distance themselves from homophobia, by emphasising their support for the protection of vulnerable (to homosexuality) children, rather than their distaste for homosexuals per se (although I would argue that this shift in discourse should not be overstated).[10] It is also important to note the considerable number of women

[8] I develop a number of examples of this construction in Stychin (1998).

[9] The quotations from debates which I use are intended as illustrative and, in many cases, innumerable similar quotations by different speakers could have been drawn upon to make the same point.

[10] I use the term 'conservative' to signify opponents of law reform, no matter what their party affiliation; and 'Conservative' to indicate the Conservative Party. For an important analysis of changes within Conservative Party discourse, see Waites (2000).

MPs who participated in these debates, largely, but certainly not exclusively, on the side of reform. Of far less significance, but still interesting, is the presence of 'out' (and 'outish') gay MPs, some of whom contributed to the debates, although usually in a way which distances the personal from the Parliamentary. That is, they tended not to draw explicitly upon personal narrative and experience, a discursive strategy which was quite common amongst (ostensibly) heterosexual MPs (both reform and opposition minded), who usually heterosexualised themselves explicitly in the debates. However, in one exchange, the homosexuality of Parliamentarians was itself brought into the spotlight in an exchange between two reform-minded MPs:

> Mr Bill Etherington (Sunderland, North): . . . I must say in all honesty that I do not think I have met half a dozen homosexuals in my life, although I have read a lot about them and have heard people speak about the subject.
> Ms Oona King (Bethnel Green and Bow): There are half a dozen on these benches.
> Mr Etherington: I should be grateful if my Hon. Friends would give me a count. It is good to get a bit of information (Commons, *Hansard*, 10 February 2000, col 459).

In this moment, the presumption of compulsory heterosexuality is displaced, in a move which perhaps indicates a hegemonic shift in the extent and degree to which homosexuals are viewed as 'outsiders' to this imagined community. But, as I will show in the next section, the inside/out dichotomy would be deployed in interesting and novel ways in the debates when it came to the construct of 'family.'

RECENTRING THE FAMILY

Of all the discourses deployed by law reform advocates, none is more central than the 'family' and its defence. This is perhaps not surprising, given that the debates focused centrally on teenage sexuality (in that the section 28 debate was—wrongly—assumed primarily to involve sex education in schools). However, the extent to which—and, more crucially, the *way* in which—family was deployed remains significant and somewhat surprising. The invocation of the family as a justification for reforming the law also raises the related issue of 'who is a family?,' a question that has never troubled conservative politicians. In New Labour speeches, we find the family centre stage. This is particularly and predictably apparent in the various speeches of Ann Keen MP, who played a leading role in all of the debates, and who explicitly takes her position as the mother of a gay son. She is one of the few politicians who does not distance gay sexuality from her family.

The use of familial discourse, however, does not prove to be a strategy whereby the family is redefined or radicalised. Rather, what proves interesting and significant, is the degree to which the traditional heterosexual family is recentred in the debates. Within these narratives of family life, gays are placed, not within families of choice, but back from whence they came: in their families of birth. They are centred in the nuclear family home: 'every homosexual man or woman *comes from* a family, and depends on the love and support *within that* family' (Commons, *Hansard*, 25 January 1999, col 77, Mr Borrow (emphasis added)). For many reformers, any discriminatory law (be it an unequal age of consent or section 28) undermines the traditional family to the extent to which these laws foster negative and hostile attitudes towards gay members within it. Such bigotry becomes an attack on the family as a unit (and as a community). Thus, we find an appropriation of the discursive terrain previously occupied largely by conservatives, by the law reformers. Discriminatory laws become an affront to the family, as it has been traditionally understood. And the family is itself chastised to the extent that it does not accept and love its gay children, who have been forced to leave their families in some cases. Of course, the possibility that gay youth may choose to reject their families is itself never seen as a possibility, nor is family seen as something from which you might want to escape.

Consequently, one of the important benefits of law reform is that it will protect and strengthen the family unit—a central Third Way institution—which plays such an important role in the inculcation of the values of citizenship. In this moment, the traditional family is seen to have failed to some extent (by not being inclusive enough), but this is correctable through education and enlightenment. That is, we can make families more democratic and inclusive. Familial discourse also provides law reformers with an important rhetorical device; speakers continually justify their positions 'as a mother' or 'as a father' (as a position of both authority and experience).[11] Indeed, at some points, discriminatory law is explicitly described as being offensive to families (Commons, *Hansard*, 10 February 2000, col 448, Ms Keen), and law reform will be 'a relief for parents and a modest contribution to family life' (Commons, *Hansard*, 25 January 1999, col 65, Mr MacShane). Thus, the homosexual is occluded completely by the family to which he has been returned. The individual has become embedded in a social unit, and is defined only in terms of membership therein.

The debates focus to a large extent on gay youth within families. For reformers, unlike conservatives, the idea of 'gay youth' is quite commonplace and even 'normal.' Rather, the problems arise from law and social attitudes, particularly manifested by bullying (which is an important justification raised for the repeal of section 28). Gay youth sexuality is itself seen as very unproblematic, and the reason why, it is clear, is that it is consistently essentialised and, usually, biologised by law reformers.[12] Sexual identity is described over and over as not being a choice, and it is certainly not a matter of any ambiguity, flux or the so

[11] For example, 'I shall revert to the position of a mother who must consider as her children grow the sort of world that she wants them to occupy' (Commons, *Hansard*, 25 January 1999, col 55, Ms Mountford).

[12] This use of essentialist discourse has been a strategy engaged in by law reformers throughout the history of law reform.

called 'grey area.'[13] As Epstein, Johnson and Steinberg (2000: 17) have characterised it, law reformers draw upon the belief in an 'age of fixation'—assumed to be prior to 16 years—when sexuality is fixed in stone. This creates an *essentially* fixed group within society; another minority in need of protection.[14] The importance of equal treatment of minorities (and families) then justifies reform of the laws. While conservatives have long argued that there are two essential types of homosexuals—the congenital and those converted by a homosexual experience during adolescence—reformers claim that only the first type actually exists. In this way, they seek to answer conservative claims that 'youth' is a particularly vulnerable moment at which childhood innocence may be corrupted and perverted (see Moran, 2001: 82; Monk, 1998), as a fixed homosexual identity now becomes 'a signifier of maturity achieved and of rational identity' (Epstein, Johnson and Steinberg, 2000: 17).

Gay male youth—who thus have no choice as to their sexual *orientation*—do have choices, however, as to their relationships (and, for reformers, these relationships must not be criminalised by the age of consent). While conservatives draw on the figures of the predator and the wayward teenage boy, reformers construct a remarkably romanticised (and, indeed, romantic) picture of gay youth. In so doing, gay youth are largely desexualised, but they must also be taught responsible behaviour through open and honest sex education, leading to a delay in embarking upon sexual activity (Commons, *Hansard*, 5 July 2000, col 365, Mr Hall), and, it seems inevitably, leading to monogamous long-term relationships. Rights and responsibilities are thereby connected. This also underscores how youth more generally are increasingly seen as active agents—bearers of rights and responsibilities—capable of good citizenship and dangerous deviance (while also capable of romanticisation as innocents, at the same time) (see generally Vaughan, 2000). Thus, as a consequence of the lowering of the age of consent, 'for the first time, 16-year-old *citizens* will be absolutely clear that they are responsible for their own sexual behaviour' (Commons, *Hansard*, 22 June 1998, col 778, Mr Allan (emphasis added)).

Youth are also seen as *knowing*—as saturated with information—but lacking in appropriate teaching on responsibility. They are no longer innocent children, devoid of knowledge (nor, therefore, should they be easily corruptible). For reformers, youth is a stage of development quite distinct from childhood, and much closer to adulthood.[15] What is seen as necessary, then, is 'the cultivation of a more active subjectivity within young people who will be required to take more responsibility for their lives' (Vaughan, 2000: 348).

[13] For example, 'All the experts agree that the vast majority of people's sexual orientation does not have that element of choice, so we should stop even talking about lifestyles' (Commons, *Hansard*, 25 January 1999, col 23, Mr Bradshaw); 'sexuality is a genetic trait' (Commons, *Hansard*, 25 January 1999, col 58, Ms Mountford).

[14] And, once constructed as a minority, it does not challenge the idea of a coherent, fixed, naturalised majority population.

[15] Conservatives, by contrast, almost always characterise the issue as centred on 'children': Moran (2001: 84).

Interestingly, by contrast, within New Labour discourse, *heterosexual* youth, while also romanticised to some degree, are increasingly constructed as quite dangerous, out of control figures.[16] Straight male youth are in danger of being drawn into delinquency, and of ignoring the importance of education and work. Straight female youth are in danger of getting pregnant by the irresponsible straight male youth. Thus, in a discursive switch, young heterosexuals are seen to be hypersexualised—and in need of more intensive regulation at various sites—while young gay men are quite desexualised. Young lesbians, for the most part, seem not to exist at all.

This same rhetorical trope of desexualisation is found in reformers' descriptions of gay male sexuality more generally (and not just youth) (and, even in the section 28 debates, gay women's sexuality is largely erased, a point of importance). Thus, for example, in answer to the usual conservative refrain about HIV infection, one reformer explains that 'only a minority of gay men engage in that activity' (Commons, *Hansard*, 25 January 1999, col 93, Ms Blears). And, as an aside, heterosexual sex is often described by reformers as being itself dangerous to health (rather than 'natural'), not only in terms of HIV, but also with respect to pregnancy (see eg, Commons, *Hansard*, 25 January 1999, col 97, Ms Hughes). No doubt some of this rhetoric is strategic, in that law reformers seek to answer conservative claims of homosexual hypersexualisation and perversion, through a strategic desexualising. That is, they emphasise an essential 'sameness,' while also emphasising respect for 'difference,' which is justified because underneath the difference is a sameness in terms of, for example, relationship forms. This combination of sameness and difference is to be found in many contributions by law reformers: 'no choice is made, other than that of a particular partner' (Commons, *Hansard*, 25 January 1999, col 58, Ms Mountford); 'they will be able to plan long-term relationships and feel that they can play a full and open part in the wider community' (Commons, *Hansard*, 25 January 1999, col 78, Mr Borrow); 'it is about time that families were all equal' (Commons, *Hansard*, 22 June 1998, col 762, Ms Keen). But, at the same time, we find limits to acceptable social change within reform discourse: 'Nobody in Britain wants the promotion of homosexuality. People in Britain want tolerance, fairness and understanding' (Commons, *Hansard*, 25 July 2000, col 1053, Mr Woodward).

Thus, for reformers, homosexuality should not be (but then it cannot be) promoted. It is a condition that demands toleration, and it cannot be dangerous because it is not contagious. But it is also non-threatening because it can be, *and it needs to be*, channelled into relationships that are about romantic love; part of a process of normalisation which I outlined in chapter 1—'a banalised respectability' (Warner, 1999: 66) or as Katherine O'Donovan (1993: 59) has put it, 'a kind of uniform monotony to our fates'. But, then again, heterosexual

[16] See, eg, the Crime and Disorder Act 1998, and, for an analysis of the construction of youth as dangerous in relation to that legislation, see Vaughan (2000); see also Morris and Gelsthorpe (2000).

young people are seen as even more in need of normalisation because they are particularly out of control.[17]

Who must normalise the young into citizenship? The answer is clear: the traditional family, which is central, and an institution that has been failing. It has failed its gay youth by ostracising them, not recognising that children are split into two groups upon the age of fixation and that they need to be treated as separate but equal (and parents must just accept this essential 'splitting of gay from straight as separate communities') (Epstein, Johnson and Steinberg, 2000: 20).[18] This gay friendliness characterises the modernised New Labour family, and many Parliamentary speakers—who have young children—go on at some length about how they will accept their children should they turn out gay. Other elements of New Labour's modernised family include: two working parents; egalitarianism and negotiation of roles; contractualism between adults (a 'deal'); and, a public, hopefully democratic institution in which the state has a managerial role because of the family's public importance (Fairclough, 2000: 43).[19]

Richard Collier (2000) has described these developments as producing a kind of de-essentialised family—a 'queering' of the family—in which the heterosexual, nuclear family has become quite plastic, in that it is open to being shaped so as to meet individual wants and needs (and this connects to some of the Third Way intellectual labour provided by Anthony Giddens (1992)). As Collier (2000: 66) has argued, 'the diverse practices which presently constitute "the familial" are being transformed, fragmented and reconstituted' (see also Fineman, 1995). While this may be true to a considerable extent, what has not been de-essentialised is the assumption that child raising is the primary function of the family, and that is why the family must be upheld and strengthened. The family, after all, is the production site of good citizens. Thus, it becomes understandable why the 'lesbian mother' (and, perhaps more generally, the lesbian) as a subject seems not to exist in reform discourse. Children are assumed to be raised by heterosexual parents (and young women seem only to enter public discourse as pathologised heterosexual single mothers). While gay children ultimately may form long-term partnerships which reformers might be prepared to characterise as families, the assumption is that these families are childless. In that sense, the heterosexual nuclear family remains firmly centred in reform discourse,[20] and the

[17] Warner (1999: 56) usefully provides three definitions of normalisation: 'certified, approved, as meeting a set of normative standards'; 'authorizing people as full members of society'; 'a standard, a criterion of value'.

[18] Of course, this discursive move erases the possibility of bisexuality, let alone bisexual youth.

[19] The interventionist role for the state in family life can be seen at other sites, particularly concerning the treatment of delinquent children (and their parents) in the Crime and Disorder Act 1998; see Fionda (1999: 46).

[20] In fact, the spectre of lesbian motherhood seems to have lost its discursive power in conservative discourse, compared to the debates of the 1980s. The demonised 'single mother'—assumed to be heterosexual—may well have replaced lesbian mothers in this regard. Perhaps this is because lesbian mothers are assumed to be coupled with at least one partner in employment. Moreover, the category of lesbian mother raises the spectre of spousal benefits for same sex couples, which New Labour would prefer to avoid. Thanks to Davina Cooper for this point.

couple form remains the normalised basis for many citizenship entitlements, such as some aspects of welfare provision (Bell and Binnie, 2000: 67).[21]

SOCIAL INCLUSION AND THE MAKING OF AN INSIDER

> Although [the Third Way] purports to govern while respecting the autonomy of individuals and associational life, this strategy to sustain civility through community actually seeks to inscribe the norms of self-control more deeply into the soul of each citizen than is thought possible through either disciplinary technologies such as mass schooling or through social technologies such as those of welfare states (Rose, 2000: 1409).

The construct of good citizenship is linked to the idea of social inclusion, the second theme of Third Way ideology which is central to the sexuality debates. Much has been written on the uses of social inclusion within New Labour discourse, and the fact that it is a particular kind of inclusion that is emphasised; one in which participation in paid employment is the defining feature of the social and of inclusion (see eg Barlow and Duncan, 2000a; Levitas, 1998; Driver and Martell, 1997). Citizenship and paid work go hand in hand. In fact, there has been considerable feminist critique of how, while New Labour emphasises the role of child care in the family, it devalues unpaid caring work as not being key to social inclusion (see eg Perrigo, 1999: 174). Rather, the working two parent family is the most efficient, economical and (according to statistics being used) effective means of raising children and inculcating the values of citizenship. Strengthening these families is a means of restoring social cohesion and social inclusion, again providing the antidote to the individualising impact of the market (Bell and Binnie, 2000: 111).

This role of the family in social re/production might suggest that gays will play no significant role in a discourse of social inclusion. To the extent that they are (often wrongly) assumed not to be producers of children, gays are not a factor in social production in that sense. Rather, they become associated with waste rather than production (Bell and Binnie, 2000: 74). It has also been argued that the normalisation of the heterosexual nuclear family—and the hetero-homo binary itself—was historically related to the importance of that family form to a capitalist economy (Morgan, 1998). That position, however, is not particularly relevant to the debates. It comes up in some conservative discourse (ie having children is what makes you valuable to society), but not having children is less problematic for New Labour than having children irresponsibly.

[21] With respect to the family, I would distinguish the UK experience from Bech's (1997: ch 6) analysis of Danish partnership law. Bech argues that it is only with the 'decline' of marriage and the family that the introduction of registered partnerships became politically possible (202). In the United Kingdom, by contrast, I would argue that it is the perception of crisis in, and the importance of 'rebuilding' the family, that is key to New Labour's incorporation of lesbians and gay men within the 'national' family (although not yet through partnership legislation).

Indeed, some reformers emphasise that normalcy does not demand being married with children (Commons, *Hansard*, 10 February 2000, col 471, Ms King). One reform argument is that a climate of homophobia—which is continually connected to discriminatory laws—leads inevitably to 'sham' marriages, unwanted children, and broken homes (Commons, *Hansard*, 10 February 2000, col 480, Dr Harris). These are the worst acts of citizenship. Much better is a situation where there is no sham, in which gays are in long-term (same sex) relationships (but not married), and know their proper, private place on the right side of an essentialised hetero-homo binary. And the pay off will be social inclusion (although, of course, not access to public institutions such as marriage). Consequently, there will no longer be a need, either, to 'make a fuss' through protest.[22] That is, with social inclusion, there will be no reason to advocate radical social change or social transformation—since society is not really in need of anything except greater inclusion (Fairclough, 2000: 65). This is quite an important device in Third Way ideology: an appropriation of some elements of reform agendas developed by new social movements (particularly feminism), but in a deradicalised and depoliticised form (a tactic deployed not infrequently by Giddens himself) (McRobbie, 2000).

Of course, the other social inclusion function played by lesbians and gays is paid employment. Indeed, this citizenship role can be performed better in the absence of children, given the importance of 'family friendly' employment policies—advocated strongly by New Labour—as a means of strengthening the family and child raising (Pascall, 1999: 263). The childless worker provides a vital function, ensuring that the workplace remains internationally competitive (another key New Labour trope), and also performs the citizenship role, not only of producer of goods and services (if not children), but also of *consumer* of goods and services (Bell and Binnie, 2000: 74). The trade off for fulfilling these citizenship functions is, again, social inclusion. To work is to *deserve* inclusion, and to consume is to deserve to be treated equally as consumer. Work is the fundamental social responsibility from which rights flow, and it is the condition upon which rights are granted.

This creates a certain tension around rights discourse. On the one hand, New Labour displays a commitment to fundamental human rights (in the form particularly of the European Convention on Human Rights and the Human Rights Act 1998), as absolute, cosmopolitan, universal claims that are, in some sense, unconditional (unlike the government's position on much *European Union* legislation, such as that designed to protect employment *rights*). That commitment is also apparent in the debates, in certain moments, when law reform is said to be inevitable in order to comply with the Convention and the Human Rights Act, and the issues are described as centred on human rights and equality.[23] But

[22] Thereby not only taking the sex out of homosexuality, but the politics as well!

[23] For example, 'why do we not draw a line in the sand on this fundamental issue of human rights?' (Commons, *Hansard*, 25 July 2000, cols 1046–47, Mr McDonnell).

this underscores how New Labour is a blending of liberal and communitarian elements (and that, in practice, there are no pure forms of either).

However, despite the importance of the discourse of equality rights to the debates, the use of the language of equality is matched by the deployment of the theme of social inclusion plus responsibility. As one reformer, during an age of consent debate, put it: 'by amending the law, we will make them part of a civil and civilised society' (Commons, *Hansard*, 25 January 1999, col 48, Mr Woodward). This phrase is unintentionally loaded with significance, indicating not only the importance of inclusion per se, but also the civilising function of inclusion and recognition (a point which I will develop further in Chapter 3 in the context of French republicanism). Reviewing the debates, inclusion seems to embrace the following ideas: long-term relationships; monogamy; no promotion of one's sexuality; remaining in a respectable sphere; avoiding *that* practice; avoiding heterosexual sex (since it is beyond one's nature); working hard; refraining from protest. These appear to be the indices of civilised citizenship behaviour, and this is also manifested in the debates through the positive characterisation of the organisation Stonewall, which acts metonymically for the civilised, gay citizen, even among some anti-law reform members (and, interestingly, campaigner Peter Tatchell is repeatedly the demonised other to civilisation) (Epstein, Johnson and Steinberg, 2000: 19).[24]

This focus on conduct and civility (as well as propriety) neatly demonstrates how, as Nikolas Rose (2000: 1399) has cogently argued, the Third Way embodies a new 'politics of behavior,' which he terms 'ethnopolitics.' The sexuality debates underscore various ways in which 'citizenship becomes conditional on conduct' (1407), through 'the micromanagement of the self-steering practices of its citizens' (1408). The flipside of the promise of inclusion is, of course, exclusion, which Rose (2000: 1406) describes as 'the absence of the stabilization of conduct and self-control,' which can easily be inscribed on uncivilised sexual subjects. My argument here is that this ethnopolitics is implicit (and often explicit) in 'liberal' Third Way sexuality discourse.

At this point, a provisional conclusion that there is a shifting in the hegemonic construction of the good homosexual, in the period since the 1980s, can be drawn. As I explained at the outset, in the 1980s, the good homosexual (as drawn by many conservatives) was a completely closeted, lone figure on the secret fringes of society, who knew that he belonged there, and accepted his lot. He entered the public sphere only as a completely desexualised subject. By contrast, the new respectability—at least from a reading of the House of Commons debates—sugggests a somewhat different good homosexual (now drawn by many progressive-minded politicians). In large measure, this may be due to a generational change amongst Members of Parliament, and a recognition that

[24] This construction of acceptable homosexuality illustrates Bell and Binnie's (2000: 30) observation that rights and citizenship claims seem only to 'work' through 'replicating heterosexual articulations of the "good citizen".'

gays are one of the constituencies/social groups to be managed, included and represented; one more community in a multicultural society; one more (no doubt sophisticated) focus group. This is a shift, and it is here that some important strategic space may be opened up by New Labour discourse and, particularly, as I will develop in the next section, in its use of the language of community.

MANY COMMUNITIES/ONE NATION

Many have argued that community, for New Labour, carries a multiplicity of meanings depending on the context (see eg Freeden, 1999: 45). It can mean the local; civil society; the nation writ large; the state; or communities of interest. Within the debates, lesbians and gays become, for reformers, a community group, and this is facilitated, to a considerable degree, by New Labour's focus on the individual as part of communities rather than as isolated. Reform-minded politicians speak frequently of the gay community, diversity, and multiculturalism.[25] This is significant to the extent that it may suggest a recognition of 'group membership as a definitive component of social life,' rather than abstracting individuals into ' "universal" citizens' (Rahman, 2000: 168; see also Ball, 2000: 468). The recognition of sexuality as constitutive of group membership has the potential, it has been argued, to 'trouble' heteronormativity—representing, as it does, a shift from the idea of afflicted individuals to a recognised segment of the wider community, seeking recognition, resources, and representation on that basis (Rahman, 2000: 192). Third Way discourse facilitates that move, although it needs to be acknowledged that with recognition comes an expectation that communities will regulate and manage themselves—become self-disciplinary—and it can also result in a 'downloading' of the obligations associated with the state on to the voluntary sector in the form of community groups (who, in the process, become 'responsible' members of their community and have a responsibility to police that community).[26]

However, community within New Labour discourse, as I have suggested, is a mobile concept, and it is often invoked to signify 'nation' (as itself the local) within an inevitably globalising, economically neoliberal world order (see Bell and Binnie, 2000: 111; Fairclough, 2000: 15). This construct of community emerges in a number of my case studies. In this moment, community is seen as crucial for success in the new world order and, of most importance, is the idea(l) of community as a conflict free zone. This imagined national community has no deep-seated, structural conflicts of interest. Rather, there is a common interest in competitiveness in the world which transcends differences within (and, in

[25] For two of the innumerable examples, see Commons, *Hansard*, 5 July 2000, col 360, Mr Borrow; Commons, *Hansard*, 22 June 1998, col 756, Ms Keen.

[26] Community groups promoting safer sex practices might well exemplify this point.

that sense, the nation is inclusive in that all should contribute to its competitiveness) (McRobbie, 2000: 102). Notions of fairness and social cohesion are seen as key to the achievement of competitiveness; thereby bringing the different strands of New Labour discourse together. In this moment, equality discourse assumes a heightened significance, as a key signifier of the New Labour, New Nation project of a modern, civilised, progressive society (Epstein, Johnson and Steinberg, 2000: 20).

This construction of nation/community is frequent and important in the debates, and can also be connected to New Labour's conception of a '*New* Britain.' Within conservative discourse, the construct of nation is often manipulated in the service of heterosexuality as norm. For example, within Thatcherite discourse, to repeat, gays were constructed both as outside the space of nation and as the enemy within, as were ethnic minorities (and now so called bogus asylum seekers) (see Smith, 1994). The nation is constituted as a space of tolerance for respectable homosexuals, as long as they know their (closeted) place within it.

But within New Labour discourse, we again find both continuities and ruptures with the past. Law reform itself becomes implicated in the process of reconstituting the nation as progressive, modern, civilised, enlightened and inclusive; all of which are necessary in order for it to be competitive. Conservatives have been 'intent on dividing our society' (this time along sexual lines), and progressive law reform is now necessary to repair that damage (Commons, *Hansard*, 25 July 2000, col 1036, Ms Armstrong). Reform is described by numerous speakers in terms of progress, modernity, and the creation of a civil and civilised society. It is hardly surprising that conservatives respond to this one new nation discourse with the claim that these ideas represent, not one nation, but 'government's metropolitan attitudes [and] their domination by a liberal elite' (Commons, *Hansard*, 3 July 2000, col 343, Mr Waterson), as well as by the 'chattering classes' (Commons, *Hansard*, 25 July 2000, col 1039, Mr Waterson).

This inclusive, conflict free society is achieved through finding a consensual, middle road: the Third Way.[27] This characterisation of the law reform initiatives is apparent in the debates. With respect both to the repeal of section 28 (but, more importantly, the implementation of what are highly conservative education guidelines around sex education[28]), and in the equalisation of the age of consent (but also in the child protection measures which accompany it), New

[27] It is worth recalling that the Conservative Party of the 1980s characterised its own policies, such as s 28, as creating consensus through a middle ground: Smith (1994: 226).

[28] See eg the Guidelines issued on 7 July 2000, which impact *directly* on schools: 'pupils should be taught about the nature and importance of marriage for family life and bringing up children'; 'pupils should learn the significance of marriage and stable relationships as key building blocks of community and society'; 'teachers should be able to deal honestly and sensitively with sexual orientation, answer appropriate questions and offer support. There should be no direct promotion of sexual orientation'.

Labour characterises its position as one of balance between competing, untenable, divisive extremes. It is balancing the protection of children, on the one hand, with promoting equality and inclusion, on the other; or balancing the importance of the institution of marriage with pluralism in relationships. This is consensual politics, to the extent that anyone who differs is an extremist: either against equality or in favour of the promotion of homosexuality (and both become similarly beyond the pale).[29]

The constant refrain of diversity, multiculturalism, and equality is also meant to signify that we are in the midst of an evolutionary process whereby all (who are law abiding) can be brought within the national space as part of a process of modernisation and progress. And this narrative of progress is also developed by connecting it to processes of European integration (a theme which is central to many of the chapters in *Governing Sexuality*). The reform of the age of consent is described as 'catching up' to other EU Member States in terms of an equality agenda (Commons, *Hansard*, 22 June 1998, col 756, Ms Keen). Moreover, legal change is justified in terms of the importance of compliance with the European Convention on Human Rights, which is itself seen both as a marker and measure of a civilised society. Interestingly, the Convention is consistently described as having been British in origin and as having been re-made as British through the Human Rights Act 1998 (Commons, *Hansard*, 28 July 1998, col 209, Mr Straw).[30]

Ironically, the New Labour language of community, multiculturalism, inclusion and diversity, has an antecedent in the policies and discourses of the Greater London Council of the 1980s, and the 'loony left' local government politics of the time (which, after all, was the claimed justification for the introduction of section 28 in the first place).[31] The difference, however, is that while New Labour's sexuality politics may entail the granting of *rights* (albeit with responsibilities attached), there is little evidence that recognition as a community results in the allocation of public *resources*. While the acceptance of the appropriateness of the language of community for sexual dissidents opens a discursive terrain for making claims to resources, the likelihood of actually obtaining them (for any community) is another matter. Rights and social inclusion—in the way in which they have been formulated in this context—lack an obvious

[29] See eg Commons, *Hansard*, 22 February 2000, col 1356, Dr Reid: 'we are required not only to defend ourselves against those whom he mentioned who would proselytise and promote homosexuality, but to protect children in our schools—all children.'

[30] With respect to this deployment of nation, interesting contrasts might be drawn to the Scottish Parliament debates on s 28 (and the process of devolution itself sits uneasily with the language of 'One Nation'). A detailed analysis of those debates is beyond the scope of this chapter, but it is clear from reviewing them that the language of nation is repeatedly invoked by law reformers, in a much more explicit way than was the case in Westminster. But, interestingly, the reform agenda is described, not so much as a Third Way consensus between reasonable people, but much more about the need to make choices about how 'nation' is to be constructed: whether a progressive or regressive nation; whether it will be rational or emmeshed in stereotypes.

[31] Thanks to Anna Marie Smith for bringing this point to my attention. For an analysis of the politics of that period, see Cooper (1994).

financial cost to the state. This dichotomy between a politics of recognition and a politics of redistribution is central to my argument throughout this book.

Opponents of the repeal of section 28 repeatedly sought to draw upon the (heavily overdetermined) legacy of 'loony left' politics, and the fear that the (presumed heterosexual) taxpayer would end up funding 'homosexuality on the rates' (Moran, 2001: 81). In this way, blatantly homophobic discourses could be replaced by a defence of the taxpayer and the particular fiduciary duty of local government to that taxpayer (and, as Moran argues, 'taxpayer' stands in metonymically for the normalised, heterosexual, middle class family) (82). However, given the changed political climate of the left since the 1980s, and New Labour's ongoing courtship of the heterosexual family, such fears of public funding of gay sex lessons seem rather far-fetched today.

THE EFFICACY OF LAW

The final theme emerging from the debates—which again mirrors broader New Labour ideology—is the way in which law itself is perceived in the 'project'; and, specifically, the important role for law in promoting community, family and nation.

Within the sexuality debates, the role of law has a somewhat ambiguous and, at times, contradictory position, a point which is frequently commented upon by opponents of law reform (Commons, *Hansard*, 3 July 2000, col 341, Mr Waterson). On the one hand, reformers point to an array of consequences which are attributed directly to section 28 and to the unequal age of consent: homophobic bullying in schools; nail bomber attacks and other acts of homophobic violence; youth suicide; the criminalisation of teenage boys simply for having sexual relations with their teenage boyfriends; inadequate and ineffective sex education leading to the spread of HIV. As a consequence, the reform of the law is seen as a major initiative filled with significance. It becomes a landmark moment in a linear tale of progressive law reform; earlier signposts of which were the ending of the slave trade and the emancipation of women (Commons, *Hansard*, 25 January 1999, col 47, Mr Woodward). Indeed, law reform is described as a means of ending 'sexual apartheid' (Commons, *Hansard*, 11 April 2000, col 249, Mr Woodward). But, at the same time, reformers argue that the laws are completely ineffective as they stand. They consistently make the claim that the age of consent never stopped anyone from having sex (Commons, *Hansard*, 25 January 1999, col 29, Mr Straw), and that section 28 applies to local authorities, who no longer have a role in what schools teach anyway (Commons, *Hansard*, 5 July 2000, col 366, Ms Armstrong). Thus, the laws are seen as both extremely powerful (making their repeal full of significance), and also completely impotent.

However, we may be able to glean something about New Labour ideology from this consideration of the power of law. And what we find is an enormous faith in the power of progressive law reform: 'the redemptive power of good law' (Epstein, Johnson and Steinberg, 2000: 12). But law reform needs to be thought through 'rationally,' with reform embarked upon only by first turning to expert discourses for guidance (as opposed to emotions and stereotypes). Law becomes a tool of management (one of many for the state), in which the goal is the shaping of individual behaviour to conform to wider needs of community and nation (ie making good citizens) (Barlow and Duncan, 2000b: 141). An expectation of individual self-governance thereby is combined with the use of law and other regulatory and normative tools by the state.

Thus, we see, in both sets of debates, reformers continually drawing upon scientific or, preferably, medical knowledge, as the final trump card, and such knowledge becomes 'fact' which must override the prejudice of the uninformed (eg Commons, *Hansard*, 22 June 1998, cols 758–60, Ms Keen). Scientific/medical fact is asserted as proof which justifies law reform. Of course, many of these facts are far from capable of scientific proof, but then again, there is never any reference provided for the proof of the fact anyway. For example: 'It is now medically accepted that homosexuality is fixed at an early age and not at an age greater than 16' (Commons, *Hansard*, 22 June 1998, col 797, Dr Harris); and 'European countries that have a lower age of consent do not have a higher rate of homosexuality' (Commons, *Hansard*, 22 June 1998, col 798, Dr Harris).

Such 'facts' not only are incapable of proof, but they are also loaded with a series of premises about what sexuality *is*. Interestingly, the comparison with the age of consent experience in 'Europe' is expounded upon by former Home Secretary Jack Straw in the age of consent debates: 'In those other European countries, there are other norms, which ensure that the kinds of conduct about which people would be extremely anxious do not, on the whole, take place' (Commons, *Hansard*, 25 January 1999, col 22, Mr Straw).

The implication here is that there can be little justification for an age of consent at all if it has no deterrent effect. Should we have an age of consent at 14, as in some European countries (thereby promoting legal harmonisation)? However, there are further 'facts' which distinguish the United Kingdom from continental Europe in terms of sexual mores. As Jack Straw explained, within 'Europe' we find strong family norms that control sexual behaviour amongst youth. This makes the age of consent of much less significance—so it can be set low. Here again, we find the failing of the family reappearing. Within the United Kingdom, law becomes a necessary means of social control, as the family (or, perhaps, the single mother specifically) has failed to curtail wayward homosexual behaviour amongst young people; just as it has failed to curtail so much other wayward behaviour amongst youth.

The point being that it is the current law which is ineffective, but law itself (if rationally thought through and based on expertise) is highly efficacious in shaping citizenship behaviour (and that behaviour is itself assumed to be based on a highly rational individual subject making rational choices) (see generally Barlow and Duncan, 2000a; 2000b). The current laws are ineffective, not because of the inherent limits of law, but because they run counter to fundamental facts: sexuality is fixed by age 16 and once people know who they are, they want to engage in responsible sexual relationships. You cannot promote homosexuality because there is no choice involved.

CONCLUSIONS

In this chapter, I have attempted to demonstrate, through the sexuality debates, the limitations to the ideal of liberal progress. First, I have suggested, drawing on the argument raised in chapter 1, that a complex dynamic between legal liberalisation and the normalisation or banalisation and management of the self is apparent. This dynamic is characteristic of citizenship and social inclusion rhetoric more broadly. To be socially included is also to be manageable, and to agree to manage oneself, and to be an object of surveillance; and it is to enter voluntarily into that field of surveillance, as a socially included subject. As Bell and Binnie (2000: 2) demonstrate, resort to the discourses of citizenship, rights, and social inclusion inevitably carries 'the burden of compromise . . . the circumscription of "acceptable" modes of being a sexual citizen'; creating both opportunities and limitations in the process.

Secondly, what the debates reveal is that it may well be fallacious to assume that communitarian discourses will necessarily lead to a conservative vision of family and nation, and that liberalism (and rights) is the richest discourse for gays to mine. Obviously, in the world of practical politics, there are no pure forms of either. But liberalism and rights have their clear limitations (which have been well analysed), and communitarianism does not necessarily have to be of a kind that excludes lesbians and gays from an imagined community. Historically, it usually has taken such a form, but in a progressive mode, communitarianism does highlight the importance of community membership in identity formation and its importance to civil society. The recognition of sexual communities of choice—as constitutive of individual identity in a multicultural society—may well be a strategically important move for lesbian and gay politics (but also has its own limitations and problems).

Thirdly, an analysis of the sexuality debates underscores, in my view, that a hegemonic shift is occurring, in which conservative discourses—which were historically dominant—are being increasingly marginalised. This is not only due to the New Labour majority in the House of Commons. Rather, I think that what 30 years of coming out has achieved is a change in the way in which processes of distancing and proximity with respect to homosexuality, for heterosexuals, are experienced. To a large extent this is a generational shift. Distancing still occurs—MPs continually speak from their positions within the heterosexual nuclear family—but the proximity of homosexuals to them is closer, and that proximity is no longer pathologised to the same degree. However, at the same time, as Epstein, Johnson and Steinberg (2000: 20) point out, the essentialising of sexual identity, so prevalent amongst law reformers, does allow lesbians and gays, and their experiences, to be kept 'at a distance', as society is split into essentially different communities.

Yet, that brings me to the final point, which is an inversion of the proximity issue. Rather than focusing on the perspective of how near gays are allowed to come to the family, my interest in this book is in what happens—not to the heterosexual family due to the proximity of lesbians and gays—but to sexual dissidents when they are welcomed within the national 'family.' Like many others, I have argued elsewhere that the language of liberalism and rights is enormously seductive despite its disciplinarity (Stychin, 1998). But communitarianism in the form of social inclusion is also, I think, no less seductive: social inclusion in a consensual, conflict free space is on offer. And, as Bell and Binnie (2000: 146) query, with such an overwhelming emphasis on inclusion as a good in itself, will 'the choice to disidentify' from the social (and from the family, for that matter) be completely devalued? If the Third Way aims to govern through the 'micromanagement of the self-steering practices of its citizens' (Rose, 2000: 1408)—whether through legal or other means—then what forms can and should resistance take, to this new and invasive form of disciplinary power? Is the effectiveness of this form of management of the self to be found in the seductiveness of its promise of inclusion and acceptance? These are key issues to which I return, in other legal contexts, in subsequent chapters. Moreover, this analysis raises (but I leave unanswered) two further difficult questions that have been the focus of this chapter. First, on what (or whose) terms is inclusion offered? Secondly, if exclusion is always constitutive of the discourse of social inclusion, then the promise of social inclusion should make us ask: who has been excluded in this process of inclusion? Who remains outside the bounds of community?

All of these questions arise in different legal and cultural settings throughout *Governing Sexuality* and, while my focus in this chapter has been on the ways in which inclusion may be disciplinary, I do not wish to diminish the ways in which it may also be enabling (these are the two sides of citizenship discourse that I considered in chapter 1). In the next chapter, I continue my examination of these same fundamental questions, but within what proves to be a very different sexual/national cultural context: France.

3

Civil Solidarity or Fragmented Identities?: Sexuality and Citizenship in France

INTRODUCTION

IN RECENT YEARS, it has become common for lesbian and gay legal rights advocates to survey developments on a global basis: from decriminalisation, to anti-discrimination legislation, to the legal recognition of relationships, to the opening of the institution of marriage. These cross-cultural comparisons are said to tell a straightforward tale of legal progress, in which repressive regimes are explained away as anti-modern resistance to the globalisation of human rights around sexual identities. Variations thereby become reduced to matters of local interest. They are secondary to the similarity in the stories of progressive legal and social change unfolding worldwide, benefiting lesbians and gay men (see eg Herdt, 1997; and, for critique, see Bell and Binnie, 2000).

This chapter resists this approach to the study of lesbian and gay rights discourse, through a comparative analysis of a legal development in France, which is explicitly framed, not as a 'gay rights' victory, but as a means legally to recognise (and benefit) relationships which exist outside of the institution of marriage: the *pacte civil de solidarité* (or PACS, as it is commonly known). Through a genealogical study of the PACS, focusing on Parliamentary debates, media commentary, and analyses by intellectuals and activists, in this chapter I seek to demonstrate that a more complex relationship exists between discourses of the 'global' and the 'local' when faced with legal struggles around sexuality. This dynamic is best understood by focusing on the way in which arguments raised in the debate, both by proponents and opponents, were consistently grounded within the dominant discourse of French national identity: republicanism. The contrast to the UK Parliamentary debates analysed in chapter 2 should become obvious. In the French debates, the manipulability of the tropes of republicanism are readily exposed, as well as their centrality in framing political issues. Moreover, the focus on the compatibility (or not) of the PACS with republicanism was reinforced by the ways in which all actors in the debates articulated the relationship of the PACS to wider issues of globalisation and transnationalism. In this way, the national specificity of the PACS—which emerged in a nation state which is a central player in the European integration project—should raise scepticism about simple tales of the globalisation of legal struggles around sexuality.

I include an analysis of the PACS in *Governing Sexuality* for several reasons. Any study which claims to look at citizenship in a European context should benefit from interrogating the French experience, given the historical centrality of citizenship discourse within France. Moreover, from a comparative perspective, the French experience underscores the specificity of the 'Anglo-Saxon' discourses of *both* sexuality *and* citizenship, demonstrating how both can be understood otherwise (and so too can the relationship *between* sexuality and citizenship). Finally, the French experience of the PACS provides an interesting example of the complex relationship between the development of uniquely national responses to perceived social 'problems,' and the transnational context of ever greater integration within the European Union (and from within a mainstream French political discourse that supports the European integration project). The PACS thus is related closely to the themes of this study, and provides (as is so often the case with France) a sharp contrast to a UK perspective on sexuality and citizenship.

This chapter begins with a short history and legal analysis of the PACS, followed by a consideration of the centrality of republican discourse, both to French political identity, and in the PACS debate. This analysis will be connected to the way in which marriage is understood within republicanism, as well as to how French national identity is constituted through an oppositional relationship to an 'Anglo-Saxon' politics, and also to wider, EU legal developments. I then show how legal discourse proves central to the construction of national identity, and how this manifests itself in the PACS debate. I conclude the chapter with an exploration of what the PACS suggests about the relationship between universalising and particularist currents in the construction of sexual identities within France today.

BACKGROUND TO THE LEGISLATION

The enactment of the PACS is the culmination of many years of mobilisation and struggle, which emanated from certain segments of the gay community in France. It was triggered in large measure by the severity of the AIDS crisis, and the material consequences which flowed for partners left without any legal protection. There were a number of attempts by various organisations to promote legislation during the 1980s, most of them having links to the Socialist Party. The PACS model emanated from the leadership of what had been a gay activist group, the *Comité d'Urgence Anti-Répression Homosexuelle* (CUARH); an organisation which dissolved in the mid-1980s (Bach-Ignasse and Roussel, 2000: 126; Martel, 1999: 337). By the early 1990s, the need for succession rights, social security benefits, and the right of surviving partners to continue occupying a residence, became increasingly urgent. This was exacerbated by two judicial rulings in 1989, which held that cohabitants' legal rights were not available to same sex couples (*X v Air France*; *Mme X v Caisse primaire d'assurance maladie de Nantes*, *Recueil Dalloz*, 1990, J582; see also *Vilela v Mme Weil*, *Recueil Dalloz*, 1998, J111). This status, known as *concubinage*, amounts to 'a scattered set of rules regulating unmarried cohabitation,' rather than any systematic legal recognition of the relationship (and many cohabitants choose not to take advantage of the legal rules on *concubinage*, by not registering their relationships) (Steiner, 2000: 3). Although some limited protection in law was accorded to same sex couples in legislation on an incremental basis, the package of rights possessed by cohabitants was not available (Barlow and Probert, 1999: 477). While some municipalities have allowed same sex couples to register as cohabitants, this has been largely a symbolic gesture (David, 1995). A campaign for the legal recognition of same sex relationships through the legislative branch thus assumed a heightened priority.

The campaign was waged over the 1990s, and the proposals went by various names: the *contrat d'union civile* (CUC); the *contrat d'union sociale* (CUS); the *contrat d'union civile et sociale* (CUCS); and, ultimately, the PACS (Bach-Ignasse and Roussel, 2000: 131). It was orchestrated by the *Collectif pour le contrat d'union civile* (subsequently *Collectif national pour le pacs*), an activist lobbying group which included gay activists, but was not identified as a gay movement. Importantly, the strategy adopted by campaigners for civil unions was always to construct reform proposals in universalising terms. That is, civil unions would be available to any couple—heterosexual or homosexual—who wished to enter into this relationship. Although early proposals replicated a model of marriage, activists made a tactical switch by focusing on cohabitation as a basis for union, disconnecting it from any requirement of a sexual dimension. In this way, the campaigners sought to avoid claims that they were proposing 'gay marriage' in the disguise of universality, although the focus on cohabitation would also open them to the charge that this was a purely utilitarian conception of the couple, removed from any 'higher' notion of romantic love. So too, some gay groups were sceptical of the 'desexualisation' of relationships under the proposals. These tensions would remain central throughout the legislative history of the PACS (see Bach-Ignasse and Roussel, 2000: 136).

The turning point was the return to power of the Socialist Party in 1997. Despite earlier scepticism, it appropriated the issue in the 1990s, along with the somewhat related issue of the representation of women in elected assemblies (*parité*).[1] This was most graphically demonstrated in June 1996, when several prominent politicians of the left signed a petition for the CUS on the day of the Gay Pride Parade in Paris (Martel, 1999: 374). After commissioning reports and proposals for

[1] *Parité* refers to the political programme which supports the greater representation of women in public office through the reform of the party list system in elections. It has been a controversial issue—characterised as a 'quota' by opponents—which ultimately led to a constitutional amendment.

reform (most notably by sociologist Iréne Thery and by law professor Jean Hauser), the government introduced legislation in 1998. In so doing, a clear choice in the direction of law reform was made. The government rejected the proposal of Thery, for a special status for same sex couples, in favour of a new legal status carrying both rights and responsibilities—the PACS—which would be available to any two people, whether or not they formed a conjugal relationship.

The proposed legislation was subject to fierce debate, which split along left-right lines, with a coalition of the left ensuring its ultimate success in becoming law in November 1999. Most politicians of the right opposed the PACS. Opponents in the Senate proposed an alternative, which ultimately (and ironically) led to the amendment of the Civil Code, opening the status of *concubinage* to same sex couples. This reform occurred alongside the PACS legislation, which itself necessitated reform of the Civil Code in several respects, most significantly in the inclusion of a new part, *Du pacte civil de solidarité et du concubinage*, in the chapter devoted to marriage. The reforms came into effect in the year 2000. The ferocity of the debate provides evidence for the claim that within French politics today, ideological distinctions are increasingly grounded 'primarily on moral or cultural grounds,' as economic liberalism has become 'the chosen government' favoured both by the Socialists and the right (Martel, 1999: 136–37). The recent electoral success of the right, as well as the far right, would seem to provide further support for this thesis.

In brief, a PACS allows two people, whether living in a conjugal relationship or not, to register a contract in a municipality, which reduces to writing their commitment to each other, and which must include the obligation to provide mutual assistance and support. The parties are able to contract over most of the terms of their relationship, although there will be an obligation to share debts incurred for their joint lives, and the contract cannot be amended unilaterally. It *can* be ended unilaterally, on notice to the other party. The parties require a common address, although the legislation appears not to require that the couple must be sharing a dwelling. The PACS is available to same sex or opposite sex couples, but not to close relatives (including siblings), and not to those already married or in a PACS. It is limited to two people.

Various benefits vis-à-vis the state flow to the PACS couple, which resemble, but are not identical to, the package of benefits historically available to married couples. The PACS couple obtain an array of rights in relation to housing, social security, taxation and rights of property, priority regarding job transfers within the civil service, and simultaneous vacation time. However, the rights are not as generous or wide-ranging as for married couples. Some rights only accrue after specific periods of time, which would be automatic upon marriage. For example, a joint tax return can be filed no earlier than three years after the PACS is formed. While there are obligations imposed upon a PACS couple, these are also not as extensive as those associated with marriage. There is no requirement of sexual fidelity (since there is no expectation of a conjugal relationship), no celebration before a mayor (unlike marriage), and the protection accorded upon the breakdown of marriage, as provided by family law, is not present. So too, the cumbersome and time-consuming legal process associated with divorce is absent. Nor is there any mention of children. While the PACS may provide some assistance for a non-national to obtain immigrant status, this again is not as generous as in the case of marriage. Thus, the PACS legislation both resembles and dissociates itself from the marriage model. Moreover, it provides a more comprehensive system of rights and responsibilities than does the piecemeal protection offered by *concubinage*.

Following adoption of the legislation in Parliament, but before its promulgation by the President of the Republic, opponents referred it to the Conseil Constitutionnel (the Constitutional Council of France). Numerous arguments were made concerning the compatibility of the PACS with the constitutional principles of the Republic. The Conseil upheld the legislation as constitutionally valid, although several *réserves d'interprétation* were made (Décision 99-419 1999). I return to the significance of the decision of the Conseil later.

Two other points are worth considering as a matter of background. First, the institution of marriage has experienced a steady decline in France over a number of years. More heterosexual people are choosing to live as couples outside marriage either for a trial period or on a permanent basis. Two million live as couples outside marriage and a third of children are born to unwed parents (*The Economist*, 1996). Moreover, the (formally) secular basis of marriage—like other national institutions—must also be recognised as a cornerstone of French republican ideology. Perhaps as a consequence, public opinion was not hostile to the PACS, particularly when it was interpreted in universal terms as a status available to all couples who are unmarried (Bach-Ignasse and Roussel, 2000: 164). Although there were rural-urban and generational splits in public opinion, there was general support for a plan to 'resolve' the problems of the unmarried (and general approval for allowing same sex couples to enjoy that status). While many politicians, academics, activists, and religious leaders would not share that view, public opinion perhaps suggests the degree to which the PACS was viewed in terms of its pragmatic, rather than symbolic, effect. Thus, the PACS has proven extremely popular: by April 2000, the government had already recorded almost 14,000 PACS, with estimates that around 40 per cent are heterosexual couples (Daley, 2000). By contrast, as I want to explore in the remaining sections of this chapter, the symbolic dimensions of the PACS would prove to be the centrepiece of public debate and controversy, including numerous protests and demonstrations, as well as the longest Parliamentary debate since the enactment of the Constitution of 1958.

REPUBLICANISM AND RELATIONSHIPS

An analysis of the Parliamentary debates, academic analyses, and popular commentary reveals, above all else, the centrality of the discourse of republicanism in framing the PACS. By republicanism, in this chapter, I refer to the dominant ideology in France which privileges the nation state and its direct relationship to individual citizens, and which is founded on the principles of equality and universality (as guaranteed by Article 1 of the Constitution). The individual communes directly with the nation state, leaving little space within the public sphere for groups within civil society to become politicised entities. And there is no space for an officially recognised multiculturalism, differentiated citizenship claims, or a right to 'difference.' Claims which are made in those terms—or which are constructed by their opponents in such a way—are discredited from the outset, as they are perceived to be threats to the coherence and stability of the Republic. They weaken and fragment it (see generally Brubaker, 1992; Favell, 1998; Jennings, 2000; Laborde, 2001; Noiriel, 1996; Soysal, 1994).

The history of republicanism in France is well beyond the scope of this chapter, but a brief encapsulation demonstrates why it would prove central. The role of republicanism as a foundational political theory is far from simply a matter of historical interest. It represents the founding principles of the Republic, whereby the individual relates to the state unmediated by other corporate bodies (Brubaker, 1992: 48). Consequently, the state finds itself 'at once intolerant of constituted groups and inclusive of their constituent members as individuals,' leading to an assimilationist model of citizenship, which continues to resonate in French politics and society (106). While the Republic may not have sought officially to eliminate diverse ethnic cultural traditions, the politicisation of identities was prohibited; meaning that 'the defense of cultures of origin could, therefore, not be allowed to constitute a legitimate demand, an object of public controversy' (Noiriel, 1996: xxiii). The precondition for full citizenship for migrants thus is individual assimilation into a way of life, and *any* individual *in theory* should be capable of full membership upon assimilation; thereby differentiating the French republican ideal from an ethnic model of citizenship. This provides the justification for the refusal to recognise any racial or ethnic differentiation as the basis for group-based political claims (unlike, for example, in the United Kingdom). The republican vision of the social order has relied upon, and has been bolstered by, the central role of the state and the high degree of centralisation of state institutions (particularly education), which has helped to cement, throughout history, an abstract political ideal into practice. That is, republicanism depends upon a belief in citizenship as a national project in which individuals *in fact* will transcend their particular affiliations, towards full and foundational membership in a wider community of citizens. This, in turn, requires the preservation of a clear differentiation between the public and private spheres. Cultural difference must be privatised in order to preserve a universalist, liberal, neutral vision of the Republic and the citizen within it. Individuals, but not communities, are the bearers of rights.

The last quarter century in French politics has centred on the relationship between the theory of republican citizenship and the reality of an increasingly diverse population, as well as the pressures of regionalism, transnationalism, and globalisation (see Favell, 1998). While the far right in France always was (and remains) sceptical of the ability and desire of some to become full citizens (thereby justifying an ethnic notion of citizenship), the left in France in the 1970s and early 1980s flirted with a multicultural model which legitimated the role of ethnicity in political life. The bolstering of immigrant identities, through the formation of ethnic organisations (such as *SOS Racisme*) was seen as a means to fight racism through recognition of social diversity. Relatedly, the government of the time stressed administrative decentralisation and a cultural politics which recognised the institutional autonomy of the regions; summed up by the slogan *droit à la différence* (the right to be different) (Favell, 1998: 50). That phrase was easily appropriated by minority groups as a means to articulate their citizenship claims.

However, this modest attempt at reimagining citizenship and identity proved to be short-lived. Simultaneously, the Mitterand Government's attempt at state interventionist economic policies in the early 1980s failed in the face of the hegemony of global laissez faire. The increasingly constrained role for interventionist economic policy by an activist state brought into sharp relief the limits of economic nationalism as the basis for a political ideology. In the same period, the rise of Le Pen on the far right challenged (and continues to do so) the mainstream politics of citizenship and immigration, and centred on a questioning of whether migrants (particularly from North Africa) would ever, or could ever, assimilate. The decline of the welfare state in the face of economic austerity measures is also relevant here. Finally, membership of the European Union raised questions about the continued viability of national citizenship in the face of 'the emergence of a European legal and welfare regime' (Favell, 1998: 54).

The result, 'a crisis in the status of republicanism, both as universalist political theory and as governmental practice' (Scott, 1997: 6), has led to a significant resurgence of intellectual labour in the articulation of an ideological basis for a Republic faced by pressures from above in the form of globalisation, and from below, in the form of differentiated citizenship claims turning on a right to difference (Crawford, 2000: 45). This has led to a reinvigoration of 'classic' republican political theory (especially on the left). Propagated by 'a new 1980s generation of media-wise, self-promoting public intellectuals seeking to distinguish themselves from the dominant intellectual currents of the 1960s and 1970s', the philosophy has centred on individual integration as the basis of citizenship, secularism in politics and the state, and 'equality', meaning the rejection of any differentiated treatment (or special recognition) of individual citizens by the state on the basis of particularist identities and affiliations (Favell, 1998: 57–58). Republicanism in this guise is wedded to the language of universality, in that it claims that citizenship as the singular political identity is equally open to all, 'providing there is a wish of the *de facto* resident to become French in a substantive sense' (60). The reward for this form of integration is access to universal services and institutions emanating from a strong central state apparatus (Soysal, 1994: 59). Thus, by 1990, the slogan *droit à la différence* came to be replaced by an official policy of *droit à l'indifférence* (the right of minorities to be indifferent), representing 'the reconciliation of cultural diversity with universal rights and equality' (Favell, 1998: 155).

Republicanism thus provides the ideological basis for resistance to any claims to difference, which are constructed as contrary to the Republic itself, and as exemplifying *communitarianism*. Most famously, this was demonstrated in the Islamic schoolgirl headscarf controversy, in which claims to cultural difference in dress within schools (a central institution to further republican principles), could be unequivocally rejected by a leftist government and leftist intellectuals alike. It challenged 'the French Revolutionary national heritage of secular Republican education' (Moruzzi, 1994: 659), because it was seen as an attempt to gain official recognition for particularist religious identities within the public sphere. It was thus contrary to the principle of equality (since head coverings were universally forbidden).

While republicanism is constituted so as to provide ready answers to citizenship claims grounded in claims to difference, it equally must engage in ideological labour in its response to claims from 'above' the nation state, in the form of transnational and globalising pressures (Crawford, 2000). And to do so, republicanism must replace its use of a discourse of universality with a focus on the particularity of the French nation and people (Laborde, 2001: 726).[2] While subnational identities must be rejected as a basis for politics because of their 'inevitable' ability to fragment the nation state, globalising (universalising) pressures on the nation state must be resisted by cultural nationalism: the 'French exceptionalism.' In this moment, republicanism favours the defence of particularism against global culture, especially an individualist, consumerist culture, which atomises and undermines the social body and destroys social solidarity (730). Thus, a politics of subnational identities is dangerous because of its potential to fragment the Republic into a series of competing, essentialised, politicised groups. Global culture is dangerous because it fragments the bonds of national social solidarity through an individualising pressure whereby the connections between and among citizens and the state will be fragmented. The Republic (and republican ideology) must resist both.

It is therefore predictable that republicanism should frame the public and Parliamentary discourse on the PACS. It is invoked on all sides as their fundamental justification. For supporters (both within and outside Parliament), the defining features of the legislation are its universal availability, that it facilitates individual autonomy through allowing parties to contract (largely) as they wish, and it recognises a social reality. Promoters go to great length to stress that the PACS is not communitarian, in that it is not designed simply for the gay and lesbian communities: 'we refuse to institute a special communitarian framework.

[2] I think that this neatly exemplifies Peter Fitzpatrick's (1998: 28) thesis that the 'nation exists in-between the universal and the particular'.

Our Republic is one' (Catherine Tasca, Assemblée Nationale (hereinafter AN), 3 November 1998, 7943).

For advocates, its purpose is not only the promotion of a range of rights for couples who choose them, but these rights have a social utility that is directly connected to the goals of republicanism. As a consequence, the PACS is not a means to regulate matters which should remain in the private sphere. Rather, it touches upon issues which are at the heart of the public good:

> This newly found freedom and this mutual commitment do not simply concern private life. They also concern the Republic and society, as they recognise the couple and institute a greater stability in relationships (Tasca, 1998).

Along with the enjoyment of rights, 'legal recognition will change the life of interested couples by changing the way our law considers them' (Tasca, 1998). They will become full citizens of the Republic. Social cohesion and solidarity will be affirmed and strengthened.

The secular, contractual and, indeed, rational basis of the PACS is also linked to republican ideology. For supporters, 'the PACS has not been created out of passion. On the contrary, it is a product of both reason and higher principles to which we, on the Left, are attached: liberty, solidarity, secularism, dignity of the individual, the Rule of Law' (Tasca, 1998). Republican ideology assumes a high degree of individual rationality and autonomy and, for supporters, the PACS furthers those qualities, along with secularism, equality, assimilation, and universality. Rather than promoting an (un-French) 'ghettoisation' or 'special status' or right to difference for homosexuals, the PACS does the opposite by creating an exceptionally French, universally available status, allowing for the integration of all, equally, into the Republic. French exceptionalism thus promotes universal equality. As one supporter neatly summarised:

> The Republic represents, above all, three fundamental values: liberty, equality, fraternity. Let us question ourselves about the PACS. Does the bill reinforce liberty, does it guarantee equality and does it encourage fraternity between the citizens of this country? In our opinion, the answer to these three questions is clear: yes, the PACS does reinforce liberty for each individual; yes, the PACS does guarantee equality for all, and finally yes, the PACS does encourage fraternity and solidarity within our Republic (Yves Cochet, AN, 8 June 1998, 5532).

Similarly, another eloquently stated:

> This is a liberal text, which is both secular and republican. It takes into account the social realities of today and endeavours to offer a solution for the various ways of life that coexist. In doing so, it brings back within a legal framework a great number of our fellow citizens who had previously been excluded therefrom. It allows for the reinforcement of the social bond. And this, indeed, is the most essential role of the legislator (Jean-Pierre Michel, AN, 3 November 1998, 7939).

Parallels can be drawn to the discursive use of republicanism by proponents of the principle of *parité* to further more equal political representation on the basis of gender. In both cases, advocates of reform have been careful to avoid communitarian-based claims in favour of universalist language:

> The purpose is to integrate, in the same way, women into political life and homosexuality into social life. Far from threatening national unity, these two projects reinforce the civic bonds. Far from setting up legal and political minorities, they accomplish, each in its own way, a universal programme (Fassin and Feher, 1999: 22).[3]

The rhetoric exemplifies how, in France, 'movements based on particular collective identities demand *equal*, rather than *special* treatment . . . those groups that are proud of their unique identity often formulate their pride in general, universal terms' (Fillieule and Duyvendak, 1999: 186). It also demonstrates that in order to achieve political results, progressive new social movements in France must 'speak the language of the left-wing political family' (187).[4]

Turning to the way in which opponents of the PACS articulated their claims, here again it is republican ideology which provides the justification. The PACS is a special status for gay couples which has been cleverly disguised in universal terms. Opponents consistently point out that heterosexual couples have never asked for a new legal status. By opting out of the institution of marriage and, often, by refusing to register as cohabitants, they have indicated their intention to avoid state regulation. As a consequence, the PACS can be branded as communitarian, aimed at a special interest, which will fragment and undermine social solidarity. Describing the Socialist Government, one opponent stated:

> Your policy in relation to society deals with different segments of society separately, and each time you legislate, you do so for certain specific categories of citizen. . . . But it is in fact your vision of society which is communitarian. On the Right, we think that the Republic is universal (Patrick Devedjian, AN, 8 June 1998, 5537).

The result of communitarianism is inevitable: 'the progressive fragmentation of the coherence of society into as many separate categories as groups coming to claim legitimation from the state' (Bernard Seillier, Sénat, 17 March 1999, 1527). More dramatically, 'the PACS is a time bomb as well as a cluster bomb for our society' (Jean Boyer, Sénat, 30 June 1999, 4693). It will lead to 'a patchwork of small communities with limited emotional liability' (Jean-Claude Carle, Sénat,

[3] In other ways, it has been argued that the PACS and *parité* differ in terms of their conception of gender roles. In the case of *parité*, advocates focus on 'natural' sexual difference, a discourse which can easily be appropriated by opponents of the PACS: see Pisier (1998).

[4] Another similarity between the two programmes is that they were *relatively* inexpensive as the basis of a political programme for the then Socialist Government. Although cost would be an issue raised by opponents of the PACS, both *parité* and PACS are far removed from a redistributive politics once favoured by Socialists. While parallels can be drawn here to New Labour in the United Kingdom, the differences between the two parties—in terms of their visions of the role of the state in the economy—are also important. See generally Clift (2000).

30 June 1999, 4694). This will produce intolerance, ghettoisation, and the decline of social solidarity.[5]

Moreover, by extending individual rights to a minority community (rights which are interpreted as largely financial in character), the law privileges the individual at the expense of the social. Solidarity is located, not surprisingly, in the heterosexual family as a microcosm of the nation as a whole. In this way, the PACS is interpreted as both anti-republican and anti-family, as both individualistic and communitarian, all simultaneously (see evidence of Guy Coq, *Sénat Rapport* (1999) 173–76). The individual becomes the consumer of rights for financial gain. As the leading opponent of the PACS in Parliament, Christine Boutin, explained, it all goes to the kind of society being advocated:

> A society composed of a juxtaposition of individuals, each one being solely responsible for himself or a society which puts the family as its first and foremost foundation? A society founded on individualism or a society founded on solidarity? (AN, 8 June 1999, 5540).

The PACS furthers an individualist, consumerist, rights-oriented society, in which relationships are reduced to material well-being, and in which they can be discarded easily and unilaterally. In keeping with republican tradition, many opponents of the PACS argued in favour of tolerance of individuals, but against the institutionalisation of their particularities. This argument was articulated through the public/private distinction and the assumption that same sex relationships do not make the same sort of contribution to the public good as the heterosexual family (primarily because children are assumed to be exclusively located in that family). This point then would be deployed to refute the use of equality discourse by advocates of the PACS.

Furthermore, opponents (like proponents) drew on the republican discourse of secularism. For them, the PACS opens up a veritable Pandora's Box of divisive claims regarding marriage and the family. The spectre of religious (ie Moslem) marriages was frequently invoked, which is assumed to pose a grave danger to the future of the Republic. As one anti-PACS activist explained to a Senate Committee:

> The existence of another danger has been put forward . . . which is that the PACS opens the door to a multiplicity of recognised relationships: each community is going to make claims for its own system of marriage. . . . It will not be possible to refuse it once a 'community'—which presents itself as such—has obtained the status. At the end of the day, we will move from national unity to a juxtaposition of communities (*as in some countries*) (evidence of Marguerite Dovolvé, *Sénat Rapport* (1999) 222, emphasis added).

[5] For an excellent analysis of this point, see Eribon (2000: 39):

> By refusing the issues imposed upon us by the dominant discourse, such as 'are you communitarian or universalist?,' I am trying to deconstruct those dominant discourses, by proving that behind the apparent neutrality, or the apparent obviousness of these questions, one can find, in reality, the fruits of ideological labour which tend to perpetuate the force of the old homophobic discourses.

The PACS thus undermines all of the foundational principles of the Republic:

> With the PACS, you are putting into question a boundary which has been the expression of a continuous Republican tradition, the boundary between private life and public life. You are forcing people to render public their choices made in private. And you are doing so particularly when it comes to the homosexual community. The PACS does not represent an increase in liberty; but on the contrary, it represents a decline in liberty because it marks the intrusion of the state and the legislator into questions which strictly concern the life choices of each individual. . . . Finally, you are talking about fraternity. However, if you are talking about Republican fraternity, then how can you support legislation inspired by communitarian principles; legislation which is the very opposite from our tradition, and which leads you to place artificially—under the same status—couples that emerge from situations that are totally opposite (Henri Plagnol, AN, 8 June 1999, 5533).

In this way, the PACS runs counter to liberty, equality, and fraternity. Its communitarian origins undermine the principle of fraternity; its invasion of the private sphere undermines the liberty of individuals (despite the fact that they can always choose not to register their relationships); and it undermines the principle of equality by treating unlike relationships alike.

The question of equality, however, demands closer interrogation, given its central role in the debates. The use of equality discourse underscores the dominance of a formal, Aristotelean conception of equality in French politics and law (see generally Wallace, 1999). For PACS supporters, equality is applied in a straightforward fashion. Like cases should be treated alike, and all unmarried couples are essentially alike. Therefore, those who wish to, should have access to the universally available institution of the PACS.

But the PACS debate underscores the manipulability of a formal conception of equality, depending, as it does, on deciding what two things are *essentially* alike. Much like republicanism, equality proves eminently manipulable, and it is used to considerable effect by PACS opponents. They argue that the PACS promotes inequality and that it is discriminatory in several respects. First, if the PACS is the legal recognition of a contractual relationship (unlike the status of marriage), then what justification can be put forward for restricting its availability: why is it limited to 'duos' and not available to groups greater than two who wish to share a common life? Why not open the PACS to family members, such as siblings, who may live jointly?[6] These restrictions cannot be justified if the PACS is constructed as the recognition of a social reality and the public enforcement of a private contractual arrangement. Rather, the PACS appears instead to constitute a legally recognised *status*, based upon and resembling the institution of marriage. Thus, one cannot form a PACS with a close family member and one cannot belong to more than one PACS at the same time (see

[6] In earlier versions of the legislation, the PACS was available to *frateries* (siblings), but this was subsequently removed; one justification being the fear of promoting incest. The point highlights the way in which, despite protestions to the contrary by supporters, the PACS does bear resemblance in some respects to the institution of marriage.

Cabrillac, 1999). While there may be no official ceremony associated with the PACS, the registration is itself interpreted as a 'parody of marriage' (74). It 'institutes a certain solemnity and it establishes rules that are close to those of marriage in relation to the ability to enter into a contract, the requirement of a common life, and even the rules on succession' (Patrice Gélard, Sénat, 17 March 1999, 1519).

This claim is then developed at length by PACS opponents, who argue vociferously that the PACS is a form of 'gay marriage,' but without the social and interpersonal responsibilities associated with that institution (and there are similarities here to the UK debates surveyed in chapter 2). They point to a false equality between unmarried same sex and opposite sex couples. The latter have opted out of marriage (and can always opt into it), and the former are assumed to want access to the institution of marriage (eg Alain Lambert, Sénat, 17 March 1999, 1526–27; Cabrillac, 1999). Given that dynamic, the PACS legislation *must be* a form of de facto 'gay marriage.'[7] And the form it takes is 'marriage light,' or 'the Canada Dry of marriage: it looks like marriage, it tastes like marriage, but it is not marriage' (Cabrillac, 1999: 72). It gives to homosexuals the benefits of marriage, but without the responsibilities of family. It provides for easy and quick exit from relationships on demand (requiring little by way of responsibility towards partners, leaving them unprotected on breakdown), and the widespread assumption is that children do not enter the picture. In fact, the absence of children in the formulation of the PACS relationship is frequently invoked by opponents. It is the dependent relationship created by the presence of children (both of children on their parents, and the primary care-giving spouse upon the other) which justifies the benefits accorded by the state to married couples. Thus, the PACS 'creates mechanisms which institute family dependency where it does not exist' (Gaudu, 1998: 20). The law compensates for the cost assumed by the family in the interests of society, whereas providing benefits for the PACS couple 'offers public remuneration for private affection' (Phillippe Marini, Sénat, 30 June 1999, 4680). The absence of such a dependent relationship and, indeed, of contribution to the public good through the propagation of the nation, makes gay relationships essentially different from heterosexual marriage. As a consequence, the former should not be treated on an equal basis as the latter through the creation of a legally recognised status with benefits accruing to couples. In this formulation, of course, PACS = gay; marriage = straight; and unmarried heterosexual cohabitants have made their choice to avoid legal recognition (except to the limited extent that it is accorded to cohabitants) and can live with the consequences.[8] Thus, 'one cannot simply move from the principle of equality of the individual to that of relationships. These are two different concepts' (Anne Heinis, Sénat, 17 March 1999, 1534).

[7] And, by extension, the PACS will not satisfy homosexuals, who will inevitably lobby for the entire package of benefits associated with marriage.

[8] One of those consequences is the lack of protection accorded by the law to (usually) women in cohabitation upon the breakdown of relationships: see Pillebout (1987).

While some opponents conceded that gay couples were similarly placed to unmarried heterosexual couples—leading to the change to the Civil Code to recognise gay couples within the definition of cohabitation—the rights and responsibilities associated with the heterosexual married couple justify the special status and privileges it is accorded. It promotes the public good and the survival of the Republic, and thus serves a special social function (and, as with New Labour in the United Kingdom, the responsibilities of citizenship are emphasised here). A variation of this argument was also deployed by many religious leaders, generally opposed to the PACS, who argued that, while homosexuality might be tolerated, the heterosexual relationship had a particular role in the social structure (see *Sénat Rapport* (1999) 184–200).[9]

Thus, the PACS represents a false universality; it treats unlike cases alike by according them legal recognition (albeit in different forms). It promotes inequality by disturbing 'a perfect reciprocity of rights and responsibilities' (Henri Plagnol, AN, 10 December 1998, 10245), by giving rights and privileges to those who have not taken on responsibilities. In this way, it financially benefits those who are already well off (since they are assumed not to have the financial burdens of child-raising), and who have not made the social contribution of married couples. It creates, instead, a 'supermarket of the family' (Henri Plagnol, AN, 10 December 1998, 10245); a 'pick and mix' of rights and responsibilities. Indeed, the legal recognition of PACS relationships, for opponents, represents the triumph of individualism ('it corresponds to a purely individualistic application of human rights') and benefits the self-serving (and selfish), rather than republican (socially responsible) relationships ('behind the couple, there is both the family and the child') (Anne Heinis, Sénat, 17 March 1999, 1534). As one member of the Senate made explicit, 'we are being asked to redefine Republican marriage, as it stands in the Civil Code and as it has existed since the French Revolution!' (Jean Chérioux, Sénat, 18 March 1999, 1575).[10]

The PACS also promotes inequality in a different way. It privileges the PACS couple who, opponents argue, is essentially the same, in terms of social contribution, as those who remain excluded: single people, siblings who live together, single mothers, etc. None of these 'groups' benefit from the PACS, and they will end up paying for the financial (and other) benefits obtained by PACS couples, estimated by a Senate Committee to amount 'to 4.6, or perhaps even 8 thousand million francs' (*Sénat Avis* (1999) 16). While it is assumed to be reasonable that everyone should pay to uphold the institution of marriage—because of its self-evident social benefit—what is the justification for favouring the way of life chosen by the PACS couple? As Christine Boutin explained:

[9] In fact, French law in the area of taxation and social welfare has long and generously privileged families with several children, to the disadvantage of single people: see Joanny (1998).

[10] By contrast, the President of the *Collectif pour le Pacs*, Jan-Paul Pouliquen (1999), turned the republican justification for marriage on its head, arguing that 'marriage is not a sufficiently republican institution, because it excludes same sex couples and it excludes couples whose members do not keep up any sexual relations between themselves.'

The main losers of the *Pacte Civil de Solidarité* will be single people. Indeed, if it is justified that a married civil servant benefits from priority in respect of geographical transfers to join up with a spouse in order to ensure the smooth functioning of the family (being the social unit *par excellence* and a unit whose utility is undeniable), such a justification cannot be found when it comes to civil servants who have signed a PACS (AN, 8 December 1998, 10177).

There are numerous paradoxes contained within this argument. Most obviously—as many lesbian and gay activists point out—the PACS does not accord all of the benefits of marriage. While it may be a status, it is a 'second class' status, and while it may entail fewer responsibilities towards partners, the rights are proportionately less. The assumption that marriage = children is also questionable, and reveals the extent to which lesbian couples with children are erased from the debates. A claim was also raised by activists on behalf of *célibataires* (single people), who argued that *neither* married couples without children *nor* PACS couples should be financially privileged by the law (*Sénat Rapport* (1999) 228–39).[11] Finally, arguments raised by PACS opponents—with their emphasis on marriage and the family—appear disingenuous given the statistical evidence that marriage has lost much of its popularity in France, and given the preponderance of children born outside of wedlock. Either marriage *isn't really* that important for the survival of the Republic or, alternatively, many French are not proving to be 'good' citizens.[12] The early statistical evidence on the take up of the PACS, showing substantial numbers of heterosexual cohabitants choosing to register either as a trial run or as an alternative to marriage, also makes many of the arguments raised by PACS opponents ring hollow.

However, the appropriation of the discourse of equality by opponents of the PACS forced advocates to respond. They did so by appropriating the same discursive terrain (in ways not unlike some elements of New Labour discourse in the United Kingdom). In order to answer the claimed inequalities resulting from the PACS, the Minister of Justice, Elisabeth Guigou, made clear the social basis for privileging the PACS couple over other ways of living:

I also believe that it is in society's interest to favour people who choose to live together, as this breaks the solitude which is far too widespread in our society and it encourages solidarity rather than individualism. It is legitimate for the state to require from two persons that they commit themselves by a specific act, thereby asserting the existence of their solidarity openly before society. . . . To admit a contract which is of a purely

[11] This was raised in a contribution by Renée Labatt before a Senate Committee (*Sénat Rapport* (1999) 228–39). Before the same Committee, a representative of cohabitants argued that the denial of the benefits of the PACS to them was itself unequal and discriminatory (*Sénat Rapport* (1999) 223–28, evidence of Xavier Tracol). The permutations of the discourse of in/equality thus began to expand exponentially.

[12] See *The Economist* (1996): in 1994, the number of weddings in France fell to a record post-1945 low, producing the lowest marriage rate in Europe outside Scandinavia. Only 7% of the French population regards 'living in sin' as morally wrong. According to *Les Echos* (1999), the number of non-married couples rose by 60% between 1990 and 1998.

pecuniary character would amount to the denial of a specific recognition to non-married couples and would reduce the value of both the affective commitment and the solidarity which are not solely material. A couple is not a corporation (AN, 3 November 1998, 7944–45).

Thus, the justification for recognising and privileging the couple becomes clear, and Guigou sought also to answer claims made by single people. Living as a couple contributes to the solidarity of society—it is a microcosm of the social—and the special rights of coupledom are therefore justifiable in law given this contribution. Individualism runs counter to the fraternity of the Republic, and the individualism and atomisation of the life of the single person does not contribute equally; thereby justifying unequal treatment in law. Legal recognition through the PACS will encourage stability, in part, because some of the rights only accrue after a period of time following registration.

But PACS supporters in government were forced to answer other equality-based arguments. The government consistently made clear that the PACS does not interfere with the institution of marriage, the raising of children, or the rights which are granted to heterosexuals: adoption, *in vitro* fertilisation, and the status of being married itself. This bundle of rights and responsibilities—and the construct of the 'family' with which they are associated—remain privileged, not open to the PACS couple, and certainly not open to homosexuals qua PACS couples.[13] As the Minister of Justice made clear:

> Marriage is inherently different. The *Pacte* does not concern the family. Accordingly, how could it possibly have an effect upon the rules on filiation? The only purpose of artificial insemination is to cure the pathological infertility of a couple, such couple being made up of a man and a woman. My refusal to allow homosexual couples to adopt is justified by the interests of the child, and its right to be brought up in a family environment where it can shape its identity and freely develop its own personality (AN, 3 November 1998, 7946).

Thus, while the government deployed the discourse of formal equality to justify the PACS, it also drew limits beyond which the PACS couple (or, more accurately, the homosexual couple) is not similarly situated. It is at this point that rights 'run out' (justified in part by a discourse of children's rights) for the PACS couple.

However, opponents of the PACS seized upon this point, arguing that PACS (homosexual) couples will inevitably claim all of the rights which accrue to married couples, and will do so in the language of equality (which is precisely the argument that many activists make). Given the decline in marriage, and the take-up of the PACS by heterosexual couples, there is some merit to this argument. Will not PACS couples make rights claims in terms of adoption and IVF? Given the number of children likely to be raised by PACS couples, how forcefully can a government resist the claim that they are 'families'? And, then, given

[13] Although, interestingly, single people can adopt children in France.

the fact that the ideology of republicanism has led to a universally available status (identical for straights, gays, and non-sexual cohabitants) how can distinctions be justified, as between PACS couples, in defining who is a 'family'? This was recognised by the sociologist Iréne Thery, who recommended a special (but less than equal) status for homosexuals as a way to preclude such arguments (*Sénat Rapport* (1999) 156). The discourse of universal equality, linked to the ideology of republicanism, thus may prove a powerful discursive weapon in the hands of lesbians and gay men, and may well be facilitated by the PACS.[14]

REPUBLICANISM AND INTERNATIONALISM: THE CHALLENGE FROM 'ABOVE'

Republicanism—like all discourses of national identity—draws upon and deploys the idea of 'foreign' ideologies which run counter to an essentially French political outlook. This has proven to be an important means by which republicanism has resisted the currents of globalisation and what they are frequently seen to represent in France: an Anglo-American cultural and political imperalism. Although French culture may have been hit by the 'shock of globalization' (Garapon, 1995), the capacity of the French state and ideology to resist should not be underestimated. Described by one commentator as 'a backward-looking nationalism . . . that implicitly places France's victimization by the U.S. culture industry on the same plane as Brazil's or Mexico's' (Woodhull, 1993: 140), republicanism frequently has deployed anti-Americanism in different forms. This 'displacement' of the United States (Scott, 1997: 17) within republicanism is central to the way in which the wider ideological implications of the PACS are characterised by both sides.

As I have already suggested, PACS proponents quite clearly seek to dissociate the legislation from special interests. Rather, the PACS is consistently represented as universal, neutral and modern. For Parliamentary supporters, it is all of those things, as well as normalising: it will de-ghettoise and integrate lesbians and gays (and this is simply *assumed* to be a positive benefit for the Republic). For opponents, it is the opposite: it will *encourage* a ghetto mentality because the PACS is specifically designed for the gay community. This kind of discursive framing around sexuality is not without precedent. Gay Pride parades, a relatively recent development in Paris, have been analogised to Islamic fundamentalism (the ultimate demonisation) (Eribon, 2000: 32). Some supporters claim in response that Pride parades are celebrations open to all (ie universal) and are not therefore communitarian (Bach-Ignasse and Roussel, 2000: 154).

These arguments are closely linked to a dissociation of French political practice from an Anglo-Saxon model of multiculturalism, in which group identities are said to have become politicised. Throughout the debates—much like the

[14] Such moves are already being strongly resisted through widespread mobilisation against any extension of adoption rights to gay couples.

debates around *parité*—there is much discussion of an Anglo-Saxon politics of multiculturalism, difference, and 'political correctness'; all of which is encapsulated by the term communitarianism. For opponents, the PACS is a clear example of this Anglo-Americanisation of politics: a special interest group is obtaining a special benefit which will fragment the Republic.

At the same time, as I have demonstrated, opponents criticise the PACS on the basis that it is too individualistic. Here it resembles the critique of the United States: it is both too communitarian and too individualistic. Like the United States, the PACS represents the fragmentation of the Republic into particularist groups (leading to 'the ethnic nightmare of racial segregation and breakdown') (Favell, 1998: 61). But also, like the United States, it is too individualistic, in that the PACS is a status from which rights flow, which are then consumed in a completely self-interested way (see Fassin and Feher, 1999: 15). As with the United States, the PACS underscores a prioritisation of the private sphere which comes to dominate and trivialise politics. This caricature of American politics and culture serves an important function in shoring up republican ideology. 'America' becomes the other to an essentially French way of life.

While republicanism opposes the globalising effect of 'America', on the one hand, it must also resist the impact of the European Union, on the other. The irony here is all too apparent. While republicanism relies upon a discourse of universalism—and a resistance to fragmenting particularity—it simultaneously draws upon cultural nationalism to oppose processes of Europeanisation which threaten to engulf French exceptionalism (Laborde, 2001). For opponents of the PACS, these dangers demand its rejection. The experience of other Member States of the European Union (especially the Netherlands and Scandinavia) is deployed in order to discredit the PACS, which is constructed as the first step towards gay marriage and adoption (Claude Goasguen, AN, 12 October 1999, 7154). But more dangerous in the eyes of some PACS opponents is the linking of the PACS to an EU-wide agenda for the normalisation of homosexuality as part of the integration project (a project which, in turn, threatens a French way of life). In this moment, the PACS (inaccurately) is linked to the Treaty of Amsterdam and its anti-discrimination provision, and to the integration project of the Court of Justice and European Parliament:

> Little by little, Europe, framed by the PACS, is being harmonised and the Treaty of Amsterdam . . . will force us on to this devastating path. Section 13 is indeed unambiguous: the European Union may take the appropriate action to combat discrimination based on, among other things, sexual orientation. You cannot fail to notice that on the basis of Section 13 of the Treaty of Amsterdam, a "pacsed" homosexual couple to whom the possibility of adoption has been refused, will have the opportunity to complain to the European Court of Justice in order to assert its rights. And the Court in Luxembourg, true to its practice of erasing the existence of national legal rules, will impose upon nation states the requirement to suppress what it considers to be "discrimination on the basis of sexual orientation." Therefore, it will consequently oblige Member States to authorise homosexual couples to adopt children. The spiral has

already well and truly begun. The European Parliament is already beginning to put pressure in many ways to that effect (Philippe de Villiers, AN, 30 March 1999, 3081).

Thus, the survival of the Republic depends upon 'holding the line,' not only against Anglo-Saxon identity politics, but also against European harmonisation, which will destroy the logic of the Republic.[15]

For PACS proponents, by contrast, some pride is taken in the fact that they have devised an 'exceptionally' French solution through a universally available status, which is (assumed to be) different from the approach taken in other jurisdictions, which have created a special status for gay couples. But proponents also draw upon transnationalism in a favourable way, citing resolutions from the European Parliament, the Treaty of Amsterdam, etc. In this moment, the PACS is a source of nationalist pride because it demonstrates that France is at the forefront of progressive legislative change within Europe (Patrick Bloche, AN, 3 November 1998, 7940).

But this deployment of European integration can also be located on a closely related terrain: the role of the civil law in the reproduction of the identity of the Republic. French legal discourse, like republicanism, 'holds out the offer of security in a monolithic and monopolistic way . . . marked by the absence of a public discourse acknowledging the existence and importance of social identities other than the abstracted *citoyen*' (Crawford, 2000: 45). As a consequence, the PACS was described by many academic commentators as a perversion of the civil law: 'an abuse of law' and 'a legal monster' (see Bach-Ignasse and Roussel, 2000: 157). It creates a second status—marriage light—which undermines the centrality of marriage in the Civil Code. By introducing what is interpreted as an alternative status to marriage, the government created:

> the presence in one field of more than one legal order which characterises legal pluralism, [which] is at odds with the French abstract conception of the law, according to which law generates from one source and takes only one form (Steiner, 2000: 5).

While the law should not penalise homosexuality or any alternative relationship form, so the argument goes, it should also not recognise it.[16] Moreover, the PACS is consistently interpreted as leading to abuse and fraud through immigration *PACS blancs*, because of the possibility that the PACS can assist a non-national in obtaining immigrant status (see Thierry Mariani, AN, 1 April 1999, 3237; Cabrillac, 1999: 74).[17]

[15] The EU Charter of Rights with its non-discrimination Article 21 (which includes 'sexual orientation') further underscores this process of harmonisation. On the development of an EU family law, see McGlynn (2000).

[16] One argument raised by a PACS proponent in response was to point to the example of Quebec, a civilian system in which legal recognition of same sex couples has been codified; an interesting inversion of colonial nationalist discourse (Patrick Bloche, AN, 8 June 99, 5503).

[17] Early indications are that relationships with foreign nationals will be carefully scrutinised by officials, even when there is ample evidence of the long-standing character of the relationship: see Zappi (2000).

As well, as Antoine Garapon (1995: 499) argues, 'for the French, law is the purveyor of identity' in that it provides an important 'structuring' dimension in French culture. An emphasis on legal certainty and the perfectability of the Civil Code is important here, which is contrasted to the flexibility, pragmatism, and ultimately, lack of certainty of the common law (Wallace, 1999: 407). The PACS is interpreted as a threat to that fundamental conception of legal identity as certain and predictable, not only because of the many legal questions which remain unanswered by the legislation, but also because of the way in which it allows private parties to structure the legal character of their relationships autonomously.

It is in this context that the decision of the Conseil Constitutionnel (Décision 99-419 1999) must be understood. Opponents of the PACS referred a number of constitutional questions to the Conseil to determine its congruence with the founding principles of the Republic, particularly 'equality.'[18] The Conseil upheld the PACS, albeit with certain 'reservations.' With respect to equality, as between rights accorded to cohabitants and to PACS couples, the Conseil saw no constitutional violation, because the obligations imposed upon PACS couples justified the difference in terms of rights (thereby demonstrating a formalistic approach to equality). However, two reservations are relevant. First, the Conseil clarified the meaning of *la vie commune* (a 'shared life') for the PACS couple: 'the notion of a "common life" is not merely a community of interests, and is not limited to the requirement of simple cohabitation between two persons; the common life mentioned in the referred act implies, besides a common address, living as a couple' (9). Thus, 'simple' cohabitation would not satisfy the requirement. Secondly, the Conseil made clear that parties would not be allowed to contract out of the obligation to provide mutual assistance, and one party can be found liable to the other in the event of a unilateral decision to terminate the contract (9).

These two reservations are extremely significant in terms of the way in which the French legal order seeks to reassert certainty and discipline over a situation which it finds unruly and open-ended. The reservations are an attempt to impose a particular model of the organisation of relationships—the replication of the institution of marriage—the unity of which is central to republican ideology.[19]

[18] As Wallace (1999: 406) explains: 'The *bloc de constitutionalité* consists of a group of provisions, made up of the Declaration of the Rights of Man and the Preambles of the Constitutions of 1946 and 1958, which in turn are said to refer back to the founding principles of the republic. This set of principles has been given the status of positive law by the Constitutional Council. The principle of equality has been recognised as a constitutional principle: in a decision of 5 July 1977, the Constitutional Council held that there was a requirement to treat in the same way situations that were the same.'

[19] The decision of the Conseil Constitutionnel also may be partly explained by the fear of the formation of the PACS *exclusively* as a means to achieve a benefit, such as priority for civil servants in transferring to a job in a different area of France. If the PACS is understood purely in contractual terms, it becomes difficult to understand what is illegitimate about such an arrangement. However, by strengthening the precondition of a 'shared life,' the Conseil may be attempting to impose a more stringent requirement as to what constitutes a *genuine* relationship, through the use of the marriage model.

While the PACS potentially challenges that ideal of singularity, the Conseil tries to mould it in the image of marriage. The result is that, rather than creating an indeterminate legal basis for the organisation of relationships, three legal categories have been devised: marriage; PACS; cohabitation. As Eva Steiner (2000: 7) concludes:

> PACS, resembling marriage as it does, far from promoting the legal pluralism which called for reform in the first place, on the contrary, shuts the door on an alternative way for couples to organise their domestic life. Indeed, the adoption of the marriage model in the new scheme fails to recognise the diversity in the relationships couples choose for themselves and renders ineffective the pluralism based arguments which initially demanded recognition for unmarried cohabitation.

In that sense, the argument of PACS opponents that the PACS is a form of 'marriage light,' is not without validity. What that argument ignores, however, is the way in which the PACS is a product of a particular legal and political ideology of republicanism; which provides the grand theory upon which both proponents and opponents of the PACS must rely to buttress their claims.

REPUBLICANISM AND SEXUAL IDENTITIES: THE CHALLENGE FROM 'BELOW'

As well as the challenges generated by international and transnational developments, republicanism also must face subnational movements and identities making rights claims from 'below' the nation state (see Crawford, 2000). As I sought to demonstrate in the previous section, republicanism connects the two by discrediting identity politics; claiming it emanates from a foreign, Anglo-Saxon ideology of 'multiculturalism,' which is destructive to an essentially French way of life. But while this is clearly a stereotype of Anglo-America, it leaves open the question of the relationship between republicanism and the self-constitution of social movements—in particular, gay movements—within France. What is the relationship between republicanism, multiculturalism (as the French characterise it), and gay politics?

It has been frequently argued that the history of gay politics in France has not strictly 'followed' the Anglo-American path, and that this must be understood in terms of the republican political tradition (see generally Fillieule and Duyvendak, 1999; Marshall, 1997; Martel, 1999; Rollet and Williams, 1998; Tamagne, 2000). Much of this history has been his-story, while the story of lesbianism in France often has involved considerable friction in attempts to form coalitions with gay men, matched only by the acrimony produced by working with heterosexual women within the feminist movement (see Martel, 1999: ch 2). The PACS, however, does appear to represent an issue on which there has been a certain degree of successful coalition-building between women and men.

In terms of French legal history, the revolutionary government abolished all laws of the *ancien régime* against same sex sexual practices; and they were only re-criminalised by the Vichy Government (and continued in the post-war period) (Marshall, 1997: 3). The history of a collective gay consciousness in France also demonstrates a certain French exceptionalism, characterised by the degree to which an identity-based social movement along the Anglo-American model has never truly developed.

Mobilisation in the immediate post-1968 era bears resemblance to the revolutionary liberationist movements which developed elsewhere (the Gay Liberation Front in the United Kingdom, for example), in which a universalising critique of the relationship between capitalism, heterosexuality and patriarchy was deployed through a militant politics (which largely avoided dealing with the official apparatus of the state, unless confronted by it directly through repressive measures) (Martel, 1999: chs 1–5). That revolutionary moment was not sustained through the coming years, as the countercultural positioning of homosexuality faded as a political strategy. Nor was it replaced by the movement of identity politics which characterised the American experience. Instead, France saw the growth of a subcultural rather than political orientation (Fillieule and Duyvendak, 1999: 194). Indeed, a politics of (public) identity has been resisted in France in the name of republicanism, not only by political elites, but by gay activists and intellectuals as well (see Pratt, 1998). This has meant that although consumer citizenship through capitalism has fostered a market ghetto, the fear of *political* ghettoisation has meant that this is a 'reluctant ghetto' frequented by particularised consumers aspiring to be universal citizens (Gunther, 1999: 34). Moreover, there continues to be considerable resistance to the notion of a specifically gay culture of film and literature in France—which again can be located within the republican ideological opposition to ghettoisation and difference (see Rollet and Williams, 1998: 196). In this regard, gay themed cultural productions in France have been described as inevitably 'personal dramas of existential choice,' rather than stories of gay community (Marshall, 1997: 75). The strength of republican ideology has meant that 'many homosexuals took an apolitical view of their sexual orientation' (Fillieule and Duyvendak, 1999: 203).

The election of the Mitterand Government, which immediately repealed anti-gay criminal legislation, ironically had the effect of disempowering and demobilising what remained of a gay movement in the early 1980s (and a similar dynamic was experienced by other new social movements) (Martel, 1999: 136). What emerged instead—in the face of greater tolerance and openness—was a way of life which, for some, was an increasingly individualist, consumerist existence, and 'it did not simultaneously generate a politically constituted gay community' (Ernst, 1997: 26). Rather, 'the left-wing government itself looked after homosexual interests' (Fillieule and Duyvendak, 1999: 192). This era has been described in terms of the rise of an American, global gay culture in France; and it was criticised on precisely the same basis as the more general critique of the United States: too communitarian and too individualistic (see generally Caron, 1998: 287). Once again, globalising currents threatened to sweep aside the particularity of an exceptionally French way of life.

The emergence of the AIDS epidemic can be located squarely within these developments. It is argued that the slowness and ineffectiveness of responses to the crisis can be traced to the republican ideological framework and the 'relative lack of a gay infrastructure' (Marshall, 1997: 88). That is, the absence of a gay community response—as in the United Kingdom and the United States—is a result of the absence of politicised community. And the response of the state was often ineffective, in part because the crisis could only be addressed as a universal public health issue, in which educational and other programmes could not be targeted at particular high risk groups (since that would run counter to the principle of universality and might result in the stigmatisation of groups) (Caron, 1998; Martel, 1999: 231). Moreover, homophobia no doubt contributed to the lack of response: 'the vague hope that the epidemic would remain confined within that undesirable community' (Caron, 1998: 286).

Frustration resulted, in 1989, in the formation of ACT UP Paris, an organisation subject to considerable comment and criticism for its 'American style', 'communitarian' approach (see Ernst, 1997; Martel, 1999: 304). The rise of ACT UP, in combination with other examples of perceived Americanisation of French gay culture (the Rainbow Flag, Pride parades, the gaying of the Marais district in Paris, gay and lesbian film festivals, a gay and lesbian centre in Paris, etc), have been criticised for their foreignness to the principles of the Republic (a criticism that comes both from dominant culture and from within the gay 'community') (see Martel, 1999: 355). But this claimed communitarian impulse is also matched within France by the increased use of the language of rights in universalising terms; a move which is exemplified by the social movement around the PACS. For gays in France, rights are consistently framed in terms of a right to indifference, as opposed to a right to difference, mirroring the shift I identified earlier within the Socialist Party (Gunther, 1999: 36). This deployment in itself can be seen as differentiating French gay politics from *what is perceived within France* as the Anglo-American turn to identity.

While gay activist organisations and individual activists—such as ACT UP, as well as many others—may support the PACS (and they do so within a highly universalising discourse), they make clear, using the language of equality, that the PACS does not go far enough. They argue in favour of marriage, adoption rights, and rights to IVF, all of which are claimed as universal rights of citizenship (see generally *Sénat Rapport* (1999) 240–48, evidence of Dominique Blanchon (ACT UP Paris); Daniel Borrillo (AIDES)).[20] Support for the PACS is frequently made in terms which draw upon republican ideology: it will incorporate gays, resulting in a 'banalisation of homosexuality', and it will incorporate them into society through the power of law (which itself has a mythical

[20] Of course, individual lesbian and gay people may not universally share the position of elites in this regard. For some, the PACS may provide a practical solution, while avoiding the ideological baggage of marriage. As one gay PACS couple described: 'it is such a heavy thing, marriage': Daley (2000).

ability within republicanism to achieve that end) (Martel, 1999: 359). In making these claims, the idea of a gay community is explicitly rejected by some activists in favour of assimilation within the universal:

> When it comes to marriage, I cannot accept the idea of the possibility of talking about homosexuals as a category which could constitute a political or legal subject. In the law of the Republic, there is no homosexual body, there is no homosexuality, there are no homosexual representatives, or if that is what you want, then there ought to be a body of homosexuals to talk about homosexuals. Let's not talk about homosexuals, they do not exist or, at least, they do not appear to exist within the logic of the Republic. This is why I believe that we must not draw up any special law in the name of homosexuals and for homosexuals (*Sénat Rapport* (1999) 261, evidence of Daniel Borrillo).

What is largely lacking within this discourse is the concern for the dangers of 'normalisation' (see Warner, 1999), and 'self-regulatory containment' (Pratt, 1998: 280), which I have discussed at length already in chapters 1 and 2. That is, the turn to universal institutions as a basis for the claiming of rights might be thought to lead to normalisation and disciplinarity. The relative absence of such arguments in the French context speaks perhaps again to French exceptionalism, but also to a different reading of Foucault by gay intellectuals, activists, and commentators (see especially Eribon, 2000; Hocquenghem, 1993). A 'banalisation' or 'assimilation' of homosexuality is not equated to disciplinarity, in which heterosexual marriage is the idealised basis of social relations. Rather, some argue that the virtue of the PACS is that it may open new ways of living for all—'other social models'—avoiding the constraints of identity altogether (Eribon, 2000: 83). It is also claimed that the same sex PACS relationship is challenging to heterosexual hegemony, because of the 'resemblance of the Other to the Same' (and the Parliamentary debates provide some evidence for this claim) (Marshall, 1997: 91). Moreover, the norm does not necessarily remain the same in the face of social inclusion (Fassin, 1998). Gay relationships and lifestyles, it is thought, can maintain a critical edge even while individuals may take advantage of the PACS.

But it is also argued—perhaps more so than would be the case in Anglo-American debates—that, normatively, assimilation and incorporation are goods in themselves; allowing individuals to transcend the particularities of their identities in favour of a wider social solidarity; to leave the ghetto and participate in wider projects of the national community, in which homosexuality will have 'become simply a lifestyle difference' (Martel, 1999: 316). This, of course, is the foundation of republicanism, and its embrace by gays speaks to its ideological power. It also underscores what may appear to be a contradictory relationship between the local and the global. While a gay way of life in France may appear to be increasingly globalised (from the Rainbow Flag to the claiming of rights), gays do not necessarily become 'full blown' cosmopolitan citizens, in which their (nationalist) communitarian roots are abandoned. Rather, the cosmopolitanism associated with global capitalism remains in tension with the republican dream of integration (Gunther, 1999). Although it has been argued that 'the future of the gay and lesbian movement in France in the coming years depends on the political opportunities to manifest oneself as being different' (Fillieule and Duyvendak, 1999: 205), my analysis suggests that such opportunities inevitably will be sites of contest both within and outside the gay 'community.'[21]

Finally, the continuing turn to republicanism, in the face of, or because of, the currents of globalisation, raises the ultimate question: what does incorporation, assimilation, and banalisation *achieve*? For lesbians and gays, what does it mean to be considered full citizens, officially undifferentiated and unhyphenated: 'individuals without labels'? (Martel, 1999: 359). Does it mean a society which does not privilege heterosexuality, or simply one in which the 'difference' of homosexuality is deemed to be politically and legally irrelevant? The implications of this are wide, going to the role of French cultural nationalism in an era in which the nation state is continually claimed to be in terminal decline. One prominent gay (republican) activist and intellectual suggests an answer: it will allow gays to become 'adults' (Martel, 1999: xiv). That is, to become fully rational, autonomous and reasonable beings or, in other words, to be *civilised*. This is the ideological power which republicanism continues to wield (and the state is assumed to play a central role in inculcating the values of citizenship). If republicanism can no longer fuel a colonial expansionist imaginary, and if the limited power of the nation state in the face of transnationalism (European Union) and cultural globalisation (American imperialism) becomes all too apparent, then France at least is thought to remain the (perhaps last) outpost of reasonableness, civilisation, and 'virtue', as manifested by universal rights, a depoliticised private sphere, and a monolithic, undifferentiated vision of citizenship (on 'civilisation' and the national imaginary, see Gunther, 1999: 36; Laborde, 2001; Marshall, 1997: 51). This exemplifies how citizenship 'combines membership of the particular national community with what is expansively and universally "civil"' (Fitzpatrick, 1998: 37). While others may fall victim to communitarianism, political correctness, the fragmentation of the nation state, the valuing of 'the minority at the expense of the national culture' (Martel, 1999: 356), leading to *the decline of civilisation itself*, France (*including the citizen who happens to be gay*), resists.

[21] The period since the PACS debate has seen a significant interest by the media, particularly television, in matters gay. Whether that should be interpreted as an indication of assimilation, ghettoisation, or simply mainstream curiosity (or all three), is open to debate. Whether it suggests that the PACS may provide a 'paradigm for positively figuring homosexuality as part of a valid French identity' (Pratt, 1998: 280)—which Pratt and others would argue has never existed—remains to be seen.

CONCLUSIONS

It might be argued that, in this chapter, I have 'overtheorised' a legal reform which was supported as a means to resolve pragmatic problems associated with a social reality, rather than as a means to change society. The fact that the PACS is being used pragmatically, particularly by young heterosexual couples—as a prelude to marriage, as a preferred alternative to it, or as a means simply to gain a benefit or avoid a detriment—underscores the banalisation of the PACS, more than it does the banalisation of homosexuality. While gay couples (or, indeed, non-sexual cohabitants (who might also happen to be gay)) sometimes may approach the PACS differently—often emphasising its symbolic importance through arranging a celebration for friends and family after registration—perhaps that merely underscores how a universal institution can be made flexible enough to accommodate different citizens' wants. Because the ideological grounding of the PACS is so contentious and debateable, and because of its very 'newness,' its virtue may lie in the fact that the PACS can *signify*, for the contracting parties, whatever they want from it, despite the way in which its legal form may come to be disciplined through judicial interpretation. Of course, that flexibility in itself could ultimately undermine the legitimacy of the PACS, particularly given the rapid emergence of the PACS 'of convenience' (especially useful for civil servants seeking to relocate).

In any event, contrary to what opponents may claim, I have argued in this chapter that the PACS seems unlikely to undermine the republican order and, ultimately, what opponents are unaware of, is the degree to which that ideology—especially the desire for social inclusion and acceptance as full citizens—permeates the attitudes and approaches of citizens as they make claims to rights in France, and in how they exercise those rights. While opponents may have castigated the currents of globalisation supposedly represented by the PACS, their claims are undermined by its reality. Its paradoxical combination of the universal and the particular merely replicates a uniquely French *rhetorical* answer within a globalising world order.

4

Grant-*ing Rights: The Politics of Rights, Sexuality and Citizenship Before the European Court of Justice*

INTRODUCTION

ON 17 FEBRUARY 1998, the European Court of Justice delivered its judgment in *Grant v South West Trains* (C249/96) [1998] ECR I–621, holding that a refusal by an employer to grant travel concessions to a person of the same sex with whom a worker has a 'stable relationship' does not constitute discrimination based directly on the sex of the worker, as prohibited by Article 141 (then 119) of the EC Treaty and by the Equal Pay Directive, even where such concessions are allowed to a person of the opposite sex with whom a worker has a stable relationship outside marriage. The reaction to this decision by activist and academic commentators alike was both surprise and indignation: the latter generated by the apparent 'injustice' of the decision on the basis of formal equality; the former, because the Advocate General (an advisor to the Court) had reached the contrary result in an Opinion of 30 September 1997. For the legal rights-oriented activist group Stonewall, the outcome of this litigation strategy—which they actively supported—was somewhat embarrassing as well as unexpected, underscoring how the privileging of a rights-based activist programme can lead to disappointing results. Not surprisingly, Stonewall assumed the moral high ground, describing the judgment as 'a blow to lesbians and gay men everywhere in the EC' (*Stonewall News*, 1998). Academics have found the decision in *Grant* a rich source for analysis. The decision of the European Court of Justice has been deconstructed from a queer theoretical perspective (Beger, 2000), interrogated for what it reveals about the emerging conception of European citizenship (Bell, 1999), and examined for what it suggests about the relationship between the institutions of the European Union (Armstrong, 1998b).

In this chapter, I will also touch upon some of these themes, but the focus of my analysis is rather different, in that I deploy the *Grant* litigation in order to illuminate the wider limitations and distortions which rights politics can foster when it is privileged so centrally within an activist strategy. In particular, given the absence at the time of any explicit basis for sexual orientation discrimination protection within EC (or UK) law, the turn to Article 141, I argue, was most probably a deeply flawed strategy from the outset; which, if successful, also would have distorted the meaning of this sex discrimination provision. I develop this (admittedly contentious) argument from the perspective of an emerging discourse on the *political economy* of rights, sexuality, and citizenship, which to date has been articulated primarily within North American debates on the politics of rights and sexuality (see Goldberg-Hiller, 1998; Boyd, 1998). My claim is that given the focus of European rights discourse on the 'market citizen' (Everson, 1995), and the creation of a 'transnational capitalist society' (Ball, 1996), the sometimes taken-for-granted politics of European sexual citizenship rights is much in need of interrogation for its broadly political economic implications. In so doing, the aim in this chapter is to question the privileging of rights discourse in sexual citizenship strategies, particularly within the European arena, because of its limitations as a vehicle for challenging underlying structural barriers to full citizenship (points which I have already alluded to in chapter 1). I advocate instead, as I do throughout *Governing Sexuality*, not a sceptical approach to European politics and law, but an engagement of activism with the construction of, and participation in, democratic institutions, and a politics, not only of legal recognition, but more broadly, of recognition *and* redistribution.

BACKGROUND TO THE DECISION

The facts and background to the *Grant* litigation have become extremely well known and can be summarised only briefly here. Lisa Grant, an employee of South West Trains Ltd (SWT), was refused a travel pass for a female partner, despite the fact that her contract of employment stated that 'you will be granted such free and reduced rate travel concessions as are applicable to a member of your grade. Your spouse and dependants will also be granted travel concessions' (*Grant* at I–621). It was company policy to grant 'privilege tickets' to a common law spouse of the opposite sex provided a statutory declaration was made that a meaningful relationship had existed for a period of two or more years. Grant's request for travel concessions was denied because her partner was of the same sex. She claimed that this was contrary to EC law given that her male predecessor in post had received the benefit for his opposite sex partner.

An industrial tribunal referred several questions to the European Court of Justice, all of which turned on the issue of whether SWT's actions constituted 'discrimination based on sex' for the purposes of Article 141, the Equal Treatment Directive and the Equal Pay Directive. The case received the support of Stonewall, which 'mounted an intense media campaign to raise awareness of the significance of a ruling favourable to Grant' (Armstrong, 1998b: 456). Before the ECJ, both the United Kingdom and France intervened in support of SWT.

Despite a finding in favour of Grant by Advocate General Elmer, who reasoned that this difference in treatment constituted discrimination on the basis of 'gender' (*Grant* at I-629–30), the ECJ held that the refusal to grant travel concessions did not constitute discrimination based directly on the sex of the worker prohibited by Article 141 of the EC Treaty or the Equal Pay Directive (at I-646). Nor did sex discrimination include discrimination on the basis of sexual orientation. First, the condition applied in the same way to male and female workers, and therefore could not be regarded as constituting discrimination directly based on sex. Moreover, discrimination based on sexual *orientation* did not constitute discrimination on the basis of the sex of a worker, and Community law does not regard stable relationships between two persons of the same sex as equivalent to stable relationships outside marriage between two persons of the opposite sex (at I-648). According to the Court, 'in those circumstances, it is for the legislature alone to adopt, if appropriate, measures which may affect that position' (at I-645).

Although mention was made by the Court of the International Covenant on Civil and Political Rights, and the view of the Human Rights Committee that 'sex' 'is taken as including sexual orientation' (at I-650),[1] that in itself could not give rise to a general principle of Community law:

> although respect for the fundamental rights which form an integral part of those general principles of law is a condition of the legality of Community acts, those rights cannot in themselves have the effect of extending the scope of the Treaty provisions beyond the competences of the Community (*Grant* at I-650).

In terms of institutional competence, the Court also noted that the Treaty of Amsterdam enables the Council of the European Union—by unanimous vote on a proposal from the Commission after consultation with the European Parliament—'to take appropriate action to eliminate various forms of discrimination, including discrimination based on sexual orientation' (at I-651) (and which the Council has subsequently achieved through the Framework Directive discussed in chapter 1).

It is this judgment by the European Court of Justice, and the events which led to it, which form the backdrop against which my analysis proceeds in this chapter.

THE POLITICS OF RIGHTS IN A EUROPEAN CONTEXT

The 'rights debate' in legal theory is now sufficiently well known that it need not be replayed in this chapter (see Herman, 1993). The debate concerns the political implications of (primarily) constitutional rights struggles, particularly in a North American context, and it was propelled by a recognition of the inadequacy of

[1] The Court cited *Toonen v Australia*, Communication No 488/1992, 31 March 1994. I have considered the implications of the *Toonen* decision elsewhere; see Stychin (1998: 145–193).

liberal, modernist assumptions about the inherently progressive character of rights discourse. In reaction to that traditional legal 'faith' in rights, some have argued that rights struggles tend to produce politically conservative (or more accurately) classic liberal outcomes, and that this provides the ideological underpinning of many rights 'victories' (see eg Bakan, 1997; Fudge and Glasbeek, 1992). More progressive political struggles thus come to be channelled and neutralised through the turn to rights. Others are sceptical of this position, and point to the powerful emancipatory potential of the language of rights in some forms, and its role particularly in civil rights struggles in the United States (see eg Williams, 1987). Still others see rights as having a highly disciplinary function, particularly when conjoined to the language of responsibility (a point made throughout this book; see also Brown, 1995). My own approach might broadly be described in terms of the 'critical pragmatism' advocated by Didi Herman (1994b), namely, that rights have their pragmatic uses depending upon the precise context, but that rights struggles should not be divorced from broader social, political and economic movements for progressive change. At the same time, I would concede that the case studies in this book are generally tilted towards the disciplinary function of rights and citizenship.

In fact, the *Grant* litigation contains many diverse strands of the rights and citizenship debate. Although in this chapter I focus primarily on the ideological grounding of *rights* which was articulated (explicitly and implicitly) in the case, and how potentially progressive rights discourse was largely 'transformed into dominant ideological terms' (Bakan, 1997: 117), I make no claim that this is the 'grand narrative' of the litigation. Instead, it demonstrates simultaneously that rights can function importantly as a 'heuristic device' for social movement politics, drawing attention to social struggles and, indeed, diverse 'ways of life' (Kingdom, 1996). It thus can educate people about political change, citizenship demands, and also—in the context of a European rights struggle—the potentiality and limitations of membership in a transnational community.

Moreover, an analysis of the use of EC sex equality law as a tool in rights struggles importantly demands that the insights flowing from the academic commentary on the politics of rights be contextualised in the unique circumstances of the European Union. Certainly, EC sex equality law illustrates both the practical potential and the limitations to the use of rights discourse. More broadly, the role of rights themselves in the EU legal order is specific, and should be differentiated from the rights debates that go on in North American academic communities. As Carlos Ball (1996: 333) suggests, constitutional rights in the American sense are grounded in the value of individual autonomy, and rights are ostensibly designed to facilitate the individual atomistically choosing the ends that she desires to achieve. By contrast, in the European Union, freedoms and rights have had a more instrumental role, in that their fundamental character is a result of 'their consequentialist function, namely their being necessary to achieve Community objectives' (340). As a result, the protection of individual rights has been geared, not towards a belief in the inviolability of individual autonomy, but rather, rights become a *means* 'of enforcing the positive obligation of the Community and of the member states' towards the achievement of the objectives of the integration project (344). The objectives, as is well known, have been highly economic in character: 'the creation of an integrated and "efficient" market' underpinned by a 'neo-liberal market ideology' (Hervey, 1998: 204).

Thus, while some North American academics of the left go to great pains to demonstrate (often persuasively) the ideological grounding of rights discourse, those interested in European rights need not engage in such labour. Individual rights have an *explicit* ideology, and while they can and often have been deployed towards moderately progressive ends—particularly in the context of employment related rights—such successes do not negate the claim that there is an ideological underpinning to rights discourse centred on market relations. Thus, for example, Tamara Hervey (1998: 106), argues that a hierarchy exists among EU citizens with respect to social security, and at its apex 'is the migrant EU citizen who is an employee or a self-employed person.'

The history of sex equality rights in EC law provides ample evidence for this argument. It is universally acknowledged in EC legal history that economic factors were the motivating force behind Article 141; namely, the perceived need to avoid distortions in competition between Member States which had differing levels of protection for sex equality rights in the workplace (see eg Barnard 1996).[2] Subsequently, in the landmark case of *Defrenne v Sabena (No 2)* (43/75) [1976] ECR 455, the objectives of EC sex equality law were described as twofold, embracing both the need to avoid distortions in competition, and also the desire for social progress and the improvement in the working and living conditions of the peoples of Europe.

The effect of European sex equality rights in practice has been well documented, particularly by feminist analyses which have highlighted the positive benefits of the resort to rights, but also the limitations imposed both by the structure of the rights, and the broader ideological project of the formation of an internal *market* in which rights discourse is embedded (see eg Barnard, 1996; McGlynn, 1996: 239; Everson, 1995; Hoskyns, 1996; More, 1996; Hervey and Shaw, 1998). The dominant focus on formal equality and equal opportunities in the workplace has had a 'revolutionary affect' (Everson, 1995: 209) for some women—namely, working European women, particularly around issues such as part-time work and pregnancy discrimination. And it has been through rights struggles, often by 'lone women,' that these successes have been realised as a result of often protracted litigation (Hoskyns, 1996: 78).

[2] Article 141 EC provides for equal pay for men and women, and has been supplemented by Directives concerning equal pay and equal value (75/117), equal treatment in employment (76/207), equal treatment in social security (79/7), equal treatment in occupational pensions (86/378), and equal treatment for self-employed women (86/613). For an outline of the legal framework, see Hervey and Shaw (1998, 46–47).

However, the limitations of EC sex equality law are also well known. The emphasis on 'fair' competition in the marketplace, the 'merit' principle, and 'equal' opportunities leaves little scope for the use of rights discourse to tackle the underlying structural barriers to substantive equality, many of which result from the private sphere of the home and from impediments to full entry into the labour market, such as 'the double burden of "care" and "work" for women' (Hervey and Shaw, 1998: 60; see also Fredman, 1997). This is a realm considered beyond the role of rights which, because of the ideological basis of those rights, is focused on the public sphere, employment relationship.[3] There is little recognition, for example, of voluntary work and informal care as leading to entitlements to rights such as social security (Ackers, 1996: 226).

Thus, two of the many sides of rights discourse become apparent. The language of rights has meant that 'the EU system can be politicised in the interests of the democratic majority' (Hoskyns, 1996: 210) (and, in that sense, rights prove a useful heuristic device), but, by virtue also of the explicit ideological grounding of EC law, rights struggles are channelled into an economically liberal model tied to the atomistic individual actor freely and fairly working in the competitive labour market (Shaw, 1996: 283).[4] The potential for social change through the employment relation is certainly present (and has been achieved to some degree), but the role of rights in social change is constrained from the outset.

It is on such a politically ambiguous terrain that actors engaged with sexual orientation struggles have sought to 'graft' their claims. Such a move is practically and politically problematic, however, in several important respects. Most obviously, such a move runs into difficult questions regarding the interpretation of the words of the provision, and the fairly clear intention that Article 141 was not intended to cover sexual orientation discrimination. Of course, it also can be argued that if the Treaty is a central constitutional document, then it should be construed in a purposive and teleological fashion and, if Article 141 is designed to foster social progress, then a broad interpretation is justifiable. The issue, according to Kenneth Armstrong (1998b: 462), is how two central tensions in EC law are to be resolved:

> The first is the extent to which the ECJ is willing to extend the scope of Community law beyond the domain of economic integration and to embrace the broader political dimension of laying the legal foundations for a citizenship of the EU. The second . . . is the tension between the interpretation and construction of the EC Treaty as a typical agreement between nation-states or as a constitutional text to be given meaning in the context of a process of constitution building.

[3] See eg *Ulrich Hofmann v Barmer Ersatzkasse* (184/83) [1984] ECR 3047 at 3075: 'It is apparent . . . that the directive is not designed to settle questions concerned with the organization of the family, or to alter the division of responsibility between parents.'

[4] The role of rights is undoubtedly multifaceted, and my focus is undeniably narrow here. As well, rights should not be singled out as the sole means by which the European Court of Justice pursues legal integration; on this point, see Hilson and Downes (1999).

These core tensions suggest that a victory in *Grant* was never going to be straightforward or inevitable.

As well, the question of institutional legitimacy for the European Court of Justice inevitably pushed it away from such a broad interpretation of Article 141.[5] The inclusion of Article 13 EC as a result of the Treaty of Amsterdam may have suggested that this is an area for legislative, as opposed to judicial, activity (which has subsequently taken place). That in itself may have been a reason for the Court to exercise self-restraint. As Steve Terrett (1998: 505) suggests, 'at a time when ratification of the Amsterdam Treaty [wa]s by no means a certainty, the ECJ may have felt it prudent to refrain from providing ammunition to eurosceptics in the various Member States by adopting a gung-ho approach to Community legal development,' an approach which might well have been perceived as illegitimate action on the part of the Court. Indeed, the emotiveness of the combination of sexuality, rights and judicial activism has frequently resulted in claims of judicial illegitimacy in other constitutional jurisdictions and contexts (see generally Stychin, 1998).

A third problem is closely related to the institutional issue, namely, the difficulty of finding a level of uniformity in views across the Member States sufficient to warrant judicial activism. Terrett (1998: 498) analyses this point doctrinally in terms of the way in which the ECJ was asked to widen the meaning of 'sex' discrimination on the basis of a general principle of law. As he argues, the essential requirement for recognising a general principle of law is 'that the principle should be widely accepted by the Member States,' and that it 'will require some level of uniformity, albeit short of precise consensus, before it [the Court] is willing to incorporate a principle into the EC system and offer it protection at a Community level.' One of the explicit bases for the Court's decision was the absence of such a consensus to ground a legal principle against discrimination on the basis of a person's sexuality:

> As for the laws of the Member States, while in some of them cohabitation by two persons of the same sex is treated as equivalent to marriage, although not completely, in most of them it is treated as equivalent to a stable heterosexual relationship outside marriage only with respect to a limited number of rights, or else is not recognised in any particular way (*Grant* (C249/96) [1998] ECR I–621 at 647).

This recognition of variation and difference in the attitudes of Member States might well be understandable in terms of the relationship of sexuality to the private sphere. Again, in terms of legitimacy, Catherine Hoskyns (1996: 160) argues that the ECJ has been of the view that 'intervening in personal or domestic matters is not the function of either EC law or the Court' (see also Kofman, 1995: 132). Rather, the personal becomes associated with the national, even though the precise issue—right to equal pay—is quintessentially a public,

[5] On the problem of legitimacy and the institutions of the European Union, see generally de Búrca (1996).

Community law matter.[6] The alternative approach in these circumstances would be the judicial 'recognition' (or, more accurately, imposition) of a principle of Community law. Arguably, that is the approach which the Court took in *P v S and Cornwall County Council* (C13/94) [1996] ECR I–2143, in which it took no notice of national variation in the treatment of transsexuals (see Stychin, 1997). In interpreting that decision, Larry Backer (1997) suggests that judicial interpretation can act as a form of 'normalizing harmonization' (197), in which 'subnational cultural determinism' gives way to the discipline imposed by legal standards (199). That tension between harmonisation and self-determination is common in rights claims around sexuality and, indeed, it has been argued that the politics of sexuality is characterised by a dialectical relationship between the local and the global (Nardi, 1998: 567). This tension may well have been an important factor which motivated the Court to defer to the local, and it is a factor closely related to the issue of judicial legitimacy. I will explore this tension, and the relationship between harmonisation and normalisation, in much greater depth in the context of the accession country of Romania, in chapter 6.

Finally, it has been argued that a central problem with this litigation strategy was, quite simply, 'the facts.' As is well known from the history of civil rights struggles in the United States, constitutional litigation strategies demand compelling 'test cases', and Mark Bell (1999: 78–79) has argued that the 'justice' of the issue in *Grant* was simply not overwhelmingly compelling. By contrast, a set of facts dealing with an outright, irrational dismissal from employment (as was the case in *P v S*) may well have resulted in a different outcome.[7] The granting of employment 'perks' may well seem to many a less than compelling *human* rights case, particularly when those perks are not granted to employees who are not in *any* sort of traditional spousal-type relationship and who thus continue to suffer this 'discrimination' no matter what the result of the case.

Although Bell's (1999) point is intuitively appealing, I want to argue in this chapter, by contrast, that the claim in *Grant does* fit nicely into the ideological parameters of EC law, and particularly European rights discourse, despite the fact that the claim was ultimately unsuccessful. In making this argument, I hope to illustrate again how law has an often complex and contradictory role in social movement politics, and this is exacerbated in the realm of EC law. Thus, although the facts of *Grant* may appear to lack the moral imperative of a human rights claim, that is also arguably why it fits within this paradigm of rights discourse. Indeed, it has been argued that the advantage of deploying EC law for gays and lesbians is that the economic paradigm of rights abstracts them from an obviously moral underpinning, making it easier to make claims in a morally 'neutral', economically grounded language (Ball, 1996: 387). As a consequence,

[6] On the public/private distinction in EC law, see generally More (1993).

[7] In fact, it has been argued that the Court of Justice at the time might have found in favour of a claimant in a sexual orientation employment recruitment or dismissal case: Denys (1999: 425).

'successes' will be more likely. Discrimination becomes a distortion of the transnational marketplace and a barrier to free movement, and the sort of controversies which are fuelled by gay rights litigation in other jurisdictions can be avoided. In other words, the economic teleology of rights in the European Union can 'sanitise' the claim, making it more likely that a court will conclude that it can legitimately find in the claimant's favour. Although I have argued elsewhere that such an instrumental approach to rights as an activist strategy is misguided (Stychin, 1998: 143), that instrumentalism does capture something about the ideology of rights discourse in some of its forms.

In fact, the focus in *Grant* on relationships also closely fits the ideology of the 'family' as it has developed in EC law. Louise Ackers and Helen Stalford (1999) have examined how the family is 'conceived' in EC law in the context of the free movement provisions, in which a series of social rights for the families of EU migrant workers has been recognised, providing equal treatment protection in matters of employment, pay and working conditions. The assumption made by the European Court of Justice is that there is a close correlation between the exercise of the right of free movement and the granting of free movement rights to family members (705; see also Hervey, 1998: 106). However, Ackers and Stalford (1999: 702) emphasise that 'the rationale for the Court's incursion into areas of family policy in this area of Community law is based firmly on a conceptualisation of women and children as the non-productive appendages of male workers'. Moreover, only a marital relationship can be used to underpin the claim as far as the dependent partner of an EU migrant worker is concerned. Thus, a 'breadwinner' model of 'coupledom' is assumed, in which labour mobility depends upon the ease with which the worker can move the dependent spouse with 'him' when he, as a factor of production, is more highly valued in another Member State (I consider this model in more detail in chapter 5). The facts of *Grant* tap into that same ideology, in which perks are for dependants, in a model of family based upon a breadwinner, 'family' wage-earner. Thus, *Grant* exemplifies a well known litigation strategy, in which test cases draw upon fact situations which are constructed so as to replicate very traditional gendered relationship patterns, albeit with a same sex twist. Replication is assumed to be the path to litigation success.

This strategy is problematic in several respects. For example, Momim Rahman (1998: 85) argues that strategies, such as those adopted in *Grant*, endorse, rather than challenge, institutionalised heterosexuality as a model for human relationships, which is then replicated by same sex couples. Rahman, like others, argues in favour of wider strategies for social and economic change, a point to which I return later in this chapter.

However, such arguments are clearly contentious, and the tensions within the politics of *Grant* perhaps best can be illustrated through the academic debate staged between social and cultural theorists, Nancy Fraser and Judith Butler (see Fraser, 1997a; 1997b; Butler, 1998). This is not the place to restage that debate, but suffice to say that the basic issue which divides these two theorists is the relationship between struggles around the recognition of 'sexual orientation,' and wider issues of political economy and economic transformation. In the debate, this has been framed in terms of the language which Fraser (1997b: 12) has developed regarding the relationship between a politics of recognition and a politics of redistribution. Fraser's point is that sexuality struggles are *essentially* about a politics of recognition, rather than about issues of redistribution in political economic terms. The two are separate struggles.

Butler (1998: 39), in response, has questioned the dichotomy, and has asked pointedly, 'why would a movement concerned to criticize and transform the ways in which sexuality is socially regulated not be understood as central to the functioning of political economy?.' That is, Butler claims that sexuality must be understood as part of the mode of production itself. She also presents examples to refute Fraser's claim that recognition and redistribution are necessarily separate. Most obviously, lesbians as (marginalised) women as a group are going to experience both a wage gap (an issue of economic distribution), and a lack of social recognition (41).

The relationship between recognition and redistribution claims has now begun to be analysed explicitly in legal scholarship. Susan Boyd (1998: 375–76), for example, argues that while Fraser's sharp dichotomy is problematic for precisely the reason that she seems to forget that lesbian women are gendered, and gender is central to the mode of production, Butler's position is also troubling. As Boyd (1998: 376) notes, similar to the critique offered by Rahman, 'it does not follow that legal recognition of non-normative sexualities (for example, same-sex relationships) will necessarily, of itself, constitute a fundamental challenge to the capitalist mode of production.' Intuitively, given the purpose of EC rights discourse to further a free market transnational capitalist economy, it would be surprising if legal recognition in the European context would amount to such a challenge here.

In fact, the critique which Boyd offers—which is situated in the context of Canadian equality rights discourse around same sex partnership rights—is very similar to the feminist critiques of EC sex equality law. The argument in both contexts is that rights do little, if anything, to alter underlying structures which produce gender inequality, such as the role of unpaid labour in the private sphere, and barriers to entry in the workplace. Boyd (1998: 376–77) argues that the nuclear family has a material role in capitalist relations of production, through a sexual division of labour and the privatisation within the nuclear family of the social costs of reproduction and care. It is this same model of the nuclear family which, Ackers and Stalford (1999: 709) argue, is privileged within EC legal discourse. The agenda which Boyd (1998: 381) then advances is one in which activists and academics should pay greater attention to whether that gendered economy is challenged by lesbian and gay legal struggles, or alternatively, whether the lesbian or gay subject is normalised within the political economy through the (eventually successful) claiming of rights. In this regard, it has been argued that the construction of sexual identities (and political priorities for a movement) historically has been shaped by the more privileged (in terms of social class) members of the group (see Valocchi, 1999; Robson, 1998: ch 12). Thus, the question whether sexuality is integral to capitalism cannot be separated from whether sexual identities are significantly constituted and experienced in ways which reflect individual location within that mode of production.[8]

Taking up Boyd's challenge to interrogate rights claims, my argument in this chapter is that the *Grant* litigation provides a perfect example of such a normalisation, even though the litigation ultimately proved unsuccessful. Thus, once again in this book, I am drawn to the issue of normalisation. On the immediate facts, a successful claim in *Grant* would have seen the extension of marital-type perks to 'stable' same sex couples, which presumably would have marginally increased employer costs. The actual 'take-up' of the marital privileges no doubt would vary greatly across the EU depending upon local and corporate social attitudes towards homosexuality, the prevalence of such benefits in the cultural context in issue, and, indeed, whether there was already anti-discrimination legislation in place at national level in the EU Member State which covered this field. The wider procedural right of non-discrimination in employment in itself can be seen as a means to 'perfect' the marketplace to the extent that anti-discrimination law is effective in eradicating the use of irrelevant characteristics in hiring, promotion and dismissal.

However, what is also significant, as Bell (1999: 76) points out, is that the UK Government submission in the *Grant* litigation focused on the wider implications and potential future litigation which might flow from a decision in favour of Grant. In particular, state pension and social security issues may well have been at the forefront of concern. These are areas that are expensive for the state in a capitalist economy. After all, maintaining the attractiveness of the institution of marriage and marriage-like relationships requires costly social engineering. But such institutions are necessary for the maintenance of a capitalist system with a clear public/private dichotomy, in which many costs are internalised within the domestic sphere of the home (Boyd, 1998: 377; see also Hervey and Shaw, 1998). Although the European Court of Justice often has been prepared to reject the appropriateness of economic justifications for sex discriminatory employment practices,[9] many of these decisions are themselves ideologically 'loaded' (such as those concerning protective treatment of pregnant workers), and do not in themselves refute the claim of an ideological basis to the legal order centred on the public/private dichotomy (see Mancini and O'Leary, 1999).

[8] As Iris Marion Young (1997: 154) notes, 'political economy is cultural, and culture is economic.'

[9] See eg *Handels-og Kontorfunktionaerernes Forbund i Danmark* (C66/96) [1998] ECR I–7327 in the context of pregnancy. But see also *Brown v Rentokil* (C394/96) [1998] ECR I–4185 and *Handels-og Kontorfunktionaerernes Forbund i Danmark v Dansk Arbejdsgiver forening* (C101/87) [1990] ECR I–3979 (determining that pregnancy-related illness beyond the period of maternity leave is to be treated as sex-neutral).

Thus, a decision in favour of Lisa Grant would have fitted very well with the ideological grounding of EC rights discourse, in terms of the nuclear family and privatised responsibility within that private sphere, and it would have furthered transnational cultural harmonisation through a common EU definition of 'spouse' (and I consider this ideology in more detail in chapter 5). However, the wider implications of the decision—with the resulting social costs—would not be easily distinguishable within the 'all of nothing' paradigm of formal equality in EC law. The economic costs of legally normalising the homosexual subject are greater in terms of numbers than those of normalising the transsexual subject in *P v S* (C13/94) [1996] ECR I–2143. The scale of such costs no doubt is an inhibiting factor for the judiciary. By way of contrast, Canadian courts in the past have found it much easier to make such distinctions.[10] As a result, as Claire Young (2000) argues, Canadian courts developed broad definitions of 'spouse' in the context of upholding private obligations (such as support), while constructing narrow definitions in the context of state pensions. These results in Canadian jurisprudence should also make us sceptical as to whether rights in the North American context are so far removed from the economic teleology of the EC legal system. Had the European Court of Justice seen a way to achieve this distinction, a different result might have been forthcoming.

I make this hypothesis because, on its facts, *Grant* is ideologically very attractive in terms of the underpinnings of EC law: no immediate cost to the state; recognisable model of relationships suggesting economic dependence on a breadwinner; and the cost of the perk is a product of a contractually regulated private employment relationship. It provides a clear example of 'the domestication of deviant sexualities within a safe, useful and recognisable framework,' while the cost of the relationship does not touch the state (Boyd, 1998: 377). At the same time, a standardised, normalised definition of 'spouse' modelled on heterosexual marriage creates a level playing field across the European Union (from which deviant others can then be excluded).

A central paradox in the use of legal discourse towards the recognition of same sex relationships thus becomes apparent. Social scientists increasingly are confirming through empirically based research what many have long known: that lesbians and gays construct an infinite variety of ways of living—and of relationships widely defined—which not only replicate but also resist the disciplinarity of heterosexual monogamous cohabitation (Donovan, Heaphy and Weeks, 1999). Yet, when legal discourse is deployed in activist struggles for social change, the engagement with law seems to require constructing relationships which replicate monogamous, heterosexual cohabitation as an 'ideal' to which lesbians and gays can successfully aspire, and from which benefits then flow. These two dynamics—of resistance and discipline—appear (once again)

[10] Compare, eg *M v H* (1999) (2) SCR 3 (Canada) (extending definition of 'spouse' for purposes of spousal support law) and *Egan v Canada* (1995) (2) SCR 513 (no extended definition in the context of old age security legislation).

to coexist, although I would reiterate that it is also important to avoid the privileging of legal discourse in analysing processes of social change.

While the successful deployment of rights strategies will benefit some lesbians and gays materially, and no doubt symbolically, in terms of the affirmation of relationships (for otherwise, there would never have been litigation), the underlying economic question remains: what is the relationship between such claims—framed within the context of a sex discrimination provision—to underlying gender-based structural inequalities? More specifically, is there a necessary relationship between claims to recognition and what Butler (1998: 41) refers to as the 'holy family' of the capitalist mode of production?

First, in engaging in such an analysis it is important to avoid the extreme positions which the Fraser-Butler debate produces. The particularities of any struggle are important, as is the cultural and political context. For example, relationship recognition struggles in the United States arise in a political context in which, for many, affordable health care is *dependent* upon establishing a relationship with someone who has a 'good company plan.' Particularly in the context of new HIV therapies, this is a pressing issue, in which recognition issues and the material conditions of life are inextricably linked. Of course, at the same time, 'success' through legal recognition is problematic to the extent that it detracts attention from the urgent need for universally available health care. Moreover, even in this example, rights can be politically and materially indeterminate, for legal recognition may well result in a financial privatisation of care responsibilities, onto the responsible 'spouse' (see Flanagan, 1995: 210). My general point is that the issue of health care benefits has a particularly American resonance which does not travel well, for example, to the European arena.

However, it does seem a reasonably general proposition that employment rights protection will have a differential impact depending upon the intersection of identities implicated in any individual case, and this point is also related to the distinction between formal and substantive equality. At this juncture, it is useful to recognise that rights discourse around sexual orientation will benefit *most* those for whom there are no other structural, identity-based impediments to the realisation of substantive equality; or, in other words, where there is no intersection of disadvantage.[11] But there is another dynamic at work here, for all gay men (except to the extent that they are perceived to embody cross-gender characteristics) *already* benefit 'from the institutions and social customs that hinder female entry into certain jobs, including traditional notions that women should be committed to domestic life and not to market labour' (Jacobs, 1997: 170). That is, to the extent that rights discourse can eliminate irrational anti-gay animus in the workplace (and I do not want to exaggerate the extent to which law can achieve this aim), gay, childless men can benefit tremendously from

[11] I have developed a related argument concerning 'intersectionality' in a different context; see Stychin (1995a).

patriarchal economic relations which largely privatise responsibility for the care of the young.

Meanwhile, many lesbian women qua women may well still face the structural barriers which are not rectifiable through a formal equality rights-based discourse of equal opportunities alone (although statistically as a group they may fare better in some economic respects than heterosexual women). Michael Jacobs (1997: 172) neatly summarises a political dynamic which increasingly rings true today:

> Gay families need not be modeled on the social norm of a two-adult household, but for gay male couples who do form a two-income household, the benefit of men's generally higher wage earnings is doubled. This amplifies income differentials by gender within the gay community and perhaps makes gay men more conscious of the economic benefits of male privilege and less comfortable with an agenda that challenges this privilege. To the extent that their efforts to integrate into their families of origin are successful as well, many gay men may no longer find the social dominance of the family particularly oppressive and thus may not respond favorably to a political rhetoric that describes it that way.

In addition, for those gay male couples who do not reap the benefits of a two-income household, employment perks such as those at issue in *Grant* at least will allow them to keep pace with the heterosexual single income household. The point which this analysis drives at is that the use of sex equality laws—even if successful on its own terms—will definitely benefit some more than others (ironically, men more than women), and must be considered at best a modest part of a wider strategy of social change.

Furthermore, Jacobs' (1997) point is that many gay men may well not have a tremendous stake in a wider strategy of social and economic change, particularly if they achieve the sort of formal legal guarantees which were at issue in *Grant*. Here again, the ideology underpinning the EU integration project illustrates how the construct of European citizenship, which has been widely critiqued as a limited, market-centred concept, is also one which is actually advantageous in its current form to many gay men. In fact, the subject position of EU citizenship has been described as 'archetypically male' because of its market-centredness, in which the citizen is imagined enjoying the benefits of free movement unconstrained, allowing him to sell his labour to the highest bidder transnationally, and enjoying ever widening consumer choice to satisfy his wants and desires (Shaw, 1996: 297). This citizen is highly atomistic, unconstrained by relationships of dependence, and whose primary identity is derived from paid employment. For many gay men, such a construct is very appealing, particularly if formal legal protection against discrimination ensures that they can exercise these citizenship rights without fear of irrational prejudice by others. Homosexuality then becomes simply, as Mariana Valverde (1999) suggests, a 'lifestyle choice' and 'an innocuous feature of urban consumer life' for the market citizen who can choose to *consume homosexuality* unconstrained—and across national borders. Many gay men, in this consumption citizenship discourse, are themselves archetypically male: more man than most ('new') heterosexual men who are increasingly expected to prioritise their familial relationships, and to share (albeit certainly not yet equally) in child care responsibilities. Thus, European law and social policy have been subject to critique for their 'commodification of individuals' into workers (ie producers) (Hervey, 1998: 204). But homosexuality is also increasingly criticised for its own form of commodification, centred on the consumption of goods, services and, indeed, a way of life, in which 'consumerism becomes the embodiment of identity' (Valocchi, 1999: 220).

Of course, this vision of the gay male EU citizen is also dependent upon the marginalisation of traditional familial and religious discourses of homophobia; but, here again, the underlying ideology of EC law is sympathetic to such progressive change. A modernist discourse of capitalism has little room for such irrationality, which can serve to distort competitive labour markets, and an underlying desire for cultural harmonisation demands that one should be able to cross borders freely both to produce and consume a lifestyle unconstrained by bigotry in some Member States. Historically, some lesbians and probably many more gay men have often benefited from capitalism, as the 'marketplace cleared away all sorts of traditional social formations' (Adam, Duyvendak and Krouwel, 1999: 356). As John D'Emilio (1983a) has argued, it was only when wage labour became the widespread basis by which people lived that homosexuality could become the foundation of a personal identity. Thus, for example, Peter Nardi (1998: 579) makes the claim that in northern Italy, the preconditions for a lesbian and gay movement occurred only relatively recently, with the growth of urban middle class employment opportunities, economic development and personal mobility and the growth of non-religious associations. These processes will continue and accelerate throughout the European Union, particularly with the likely widening of its borders eastward, and I explore this point in chapter 6.

The argument underscores that while capitalism has depended upon the heterosexual nuclear family to help maintain it, late capitalism can now accommodate (quite happily) a group of autonomous, unconstrained producers and consumers operating outside the traditional constraints of the nuclear family. One need only look to the 'positive' attitude of many multinationals to gay consumers today for evidence of this point. It is somewhat ironic then that within legal discourse around relationships, activists and litigants seek to discipline citizenship into something which perhaps is inevitably going to replicate the nuclear 'holy family,' at the same time as that 'holy family' is increasingly decentred in many ways.[12] More than anything, this irony demonstrates how legal

[12] In examining the Danish experience—the first country in the world to enact same sex registered partnership legislation—Karin Lützen (1998: 239) points out that marital-type benefits have come to same sex couples in a society in which 25% of couples with children are unmarried. Thus, she concludes that it is only when marriage as an institution becomes anachronistic—'a worn-out piece of folklore'—that its benefits are made available to homosexuals. A similar conclusion on the Danish experience is reached by Bech (1997: 202), who argues that ' "homosexual marriage" has become possible only on the basis of the decline in prestige and importance of marriage and the family'.

discourse functions and constrains argumentation through the demands of precedent and comparison. Finally, it suggests that Butler (1998) may underestimate the inherent conservatism of law when she suggests that same sex recognition struggles inevitably challenge the 'holy family,' for it is only by making one's self (or one's client) look like the (admittedly decentred) norm that 'success' in instrumental terms is likely to be achieved.

CONCLUSIONS

Given what I have suggested in this chapter regarding the relationship between capitalism and sexuality in the face of the decline of traditional social formations, it must be tempting (at least for those gays and lesbians who are secure in their jobs), to await the 'liberalising effect of time', particularly given the limitations inherent in the use of rights discourse to advance social change (Scott, 1998: 839). Why not 'opt out' of law, once basic privacy rights are recognised and a libertarian approach is accepted to the criminal law regulation of sexuality? In answer, it is worth remembering that while we may point to the disciplinary effect of rights, and the way in which progressive politics can be ideologically channelled into principles such as formal equality, *particularly* in a legal context such as the European Union, the potential of rights and citizenship discourse must again be recalled. Although I may emphasise the disciplinary effect of rights (and of law), I also want to repeat at this point that disciplinarity is never total. The problem seems to be that, although it may be recognised widely that rights through law provide incomplete political strategies, rights discourse seduces its users to believe in its totalising potential as a political strategy.

Another problem in the EU context, as Jo Shaw (1997: 427) suggests, is that rights remain very much a 'top-down' process, leaving little discursive space for the power of rights as an enabling device for social movement activism. Rights remain largely 'granted' from on high, rather than being perceived as the product of years of social movement mobilisation. Although I argued in chapter 1 that there is some space for NGOs such as the International Lesbian and Gay Association Europe to intervene in European rights debates around sexuality, it remains a modest space, because European identities and transnational communities are still very much in their infancy. However, as I also suggested in Chapter 1, as transnational communities, identities and affinities develop, there is no inherent reason why the European legal arena might not be one in which mobilisation and struggle from below could occur more widely.

In fact, one of the roles which sexuality politics might play is in seeking to expand that space of transnational politics, in an attempt to develop strategies of citizenship which go *beyond* the market towards a political and social citizenship of the European Union. The Union remains an important site, and there is some evidence that a notion of 'social citizenship' has increasing currency through, for example, EU funding and 'soft law' (Hervey, 1998: 205), as well as in some rights-based discourse from the European Court of Justice (see Case C-85/96 *Martinez Sala v Freistaat Bayern* [1998] ECR I–2708). It is an arena which should not, then, be seen as solely one for the pursuit of legal rights, which can then be 'consumed', but instead, as having the potential to mean something 'more.' Indeed, NGOs such as ILGA Europe do seek to combine calls for rights with democratic participation in the European Union, and this may provide a useful antidote to the privileging of rights discourse (International Lesbian and Gay Association Europe, 1998). It might be helpful here to imagine a floor of anti-discrimination rights—guaranteed through EC law—which acts as a base for the development of strategies of democratic participation within the institutions of the European Union (and within social movements themselves) (see Bellamy and Castiglione, 1996: 122).

Richard Bellamy (1995) has argued that European rights will only be made meaningful in the context of democratic political arrangements. Otherwise, 'rights prove too indeterminate and subject to conflicting interpretations to provide a constitutional basis for a European polity' (153). In the European Union, things are 'further complicated by the existence of a plurality of national political traditions' (167), and I certainly would argue that sexuality is not exempt from these dynamics. Shared democratic arrangements are therefore necessary for the creation of common rights. This, I conclude in this chapter, is a central limitation of litigation strategies such as *Grant*. Rights have been abstracted from any form of democratic politics.[13] At the same time, rights claims can appear undemocratic from the perspective of those who are members of the social group at the epicentre of the claim, to the extent that the case may not reflect what are thought to be grassroots priorities by some; and, furthermore, rights may privilege the interests of some in the group over others, and may see the manipulation of litigants by lawyers and high level activists.

Yet, at the same time, the experience of the *Grant* litigation, I have also argued in this chapter, was a valuable exercise in terms of the way in which the claim for European rights operated as, in Elizabeth Kingdom's (1996) terminology, a 'heuristic device.' The deployment of rights discourse—and most importantly its widespread publicity, at least in the United Kingdom—drew attention, not only to sexualities and relationships, but it also placed gay *women* at the forefront of a campaign.[14] It served an important function in drawing attention at least to the possibilities and potential of European citizenship claims around sexuality. In a Member State in which relatively few people are even aware that they are 'citizens of the Union,' the *Grant* litigation made one group aware that there was a legal arena in which the language of citizenship could be articulated on its behalf.

[13] On the relationship between rights and deliberative democracy, see Benhabib (1996).

[14] Although litigants can also find themselves manipulated by the organisations advancing a litigation strategy.

However, my claim is that, as a normative matter, rights and democratic participation must operate as two strands of a political agenda. The creation of spaces of engagement traditionally has been tried—not always successfully—at the level of local, urban government (see Cooper, 1994). But the transnational arena should not be forgotten. The fact that transnational constructs of citizenship and 'belonging' have been closely linked to the market up to now, and that many in the lesbian and especially gay male communities may have little personal interest in broadening the horizon of transnational citizenship, does not mean that this should not be struggled over, so that recognition questions might be connected to issues of redistribution,[15] particularly in the context of a widening European Union, and in the face of the economic disparities which inevitably will be exacerbated as a result of expansion; issues to which I will return.

[15] On redistributive politics and 'sexual orientation', see Herman (1994b); Boyd (1998). On redistributive politics and sex equality, see Hervey (1999).

5

Transnational Citizens: Mobility and Sexuality

INTRODUCTION

THIS CHAPTER EXPLORES the theme of sexual citizenship and law reform in the context of mobility and migration. I seek to build upon a body of work that has considered the centrality of free movement and mobility to the constitution of lesbian and gay subjectivities, both historically and currently. Mobility has been a powerful dimension in the construction of the lesbian and gay subject but, at the same time, movement across national borders historically has produced anxieties within the nation state which have been articulated to highly sexualised discourses, deployed in part in order to control and curtail mobility, not only of sexual dissidents, but of a wide range of people. Thus, I will consider migration and movement from (at least) two quite different vantage points: as enabling and empowering, but also as producing an historically hostile response from the state. I then go on to discuss current legal and political developments with respect to same sex relationships which cross national borders as an example.

In this chapter, I consider as well the related question of whether legal recognition demonstrates 'progressive' change in social attitudes and a hegemonic shift, particularly in an era characterised by increasingly reactionary responses to migration more generally, most obviously in the context of refugee movements. In a time in which the nation state responds to perceived globalisation through a selective tightening of border control, how might we understand what appears to be a liberalising of legal and political responses to the movement of lesbians and gay men, especially when migration is aimed at facilitating unification with a same sex partner? In other words, how might we 'map' what appear to be liberal and progressive developments onto a genealogy of legal and political responses to the sexuality-migration nexus? And, finally, I consider what these developments might suggest regarding broader concepts of citizenship, community, and cosmopolitanism, and notions of inclusion within civil society and the state. In keeping with the transnational focus, my analysis will itself take a somewhat 'nomadic' approach. Examples will be drawn from a range of national and geopolitical contexts to answer these questions, in an attempt to foreshadow possible future developments in the United Kingdom and European Union.

MOBILISING SEXUALITY

I begin this chapter by clarifying some concepts which are central to my argument. I use the term 'mobility' to refer to the idea of 'uprooting'; a concept closely tied to freedom of movement and, more generally, associated with the nomadic subject—the crosser of borders and boundaries (whether by 'necessity' or 'choice'). Thus, mobility is used not only in terms of a legal right to free movement, but also to suggest wider connotations with respect to sexuality (see Braidotti, 1994). Mobility provides a useful lens through which to analyse sexual identities, and here it is connected to migration and travel more generally: movement towards a new place and a new life(style). The connections between travel, mobility and sexuality have a long and complex history which I want now to trace, albeit in an admittedly abbreviated form.

The significance of migration in the constitution of lesbian and gay subjectivities is increasingly documented, particularly from within the discipline of geography (Binnie, 1997; Binnie and Valentine, 1999). It is a recognised historical phenomenon, especially noteworthy in the United States (D'Emilio, 1983b; Chauncey, 1994). For example, Kath Weston's (1995) ethnographic work on the 'Great Gay Migration' to American cities of the 1970s and early 1980s suggests that this period saw the movement of tens of thousands of people, and the importance of the imaginative, aspirational processes associated with this migratory flow cannot be underestimated. Moreover, Weston describes how the gay imaginary has come to be spatialised, with the city providing 'a beacon of tolerance and gay community, the country a locus of persecution and gay absence' (262). The creation of gay urban spaces is crucial to this narrative of migration, as is the way in which those spaces were and continue to be constituted (Castells, 1983: 237).[1]

Central to this imaginary is movement and travel, and the importance of a literal escape from the constraints of locality, family and history (Cant, 1997). In this regard, 'home' has often been an ambiguous signifier for lesbians and gays, suggesting for some a place not of refuge but from which they need to escape, thereby leading to the appropriation of a more nomadic or diasporic identity. Although I certainly would not universalise this experience, it does seem to resonate with many. Yet, at the same time, as lesbian and gay identities became increasingly 'ethnicised' (in part through a spatial imagining of the city and gay presence within it), lesbians and gays could increasingly see themselves (and be seen by others) as trying to construct a 'homeland' within an urban setting. But, of course, the appropriation of space around an identity in this way also can be (and has been) highly exclusionary. As Weston (1995: 270) suggests, 'from its

[1] But see also Knopp (1998: 172), who underscores how forms of urbanisation are also highly culturally specific, in his comparison of American and British developments; suggesting that 'territorially based economic and political practices' are more feasible in some countries than in others.

inception, the imagined community incarnated in gay neighborhoods has been gendered, racialized, and classed.' Ironically, though, as lesbian and gay identities become geographically grounded through urban migration, these places themselves come to be simultaneously 'delocalised' (Ingram, 1997: 50); part of a 'worldwide network of "gay villages"' possessing a homogeneity and familiarity across place and time (Evans, 1998: 141).

While bearing in mind the very important point that choices regarding travel and migration (and the two often raise very different issues) are always highly constrained—in particular by money—the discourse of migration is shaped as well by an array of variables, such as relationship to family, kin and place. While some seek escape from the constraints of family, for others family continues to be a place of refuge from a hostile world.[2] Moreover, narratives of travel and migration with respect to sexuality may be a particularly Western (or, indeed, American) phenomenon. However, the impact of globalisation, time-space compression, and increased labour mobility is wide-ranging. As Jon Binnie (1997: 242) suggests, 'contemporary transformations of the global economy have created new possibilities for the transformation of sexual cultures,' and this is occurring in a range of cultural locations, and is shaped as a phenomenon by an array of identities and constraints. My aim is to heed Binnie's criticism that 'awareness of migration as the underpinning of sexual-dissident consciousness is often overlooked in studies of sexuality and space' (241), and to suggest that legal discourse is not immune from that point either. Escape, displacement, and the search for place are important elements in lesbian and gay consciousness, and I think that this provides a partial explanation for the role of sexual mobility issues in legal discourse today. As Oliva Espín (1999: 5) suggests, regarding lesbian (as well as heterosexual) women, 'the crossing of borders through migration provides the space and "permission" to cross boundaries and transform their sexuality and sex roles.' Although much of the history of gay mobility has an American focus (and is internal to the nation state), Binnie (1997: 242) points out that 'the development of a European economic superpower [could] have consequences for the social and cultural politics around sexuality', in which the need for labour mobility has necessitated rights of free movement for workers between Members State of the European Union. Thus, I cautiously suggest that lesbian and gay migration issues may well have an increasing importance, and that they are facilitated by wider economic, political and cultural developments. At the same time, I believe that an analysis of lesbian and gay migration can illuminate the experience of immigration more generally.

But the importance of movement and travel in relation to the constitution of sexual identities has other dimensions as well, especially outside of the context of the increasingly clearly delineated gay spaces of urban United States. The recognition of the importance of sexuality within tourism studies, for example, has underscored the nexus between tourism and sexual identity (see Binnie,

[2] This may have particular importance in the context of racial and ethnic minorities.

1995; Hughes, 1997). Holidays may be significant in the construction of sexual identities; reinforcing again the relationship between identity, consumption and citizenship. But a more complex connection is also apparent. Identity can be understood not only as literally *being* a tourist, but also more broadly as experiencing an identity (for those living outside the gay village) which is located away from where most of life is lived; by physically leaving one's immediate environs through travel, for example, to a gay space which may be *far* from 'home.' Travel thus can serve as a metaphor for identity. The search for identity and 'self' becomes a form of tourism. Identity is constituted through visits to the 'scene' (being a tourist there), and in this way, it is through travel that we find our place—a homeland—which is removed from the everyday constraints of home. Mobility thus can signify freedom, and it also signifies a *need* to leave—to escape—which suggests inhospitability, danger and violence; dangerous journeys undertaken before reaching a (safe) destination.

Mobility has other metaphorical resonances as well. In relation to gender, Rosi Braidotti (1994: 256) has argued that 'mobility also refers to the intellectual space of creativity, that is to say the freedom to invent new ways of conducting our lives, new schemes of representation of ourselves.' Indeed, the experience of migration can provide 'a metaphor for the crossing of borders and boundaries that all lesbians [and gay men] confront when refusing to continue living in old ways' (Espín, 1999: 159). Furthermore, these migratory processes are operating on a virtual level. Research has shown how 'one of the most common benefits of the Internet to the gay community, according to the interviewees, is that it permits geographically dispersed minority individuals to interact with one another as if they were a local majority' (which may be reducing, in the process, the importance of physical travel to identity) (Weinrich, 1997: 58; see also Bell and Kennedy, 2000). Finally, not surprisingly, mobility can be discursively appropriated in resistance to its empowering potential for lesbians and gays. The perceived frequency of lesbian and gay travel has been deployed in the construction of gays as an 'undeserving' (because privileged) minority, who do not 'deserve' what are described as 'special rights,' because of their *upward mobility* (Herman, 1997: 111–36).

Yet, mobility should not be 'celebrated' as the unproblematic basis for the constitution of a lesbian or gay identity. First, as I have already suggested in other contexts in earlier chapters, mobility is constrained from the outset by its central relationship to consumption and class, which are all too frequently closely connected to race and gender. Thus, mobility is a limited and limiting basis for identity, and moreover, in analysing gay migration processes, there is a constant danger of 'centring' the affluent, more likely male, middle class, able-bodied, healthy, cosmopolitan citizen. Relatedly, there is a tendency to assume that lesbian and gay migrants are necessarily economic (or 'lifestyle') migrants who choose to move, thereby forgetting that many migration experiences may be more closely analogous to—or, indeed, in fact may be—those of refugees. Secondly, while movement may involve travel to a more congenial place and life, this also opens up the possibilities for disappointment with what one finds in the search for 'roots' and a 'home.' Migration involves loss as well as opportunity, and transnational migrants (especially when members of a racial or ethnic minority) are subject to intense surveillance from the state, as well as from within migrant communities, particularly when they are women, both heterosexual and lesbian (Espín, 1999: 6). Language also severely constrains participation and acceptance. Moreover, while migration may facilitate the expression of a sexual identity, it may involve leaving other identities behind.

Finally, the relationship between mobility, in the context of transnationalism and globalisation, and the constitution of sexual identities, is politically highly ambiguous. It has been argued, for example, that globalisation is contributing to the imposition of a modernist, Eurocentric, universalist sexual subjectivity and a formulaic picture of sexuality (Manalansan, 1995). That is, a 'Stonewall' model of liberation based upon the closet and 'coming out' is universalised as *the* foundation for same sex sexual identities, which is assumed to be culturally constituted in the same way everywhere. Mobility as the basis of identity can be seen as part of that same narrative, and indeed, physical mobility may well help to entrench it through the expansion of the gay global village, as a result of which spaces for local articulations are increasingly constrained.[3] This also impacts upon migrants and the way their sexual identities are constituted. After all, sexual cultures are also culturally specific. In her analysis of lesbian migration, Oliva Espín (1999: 156) has found, for example, that 'many women who identified as lesbian before the migration have to learn to be lesbian in their new cultural context. If a lesbian is from a non-European background, she also faces acculturation as a (so-called) minority person'.

The problems of tourism in relation to sexuality also need to be critically considered. Here again, global travel and time-space compression may be liberating for some: for those with the money to found their identity on mobility, and who can become part of the gay jet set on the 'party circuit.' However, this can result in the sexual exoticisation of the 'southern' and 'eastern', economic exploitation, and can impact negatively on local identities through a 'backlash' by the postcolonial state in response to the (sometimes rightly) perceived decadence of Western gay tourism (the docking of gay cruiseships provides an apt example).

Thus, this chapter aims not to celebrate migration for its own sake, but rather, I attempt to respond to the observations of queer geographers Jon Binnie and Gill Valentine (1999: 179) that 'the significance of migration in lesbian and gay lives and identities needs to receive greater attention.' As they go on to point out, 'sexualities and the state are mutually constituted at different spatial scales': the local, national, and increasingly, the transnational and global (179).

[3] See also Valentine (1996: 122) who argues that with the likely expansion of the European Union eastward and the growth of transnational mobilisation, an Anglo-American 'imperialism' can result through the imposition of an equality agenda modelled on individual rights. I consider this issue in detail in the context of Romania in chapter 6.

Sexualities have long served in the project of state and nation-building, and it is to such constructs that I now turn.

BORDER ANXIETIES AND THE GOOD HOMOSEXUAL

Mobility often triggers social anxieties and fears of disorder centred on a lack of social control of subjects who are not 'in place.'[4] This is most obvious in the context of reactions to travelling and nomadic peoples, particularly when movement is perceived, not as the product of *individual* exile, but rather of group migration: 'travel is very much a modern concept, signifying both commercial and leisure movement in an era of expanding western capitalism, while displacement refers to the more mass migrations that modernity has engendered' (Kaplan, 1998: 3). The latter certainly continues to produce severe social anxieties: fears of loss of control, of a loosening of national identity, anxieties about the non-assimilable other, etc. Those reactions have a long genealogy within the Western nation state.

However, this raises another important distinction, in terms of the degree to which movement involves the literal crossing of borders. It is the transgression of political boundaries which may be crucial to understanding social anxieties. The boundary represents the demarcation of space, and suggests that what is within, as well as what is outside, can be contained. As a consequence, 'movement within nation-states is called mobility and is highly desirable [for governments and corporate interests]. Movement between nation-states is called migration and is extremely undesirable. At the borders of nation-states the virtue of flexibility mutates into the vice of potentially criminal immigration' (Beck, 2000: 93). Thus, movement within nation states is often positively encouraged. Market flexibility demands the movement of factors of production, such as labour, to where the jobs are; and such mobility is often facilitated by the state. However, the crossing of nation state borders to achieve the same end is frequently seen as illegitimate, and leads to the construction of the identity of the 'economic migrant.'

Indeed, it is the fear of migration, and the connections that are drawn between migration, crime, jobs, and social insecurity, amongst other anxieties, that produce what has been described in the UK context as a 'pathological focus' on border control (Favell, 1998: 202). Adrian Favell suggests that this heightened anxiety is closely related to his claim that 'Britain is not and has never been a monocultural nation-state' and that it is 'not strictly bound to any cultural "imagined community"' (102). Although *Britain* may lack such a monocultural identity, Eve Darian-Smith (1999: 89) has convincingly shown how border control remains connected to identity and space in the context of *Englishness*:

[4] I recognise that these reactions may be culturally specific, and I would not claim that these observations are universally true.

'modern English identity is, above all, about inclusion and exclusion, which was intricately mapped onto the British state's spatial expression as an isolated island-nation. In turn this necessitated and confirmed the need for constant military defense of what was constructed as a national cultural space.' Again, border control seems central to understanding reactions to migration. It also explains national anxieties and tensions around free movement in the context of the European Union: 'with the free movement of ideas, goods and peoples defining the essential character of a new borderless Europe, the rising salience of territorial control emerges to oppose this characterization, particularly in the security and transportation areas' (75). One could add control with regard to immigration, particularly third country nationals, and especially refugees and asylum-seekers. The tension between movement and control is thus central to the relationship between post-national forces and the nation state (Favell, 1998: 245).

My claim in this chapter is that that these dynamics are important to an understanding of reactions by the state to sexual dissidents; that there are close connections between the historical desire for the social control of homosexuality, and control over movement and borders more generally. In this regard, the figure of the illegal alien provides a useful analogue to the homosexual. Both are produced as outside the bounds of normalcy, and of law, and they are strangers; but also the most dangerous strangers of all, in that they are *essentially* different, but also able to 'pass' undetected in the absence of close surveillance.

A metaphor of bodily containment thereby becomes relevant.[5] Both the homosexual and the illegal alien (or, indeed, the so-called 'bogus' asylum seeker) are constructed as threats to the coherence and boundedness of the national body, and as a threat to knowledge of the national self, producing a heightened state of anxiety in response. As Jessica Chapin (1998: 412) suggests in the context of American-Mexican border patrols:

> The failure of the border patrol to control entrances into the body politic gives rise to anxieties that are frequently articulated in terms of the vulnerability to penetration, and hence the feminization, of a symbolically masculine body. The defense of the nation, like the defense of hegemonic forms of masculine heterosexuality, is framed as a rigorous policing of boundaries, in this case against an onslaught of immigrants at America's "back door."

In both anti-immigration and anti-gay discourses, we find tropes of bodily production and waste, in/visibility, the threat of penetration of borders, the power to 'pass' undetected, to defy and to undermine knowledges of the self. Both the immigrant and the homosexual become problems of self-knowledge, necessitating heightened surveillance. Opening the door to either will lead down a slippery slope: if homosexuality, to a slippery slope of vices threatening the

[5] I have considered the role of containment metaphors in the constitution of nation state and sexuality in more detail elsewhere; see Stychin (1999).

existence of the heterosexual family; if immigration, opening the door to offspring, cousins, and in-laws, which threaten the essential cultural heritage of the nation state (Chapin, 1998: 414). The importance of reading and controlling bodies thereby becomes central.

These 'genealogical linkages' have been well documented in the UK context by Anna Marie Smith (1994) in the particular circumstances of the 1980s, which I examined in chapter 2. Smith shows how 'traditional articulations' concerning race and immigration get rearticulated in the context of the 'dangerous queer,' in which both racism and homophobia serve as 'symbolic nodal points' from which linkages are then made (17). These links centre on disease, foreign invasion, and the threat of unassimilable 'other' cultures, dangerous criminality, etc. Such tropes are heavily dependent upon viral and bodily metaphors. They are also highly spatialised. Thus, with respect to sexuality, we see described the 'heterosexual nation as if it were a body whose immune system had to ward off the dangerous homosexual virus which threatened to invade the nation from the immoral outside' (25). So too with immigration, as 'the unwanted foreign populations install themselves in the heartland of the "mother country's" body and establish the flow of nutrients back to the foreign bodies' (159). Thus, border control is metaphorically linked to the skin and immune system: 'the British obsession with border controls against continental rabies is in this sense an important precursor to the hegemonic discourse on AIDS. The representation of disease as originating in foreign elements also mobilizes the militarization of discourse on immigration' (200). Both become invasions of the social from outside and from within. There is also a connection to the idea of containment; both immigration and homosexuality have an unfixity and an excessiveness that needs to be contained to prevent invasion: this is a dangerous difference that threatens order, consensus, nation state, and way of life.[6] Like migrants more generally, the (particularly male) homosexual has been a threat because of an inability to know *his* borders, and these tropes were also closely connected to the idea of the homosexual as security risk in the context of the Cold War (Edelman, 1994).

[6] The manipulability of these tropes is readily apparent in the context of CJD, a deadly human disease which may well have a link to 'mad cow disease', which was caused by unsafe practices in the production of animal feed in the United Kingdom. Here we find the export of disease from the island state (which is hardly a new phenomenon, as the history of imperialism and the spread of disease to indigenous peoples demonstrates), and it is also a disease which could be articulated to similar discourses as have been prevalent around HIV. Yet, within the United Kingdom, the dominant tropes surrounding CJD are trivialisation ('only a few cases'), resolution ('problem now solved; no more worries'), and historical accident (a trope rarely employed within dominant discourses around HIV). Moreover, CJD itself becomes associated with foreignness and a European 'plot' against Britain in the attempts by continental European countries to foreclose the importation of British beef. Rhetorical tropes are then deployed to suggest that things are more unsafe 'there' than 'here,' where only the highest standards of food safety are employed. Thus, in a turn of events, the threat to nation state sovereignty comes from the European Union in the attempts by EU Member States to protect public health and safety.

But I want now to take the analysis further, and rather than considering the similarities in the discursive construction of homosexuality and migration, to consider the construction of homosexual as migrant. Of course, it is not surprising that, given the historical connections between discourses of homosexuality and migration, and given the way in which, as I suggested in the previous section, migration has played a key role in the construction of sexual identities, the state has sought explicitly to control migration of those who identify with or practice same sex sexual acts. Although it is important to recognise that transnational movements are not uniform as between different cultural locales, and that there is an uneven politics of mobilisation around migration which varies as between nation states, numerous examples can be deployed to demonstrate the relevance of migration in several different national contexts. Certainly, in the United States, the history of the exclusion of homosexuals from the nation state is extensive, and it was originally linked, not to discourses of national security, but to concerns about the health of the body politic (Foss, 1994: 446). There were close connections to race-based exclusions in immigration law, turning on a eugenic justification for the control of immigration (445). Later, the homosexual exclusion would be linked to anti-Communist discourses, but those too were articulated to threats to health and to the immune system. Once again we find clear links between nation, borders, race, immigration, sexuality, mobility, health, immunity, infection, and containment.

For example, until 1991, homosexuality was a ground for exclusion from admission to the United States pursuant to section 212(a)(4) of the Immigration and Nationality Act. However, the Immigration Act (1990) eliminated 'sexual deviancy' as a basis for exclusion, and this occurred through a remarkably 'low key' and largely unnoticed legislative reform (Foss, 1994: 462). Although I would not want to exaggerate the point, the timing did coincide with the so-called fall of Communism, and it demonstrates how the most blunt use of juridical power in controlling the movement of lesbians and gay men gave way to liberal reform (to be replaced, I would argue, by more subtle disciplinary mechanisms of power).[7]

Of course, the use of juridical power certainly has not disappeared in the context of same sex sexuality and migration. The American immigration ban on persons with HIV undoubtedly is underpinned by both racist and homophobic ideologies, which reproduce the discourses of containment, infection, and fears of loss of control of the body politic (Foss, 1994: 451). Of interest here also is the fact that the HIV exclusion is accompanied by a 'waiver' provision which allows persons with HIV to migrate to the United States if they have a 'qualifying relationship' with an American citizen or permanent resident (spouse, parent or

[7] The exclusion provision itself though operated as part of a system of procedures 'for administering sex in relation to multiform objectives (that concerned not only sex but also gender, race, class, and constructions of nation)': Luibheid (1998: 479). It would be interesting to speculate whether and how discourses of border control and sexual deviancy might be rearticulated post-11 September 2001.

child), and if the applicant can prove that he or she is not likely to become a 'public charge' (Soloway, nd). The waiver is not extended to same sex relationships. It underscores the extent to which even the powerful language of disease, containment and the transgression of national borders can give way to the discourse of relationships and their reunification, particularly with regard to 'spouses.' When that spousal nexus is explicitly grounded in the privatisation of financial responsibilities for support, its attraction seems overwhelming.

The repeal of the homosexual exclusion in immigration law may foreshadow, yet again, the extent to which we are witnessing a hegemonic shift at the turn of the century, and mobility provides a useful vantage point from which to investigate changing conceptions of sexuality within dominant discourses. In particular, I want to interrogate again the continuing relevance of Anna Marie Smith's 'good homosexual', which she contrasts to the 'dangerous queer' construction in 1980s Britain (which I considered in the context of New Labour discourses of sexuality in chapter 2). To repeat, Smith (1994: 18) argues, drawing on Parliamentary debates regarding section 28 of the Local Government Act 1988, that speakers who argued in support of legal restrictions on the 'promotion of homosexuality by local authorities': 'spoke again and again of a law-abiding, disease-free, self-closeting homosexual figure who knew her or his proper place on the secret fringes of mainstream society.' This becomes an imaginary figure who, because completely discrete and closeted, has no public identity at all. Thus, the scope for social acceptance of homosexuality was limited to the subject who completely respected the public/private dichotomy, and thus facilitated the elimination of all traces of homosexuality (and certainly any 'positive images') from public view.

Undoubtedly, Smith's analysis of the good homosexual resonated strongly in the context of the Thatcher Government's tropes around sexuality in 1980s Britain. As I sought to demonstrate in chapter 2, we can detect shifts in the construction of the good homosexual in present day 'New Britain' (and elsewhere). If such shifts *are* occurring (and I suggested that there are at least signs that they are) what, in turn, does that suggest about the continuing relevance of the notions of containment, nation, place, and surveillance? Do these concepts continue to leave *their* traces?

The importance of mobility in current political and legal developments is readily apparent. Freedom of movement, for example, is a central constitutional right in the context of the European Union legal order, and it is a powerful enabling force in the construction of identity; although it is a right which undoubtedly most favours 'affluent professional lesbians and gay men with marketable skills' (Bell and Binnie, 2000: 120). And, as I have argued, mobility is also vitally important in understanding anxieties which lead to a range of restrictive and repressive measures by the state in an effort to control and contain what are perceived to be threats to the nation state and its borders.

Thus, although much attention up to now in lesbian and gay legal strategies has been focused on the empowering potential of a discourse of equality and equal rights as a key to the achievement of full citizenship and social inclusion, one could argue that it is through claims around mobility rights and freedom of movement that we can find a powerful legal 'toolkit,' through which claims to sexual citizenship can be made, and with a fairly high degree of success. At the same time, the limitations of rights discourse, and its potential for the *disciplining* of the lesbian and gay subject (the key theme of this book), certainly do not disappear in the context of claims to mobility. Even with this 'freedom' seems to come requirements for responsibility, which are closely connected to changing ideas of what constitutes the good homosexual. In this regard, many developments concerning mobility claims are tied to the legal recognition of same sex relationships, and it is here where we may particularly witness hegemonic shifts. A liberal, 'progressive' acceptance and social inclusion is accompanied by an increasingly disciplinary regime which accompanies legal recognition; in which implicitly an excluded other is constructed who can then be re-placed outside the borders of a body politic in which inclusion is symbolised by relationship recognition. This reconstruction of the good homosexual, I want to argue, drawing on themes that I have already touched upon, is linked to wider social and political currents concerning the privatisation of financial responsibility within the family, in which 'good' relationships more generally are defined in terms of their cost-saving capacity for the state. Thus, once again, the centrality of paid employment to citizenship and inclusion (which is increasingly facilitated by mobility across national borders) is combined with the encouragement of stable relationships which are supported because they are perceived to be the basis of good, responsible citizenship.

CITIZENSHIP AND THE UNIFICATION OF 'SPOUSES'

> Nothing throws the question of the different ways in which formations of sexual citizenship are constructed by nation-states into greater relief than migration policies (Bell and Binnie, 2000: 119).

Mobility and sexuality increasingly conjoin in legal discourse in the context of the recognition of same sex partnerships which involve geographically complex facts, but which appear to replicate the legally recognised institution of marriage. The complexity arises from the fact that the relationship is between a 'full citizen' and a 'foreign national', and the latter seeks to migrate to the country of the former in order fully to 'perform' their marriage-like relationship.[8] These claims for reunification increasingly are being recognised in a number of Western nation states through immigration law and special administrative concessions.

[8] In the context of the European Union, the interesting issues revolve around relationships between a 'Citizen of the Union' and a 'third country national.'

The issue brings together a number of different cultural currents which on their face one might think would produce a politically explosive combination. First, it raises the spectre of the legal recognition of same sex relationships, a major political question in the West today. As Manuel Castells (1997: 219) has argued, 'the yearning for same-sex families became [in the past few years] one of the most powerful cultural trends amongst gays and lesbians . . . extending the value of family to non-traditional, non-heterosexual forms of love, sharing, and child rearing.' In addition, it relates to globalisation, transnationalism, mobility and travel. It underscores the increasing possibilities for the crossing of borders, and the forming of relationships internationally, suggesting a cosmopolitan form of citizenship that comes with travel.

As a consequence, we might expect to see a hostile reaction grounded in the fears of spatial, territorial and sexual transgression. Here we find a transgression of the nuclear family and marital relationship through its replication (and worse, the attempt to obtain legal recognition for such 'pretend' families through immigration law), as well as transgression of the physical boundaries of the nation state through the 'importation' of a homosexual relationship. The struggle for recognition of these relationships thus might well lead to a potent combination of discourses: national territory; border controls; sexual deviancy; immigration 'fraud'; and the opening of floodgates to sexual deviants.

Given the centrality of migration and travel to the constitution of lesbian and gay identities, it is not surprising that this issue has assumed an increasingly central place on the lesbian and gay law reform agenda. What is particularly interesting to me is the extent to which legal change is occurring with relatively little 'backlash.' Of course, the symbolic and material meanings of migration differ widely as between national cultures, but generally, liberal law reform appears to be occurring in this arena (as in many others) with an almost inevitability.

Australia provided an early example, and something of a model for what is occurring in other jurisdictions. As far back as 1991, recognition of same sex relationships for immigration purposes occurred by administrative regulation, described as 'Non-Familial Relationships of Emotional Interdependency' (Hart, 1992: 122). This allowance for ministerial discretion in immigration with respect to same sex couples followed an intensive lobbying campaign by the Gay and Lesbian Immigration Task Force (GLITF). Although decision-making ultimately rested with the Cabinet Minister responsible for immigration, the Task Force 'screened' applicants to ensure a 'commitment to monogamy and lookalike heterosexual relationships' (131). The Minister relied on the Task Force 'to ensure that genuine and monogamous relationships were presented by the couples' (126). Same sex migration has become increasingly institutionalised in Australia over the period since it was introduced by ministerial discretion, although admittedly not always in increasingly liberal and enabling ways (see Stychin, 1998: 217 n 13). Those applying in the 'Interdependency Visa Category' are now required to demonstrate cohabitation for a year previous to the application:

> It is necessary to prove that "for the period of 12 months immediately preceding the date of application" you had a "mutual commitment to a shared life"; "the relationship between you was genuine and continuing and you had been living together; or not living separately and apart on a permanent basis" (Gay and Lesbian Immigration Task Force, 1999).[9]

The institutionalisation and normalisation of same sex immigration, however, as is clear from the Australian example, occurs with a requirement to replicate an idealised model of heterosexual romance, centred upon monogamy, cohabitation, and interdependency. Of course, the Australian experience has to be placed in context: it is itself a national culture in which migration is highly normalised, and where the 'tyranny of distance' may create a *somewhat* more sympathetic context in which reunification of partners can occur (Hart, 1992: 121). Yet, at the same time, an undercurrent of self-discipline has informed the history of same sex migration. The early role of the Task Force was to ensure that only 'proper' relationships were placed before the Minister for the exercise of his discretion. Thus, while on the one hand, same sex couples were strongly encouraged to mimic the supposedly 'private' institution of marriage as the prerequisite for obtaining immigration status on the basis of their relationship, on the other, the couple subjected their relationship to detailed surveillance and examination, in order to determine whether it *sufficiently* copied an imagined and imaginary model.

Very similar patterns are now occurring in other national contexts. In the United Kingdom, immigration guidelines were implemented by the newly elected Labour Government on 10 October 1997; one justification being the concern, as expressed by the Immigration Minister, that previous guidelines (which made virtually no provision for same sex couple reunification) may have breached human rights law.[10] The 'concessions' which were introduced (which, at that time, operated outside the Immigration Rules themselves), made clear the requirements which had to be met before an application would be considered:

> (i) the applicant is the unmarried partner of a person present and settled in the United Kingdom or who is on the same occasion being admitted for settlement; and (ii) any previous marriage (or similar relationship) by either partner has permanently broken down; and (iii) the parties are legally unable to marry under United Kingdom law (other than by reason of consanguineous relationships or age); and (iv) the parties have been living together in a relationship akin to marriage which has subsisted for four years or more; and (v) there will be adequate accommodation for the parties and any dependants without recourse to public funds in accommodation which they own or occupy exclusively; and (vi) the parties will be able to maintain themselves and any dependants adequately without recourse to public funds; and (vii) the parties intend

[9] Effective 1 November 1999, the visa is no longer referred to as the 'Interdependency Visa,' the name having been changed to a 'Partner Visa.'

[10] See 'Britain Eases Immigration for Gay Partners' (nd).

to live together permanently; and (viii) the applicant holds a valid United Kingdom entry clearance for entry in this capacity (Home Office, 1999).[11]

The guidelines underscore the extent to which relationships must meet an 'idealised' vision of cohabitation, and they also demonstrate the extent to which marriage-like relationships are assumed to carry with them a financial responsibility grounded in interdependency. The message in the guidelines is clear: with recognition comes responsibility, through the privatisation of all costs of the migrant onto the relationship, rather than onto the state (thereby exemplifying New Labour's wider vision of good citizenship discussed in chapter 2). Yet, at the same time, while the expectation is that the couple will act 'responsibly' (primarily in a financial sense), through such mechanisms as ownership of a family home, it also has been made clear by the Government that these 'concessions' to same sex couples should not be taken to suggest that the relationships are on a 'par' with marriage. At the same time, they are required to act in a way which replicates both an idealised version of marriage and an idealised, class-inflected, model of familial economic relations.

Those who are legally able to marry are foreclosed from taking advantage of the concession. As the Immigration Minister, Mike O'Brien, explained:

> It has been a fundamental principle of the Immigration Rules that someone already settled in the United Kingdom may bring their spouse into the United Kingdom to join them, subject to meeting clear tests as to the genuineness of the marriage and the financial capacity of the couple. The policy which was announced on 10 October is a concession outside the Immigration Rules for those unmarried partners who are legally unable to marry. This retains the special position of marriage.[12]

But such a focus on privatisation of financial responsibility is very much in keeping with a broader ideology which underpins the goverment's immigration policies. The Immigration and Asylum Act 1999 affects all those who migrate on the basis of sponsorship by a family member:

> a sponsor's failure to support will be a criminal offence, and there will be no state support for sponsored immigrants, even in the direst of emergencies. The only exception will be destitute asylum-seekers, who can be provided with accommodation and support at a price. The asylum welfare system will be run by a new Home Office agency, in a completely segregated regime featuring compulsion and surveillance. Although the Home Office says its plan is to develop "clusters" of asylum-seekers in areas where local refugee communities already exist, the Bill expressly prohibits either location or the asylum-seeker's preference from being taken into account in allocating accommodation (CARF, 1999).

Thus, the overwhelming drive is for the privatisation of the costs and responsibility of migration, combined with heightened surveillance of those who

[11] In 1999, the four-year term was reduced to two years and, as of 2 October 2000, the guidelines have become incorporated into the Immigration Rules (para 295A–295O). The substantive issue of what constitutes an 'unmarried partner,' however, remains unchanged.

[12] HC Debates, 4 February 1998, 720.

require the aid of the state. The family is idealised, not only in terms of emotional support, but also as the provider of financial assistance. Yet, even in those cases where sponsorship by a same sex partner is offered, relationships remain subject to intense surveillance by immigration officers, often with continuing fears of deportation.[13] In Foucauldian terms, the gaining of the concessions may produce 'the appearance of advancement in the fight for equality' (Beaman, 1999: 185), while in its everyday application, the immigration system gives rise to surveillance, regulation and control of those seeking to migrate. Thus, the decision by the government to create the concession to same sex migrants (and then to incorporate it into the Immigration Rules) is not surprising, as it fits very well with the New Labour ideology considered in chapter 2. The government explicitly justifies its actions on the basis of conformity with human rights, but only by further entrenching the principle of privatisation of the financial costs of migration onto 'stable' relationships based on (inter)dependence.[14] Liberal law reform occurs, but only within a strict set of constraints as to the requirements which are imposed as the price of recognition for the good homosexual. Recognition rights, as opposed to redistributive politics, are inexpensive for the neoliberal state.

However, this is not to suggest that more overt anti-gay discourses, which easily articulate to issues of migration, have disappeared. The construction of the 'dangerous queer' described by Smith (1994) continues to resonate, albeit from a somewhat more marginalised vantage point.[15] Here we find attacks on the heterosexual space of marriage linked to literal concerns about border control and the protection of the space of the nation state, which is constructed in heterosexual terms. Thus, right-wing Conservative Party reaction to the concession was all too predictable:

> It is clear that the Government's policy is to place sodomite marriage on the same standing as the honourable estate of matrimony. Presumably now we will have to endure a succession of real or alleged homosexual partners being brought in to avoid our immigration rules: Lord Tebbit.

> [The regulation] undermines marriage and undermines immigration control. The Labour party have managed to deal a severe blow at both in one fell swoop: Ann Widdecombe MP.[16]

In addition to the tropes of border control and containment which are explicit in these criticisms of the concession, we find fears of 'passing' by the inauthentic in the perpetration of both an immigration fraud and a fraud on the institution

[13] See eg *Pink Paper* (2000).

[14] The employment of a discourse of 'human rights' contains an irony. Presumably, the human right which justifies the concession is the right to the enjoyment of 'private life'; but the impact of the concession is to require of same sex couples a public acknowledgment, and an openness about their relationship for the purposes of surveillance and regulation.

[15] The vociferous reactions of sections of the public to the proposed repeal of s 28 of the Local Government Act 1988 underscores this point (see chapter 2).

[16] See 'Britain Eases Immigration for Gay Partners' (nd).

of marriage.[17] Of course, the linking of migration to fraud is common within anti-immigration discourse. It is also connected to the idea of passing and of being undetectable (which is also deployed in anti-immigration discourse). Finally, critics of the concession expressed 'fears that "millions" will pretend to be gay in order to qualify.'[18] Here we find anti-gay and anti-immigrant tropes merging seamlessly through a floodgates argument grounded in the importance of controlling borders against a torrent of inauthentic migrants seeking to take advantage of a concession, but who cannot meet the requirements contained within the rules.

Although I do not want to minimise the impact of these rhetorical tropes, particularly in their ability to draw upon heightened anti-immigrant, border control sentiment, they do appear to be increasingly located outside of the mainstream. Although the good homosexual may have been a construct which, in 1980s Britain, could only be appropriated by the completely closeted homosexual who was good precisely because no public identity was assumed, two decades later, we may see, as I have already argued, a shift towards a somewhat different construct of the good homosexual. The importance of financial in(ter)dependence is emphasised, as is stability in relationships, and the replication of key signifiers of privatised responsibility, such as home ownership. Yet, while the responsibilities of citizenship are demanded, recognition is extremely limited: marriage remains an unattainable option, as do most of the material benefits which flow therefrom. Official recognition may allow reunification across national frontiers (with accompanying surveillance and regulation), but it seems to be justified implicitly, not on a discourse of human rights (one of the official justifications), but on the importance of stable relationships in the fulfilment of the responsibilities of citizenship. This move fits New Labour's focus on the importance of stable family life as both a prerequisite to success in a global marketplace, and as a response to 'the individualizing self-interest' of that same marketplace (Bell and Binnie, 2000: 111).

This construction of the good homosexual *citizen* also can be demonstrated by turning to another example; this time a national culture in which issues of migration are tied to constitutional rights: South Africa. In keeping with my claim that migration issues have assumed a heightened priority in sexuality politics, it is worth noting that one of the most important constitutional challenges to South African laws on sexuality has centred on the issue of migration of same sex partners, and it has been the subject of a test case before the Constitutional Court (*National Coalition for Gay and Lesbian Equality v Minister of Home Affairs* (2000) (1) Butterworths Constitutional Law Reports 39). This appeal dealt with the constitutionality of section 25(5) of the Aliens Control Act 96 of 1991, which allows preferential treatment to be given to a foreign national

[17] The irony is that the absence of such a concession leads to widespread 'passing' as heterosexual through fraudulent 'immigration marriages.'

[18] See 'Britain Eases Immigration for Gay Partners' (nd).

applying for an immigration permit, who is 'the spouse . . . of a person permanently and lawfully resident in the Republic,' but not, in the words of the Constitutional Court, 'to a foreign national who, though similarly placed in all other respects, is in a same-sex life partnership with a person permanently and lawfully resident in the Republic' (para 15). The challenge to the law was brought by the national lesbian and gay rights lobbying group, in combination with a number of applicants claiming on behalf of their 'alien' same sex partners.

It was determined by the Court that, given the wording of the statute, it could not be construed as including foreign same sex partners (para 26). Therefore, at issue was its constitutionality in terms of the rights of the South African partners. Interestingly, the Court explicitly left open the question whether the provision was unconstitutional in relation to the mobility rights of the citizen 'spouse' (para 28), instead focusing on the violation of equality rights: 'overlapping or intersecting discrimination on the grounds of sexual orientation and marital status' (para 40). The Court found the failure to recognise same sex partnerships within the statute to be unconstitutional and, in the process, it went to great length to demonstrate a *knowledge* of homosexual relationships, thereby underscoring law's continuing production of the Truth of homosexuality. According to Justice Ackermann for the unanimous Court, such relationships are defined as: 'a life partnership which entails a conjugal same-sex relationship, which is the only form of conjugal relationship open to gays and lesbians in harmony with their sexual orientation' (para 36), which is 'not distinguishable in any significant respect from that of heterosexual spouses' (para 53). Unmarried heterosexuals are left to one side in the case, as the remedy ordered by the Court is the 'reading in,' after the word spouse, of the words: 'or partner, in a permanent same-sex life partnership' (para 86).

But with legal recognition comes requirements of disclosure and surveillance, as the Court proceeds to define (or, more accurately, produce) a permanent same sex life partnership which is indistinguishable from opposite sex marriage. The Court finds that while conventional marriage, because of its legal recognition as a status, 'is capable of easy and virtually incontestable proof', same sex relationships are not (para 84). Thus, implicit again in the judgment, despite its very liberal and progressive tenor, is a fear of fraud through 'pretended' relationships. Consequently, Justice Ackermann makes plain that, 'it would . . . be permissible for Parliament and the executive to take reasonable steps to prevent persons falsely purporting to be in same-sex life partnerships from evading the provisions of the Act' (para 85). Finally, the Court explicitly defines the meaning of 'permanence' in relationships, producing the idealised relationship against which all others can be measured:

> Without purporting to provide an exhaustive list, such facts would include the following: the respective ages of the partners; the duration of the partnership; whether the partners took part in a ceremony manifesting their intention to enter into a permanent partnership, what the nature of that ceremony was and who attended it; how

> the partnership is viewed by the relations and friends of the partners; whether the partners share a common abode; whether the partners own or lease the common abode jointly; whether and to what extent the partners share responsibility for living expenses and the upkeep of the joint home; whether and to what extent the partners have made provision for one another in relation to medical, pension and related benefits; whether there is a partnership agreement and what its contents are; and whether and to what extent the partners have made provision in their wills for one another. None of these considerations is indispensable for establishing a permanent partnership. In order to apply the above criteria, those administering the Act are entitled, within the ambit of the Constitution and bearing in mind what has been said in this judgment, to take all reasonable steps, by way of regulations or otherwise, to ensure that full information concerning the permanent nature of any same-sex life partnership, is disclosed (para 88).

The decision neatly exemplifies Lori Beaman's (1999: 186) insight about the production of the truth of homosexual relationships through legal discourse:

> the public confession of one's sexual orientation becomes a part of the process of the production of the truth of sex. The 'outed' party is rewarded for his/her public declaration with the promise of equality. The law becomes the confessional, the gay or lesbian couple the penitents, properly controlled by framing their requests within the confines of legal boundaries.

The conditions of recognition for the transnational couple include the requirement to approach the idealised status of marriage in the organisation of the relationship, largely through the appearance of permanence, stability and location in a particular *place* (preferably an owner-occupied home). The transnational, nomadic potentiality of the relationship is constrained by the act of recognition through a disciplinarity of geography and place which is imposed in order forcibly to provide roots to the relationship, as the reciprocal side of the claiming of recognition rights. This ironically occurs, in the South African example, within a national context in which, historically, marriage and the family often did not comport with such a narrow model because of the forced mobility which the apartheid system imposed upon so many families. Indeed, spousal relationships often survived distance and severe dislocation and the 'standards' which the Court is now imposing would themselves have appeared 'alien' to many marital relationships. Instead, those requirements (such as common abode, pension rights, wills, etc) resonate in the language of financial privatisation of responsibility, constructing an image of the good homosexual which seems to be strongly inflected by a class-based and perhaps race-based construction of homosexuality. That is, implicit in the Court's imagining of the good homosexual may be an understanding of homosexuality as a white, middle class phenomenon and, as a consequence, a wide array of ways of living come to be erased.[19]

[19] The racial construction of same sex sexualities in South Africa is a complex issue, beyond the scope of this chapter; see generally, Stychin (1998: 52–58).

Processes of legal liberalisation through recognition seem here again to come at a price, and that is in how the homosexual must be put in *place* through the disciplinarity of relationships centring upon the privatisation of financial responsibility for oneself and one's 'life partner.' Historically, as I have suggested, the homosexual may have been constituted as the stranger, the nomad, the outsider, and the excess, in which homosexuality was foreign to the nation state. However, with changing times, we find that the good homosexual can be incorporated and assimilated into a space that is 'not-marriage' (which remains a special symbolic heterosexual space), and presumably in which children are simply *assumed* not to enter the picture, but in which a relationship is recognised which possesses the imagined characteristics of marriage and which can be interrogated and subjected to surveillance on that basis. While relationship recognition in all of these cases may be a result of increased mobility, legal 'success' produces a requirement to *settle down*, and to disidentify with the disorder and lawlessness associated with undisciplined migratory flows.

The disciplinarity of legal recognition has been observed by others. As Lori Beaman (1999: 191) argues, drawing on a feminist analysis, 'the discussion of this one form of relationship as though it were the ultimate *raison d'être* in human relations is extremely misleading. Marriage is arguably the most efficient means by which men have been able to "protect" and control what is theirs.' So too, as Jon Binnie (1997: 246) cautions, 'discussion of law reform in the area of migration can lose sight of the desirability of different forms of relationships. Many would-be immigrants are not in long-term relationships, and recognising same-sex relationships for the purpose of immigration would reinforce the ideal of long-term relationships', and would 'further the agenda of those activists who favour the politics of assimilation.' Yet, this process of legal recognition, as I have argued, seems to be 'progressing' inexorably.

I have used the examples of Australia and South Africa in this chapter to foreshadow developments which may occur in the European Union. This is evidenced already by a European Commission proposal for a directive on the right to family reunification, which would facilitate migration by 'third country nationals,' including same sex partners (Commission of the European Communities, 1999). Moreover, the European Union inevitably will need to resolve the issue of the movement of legally recognised partners between Member States (see generally Elman, 2000). Thus, moves which up to now have been occurring at the national level are beginning to 'filter up' to the transnational arena, where we may well witness EU law in the future.

CONCLUSIONS

In this chapter, I have argued that it is no coincidence that mobility has assumed such a central role in claims to sexual citizenship today. Both citizenship and mobility articulate to inclusion and exclusion. The hegemony of free movement in economic discourses of globalisation under late capitalism has proven a useful discourse upon which to graft sexual citizenship demands. However, the complexity of processes of economic globalisation is apparent in the context of sexuality. Global capital, as Jon Binnie (2000: 166) argues, desires urban spaces which are 'business-friendly controlled environments,' but not obviously queer cultural hotspots; underscoring how sexual citizenship has 'a mixed relationship with advanced capitalism' (Isin and Wood, 1999: 71).

Claims regarding mobility also provide new insights and further problematise simple binaries concerning cosmopolitan and communitarian visions of citizenship, thereby underscoring the inadequacies of such a stark choice (a key theme of many of the case studies in *Governing Sexuality*) (see also Bellamy and Warleigh, 1998). On the one hand, citizenship claims centred on mobility rights appear intuitively to emanate from the cosmopolitan citizen, and suggest a 'transition from a nation-state world order to a cosmopolitan world order' (Beck, 2000: 83). Rights are deployed in universal terms, such that they can be claimed across national frontiers, trumping local hostility and opposition in their path. Moreover, recognition rights further the flow of factors of production across borders; localism again becomes an anti-modern hindrance to globalising forces and, ultimately, to the creation of a more transnational civil society. In this way, the lesbian or gay subject, who claims citizenship rights on the basis of freedom of movement, becomes the quintessential cosmopolitan citizen. This seems appropriate given the centrality of migration, movement, and travel to the constitution of a gay identity—what Jon Binnie (2000: 166) describes as a 'queer cosmopolitanism' based on 'knowingness and sophistication.'

However, I also have suggested in this chapter that such an analysis is problematic. Rights which are being advanced, which stem from mobility, are claimed, not so much as a means to advance the values of cosmopolitanism, but as a means of social inclusion within a local/national community, where recognition within the confines of community is seen as central to citizenship. This is the desire for incorporation within a specific local culture in resistance to the historical construction of lesbians and gays as outsiders to national culture and as non-citizens.

It is perhaps ironic that mobility provides the basis upon which such communitarian-based claims are made, given that these claims are often justified through cosmopolitan discourses, such as international human rights and globalisation. Although they are resisted, to some degree, in the language of localism and community, this may become increasingly marginalised. The success of these claims may facilitate mobility, free movement and 'transnational' relationships (all of which may be associated with cosmopolitanism), but more importantly perhaps, the goal is inclusion within national civil societies through the power of law. But this, in turn, also underscores the contradictions thrown into relief by the relationship between globalisation and sexual citizenship. While strong, traditional families may be seen as a corrective to the insecurities of the global marketplace, globalisation has facilitated the emergence of transnationalism in the politics of sexual citizenship. However, that development clearly centres the already privileged within the lesbian and gay communities; which reproduces the construction of lesbians and gays as affluent, independent, unconstrained by family, and selfish. Yet, the political and legal claims that these sexual 'dissidents' make are for recognition as 'couples' located within particular communities, in which the presumed benefits of family life for communities are being reproduced. In this way, cosmopolitanism and communitarianism become inseparably intertwined.

My aim, once again in this chapter, thus has been to interrogate how recognition, social inclusion and citizenship claims come at a price, in terms of the demands of assimilation, normalisation and disciplinarity in several different guises (eg marketplace; monogamy; traditional patterns of gendered relationships; home ownership), and to underscore the role which law plays in these constructions. This has been the central theme of *Governing Sexuality*, and it is crucial to the analysis of this chapter. Clearly, changes in civil society resulting from transnational social and economic processes are shaping citizenship claims and are having a material impact on people's lives. But, at the same time, legal discourse also operates to 'tame' them; to take cosmopolitan subjects of rights and put them in their place: that is, within a recognisable, manageable, and normalisable guise (and, if not normalisable, to exclude them).

This analysis also raises the wider question of whether alternative ways of imagining a legal regime that recognises spousal-type relationships is possible. In the absence of open borders, is the disciplinary and normalising function of law an inevitable result of relationship recognition? Of course, it has been the privileging of marriage in immigration law that has led to highly effective resistance and subversion of that institution through 'marriages of convenience.' In a more 'liberal' regime, will the 'unattached' form same sex relationships of convenience? And what would be the reaction to such relationships from 'authentic' same sex couples (and from activist groups such as Stonewall)? It bears reiterating that with discipline inevitably comes resistance in unpredictable forms. The ability of law to manage and to discipline is never totalising, and subjects are not necessarily as docile nor as unimaginative as we may sometimes think. Finally, consideration should be paid to the legal status of the migrating 'dependant' who, by definition, is cast in a non-autonomous (and sometimes highly precarious) position. As a normative matter, should law produce such a status? Should lesbian and gay law reform campaigners be encouraging the reproduction of a subject position grounded in dependence? However, in the absence of greater openness to independent migration, there are no easy answers. What I have argued in this chapter, though, is that current developments underscore the way in which law, and the language of citizenship, prove again to be both constraining *and* enabling in their deployment around issues of sexuality.

6

'We Want to Join Europe, Not Sodom': Sexuality and European Union Accession in Romania

INTRODUCTION

ALTHOUGH THEY ARE still located formally outside of the European Union and the so-called 'Fortress Europe,' the accession countries of Central and Eastern Europe are far from immune from the influence and impact of the institutions of the European Union. In this chapter, I explore the disciplinary force of those institutions (as well as of other international and transnational actors) on one of the accession countries, Romania, as well as the ways in which these disciplinary forces are resisted within this nation state. Generalised claims regarding recurring themes of *Governing Sexuality*—the nation, citizenship, and globalisation—will be explored through what may appear to be a small scale example: the struggle over the legal status of homosexuality. After years of social struggle (within and outside the nation state), Romania finally repealed its criminal law on same sex sexual relations on 14 January 2002. On the same day, the Parliament enacted law preventing and punishing all forms of discrimination based on a series of enumerated grounds including sexual orientation.[1] These legal developments provide the impetus and context for the analysis in this chapter.

Romania is a nation state widely viewed within the European Union, NATO, the IMF, and the World Bank as, at best, on the 'slow track' to achieving full membership in the economic and security institutions of the West. Less charitably, it is seen as an unpredictable, unruly and 'un-westernised' country in need of economic and political discipline, and it is viewed as a state that has never fully embraced the 'values' central to the West. As a consequence, Romania provides an important site in which to examine the impact of the promise of European integration. Given that EU reports, as well as those of the IMF and World Bank, consistently argue that Romania is far from achieving the

[1] Romania has a two house Parliament (the Senate and the Chamber of Deputies). Laws must be passed by both chambers, and thereafter approved by the President of Romania.

economic preconditions for EU accession (particularly given the slow rate of privatisation, continuing macroeconomic instability, and lack of reform of governance structures), it may seem idiosyncratic at best to focus on homosexuality as the lens through which to explore the dynamics of European integration and the resistance of the nation state. However, I argue in this chapter that homosexuality and its legal status have become severely overdetermined in Romanian political and public discourse and its recent decriminalisation was read as a demand and precondition emanating from 'Europe.' Along with the anti-discrimination law, it was understood as a necessary step in order to achieve, not only the normalisation of homosexuality, but the normalisation of Romania. Many domestic actors read this development as a fundamental challenge to national sovereignty, identity, and a way of life being swept aside by the forces of globalisation. While the economic austerity imposed in the post-Communist era may have left many Romanians feeling even worse off economically than before the fall of Communism, homosexuality has served as one of several scapegoats and symbols of a difficult and slow transition, and of the painful process by which Romania seeks to integrate in its turn to the West, and to emerge from its ignoble past.

This chapter thus explores the interplay between the forces of European integration and of national identity, and the way in which the former, rather than being simply a force from 'outside' imposed upon Romania, was deployed by local actors within a severely underdeveloped Romanian civil society, through the language of human rights. I begin with a short history of these actors and the NGO which has been the driving force behind the struggle for legal and social change in this field, ACCEPT. This NGO and its history, however, cannot be understood without an appreciation of the legal context in which ACCEPT emerged: the notorious 'article 200' of the Romanian Penal Code. I document this criminal provision and I include some background and explanation of Romanian attitudes to article 200 and the campaign for its repeal. This analysis in turn requires a consideration of the regulation of gender and sexuality, not only in post-Communist Romania, but also under the Ceausescu regime for, in the Romanian context, the post-1989 era cannot be seen in terms of a clear break with the past. I also try to locate resistance to the decriminalisation of homosexuality within the wider context of the role of national identity, understood in highly ethnicised terms, in Romania past and present. I argue that it is only by centring upon the ideological role played by the nation state that we can then appreciate the significance of the challenge posed by what are seen as 'outside' influences—supranational 'standards'—within the context of the drive for an expanded European Union. This analysis also illustrates the significance of the role of civil society actors, for which there is little historical precedent in Romania, in struggling to achieve social change through a form of participation and the claiming of rights that amounts to a practice of European sexual citizenship. And rights of sexual citizenship recently have begun to be achieved in Romania both with the decriminalisation of same sex relations and the anti-discrimination law. This chapter thus aims to provide a genealogy of this historically important moment.

CREATING AND RECREATING HOMOSEXUALITY IN ROMANIA

Struggles over the decriminalisation of homosexuality, and the role of social movement actors in the process, require an understanding of the history of same sex relations and their legal and political status. As has been suggested in other European national contexts, the invention of a homosexual identity is largely a twentieth century phenomenon, and Romania is no different in this respect. The classification of sexualities in law can be traced to the Penal Code of 1936, when the Kingdom of Romania enacted article 431, which criminalised 'acts of sexual inversion committed between men or between women, if provoking public scandal', with a penalty of six months to two years' imprisonment (Human Rights Watch, 1998: 6). The framing of the law through the use of the public/private distinction is significant (and 'public scandal' is highly ambiguous in the way in which it can cut across public and private space). The law also was noteworthy in criminalising relations between women (unlike many other national contexts), and also for *potentially* creating a private sphere free of legal regulation for both men and women. The 1936 Penal Code would not be revisited comprehensively until well into the Ceausescu era in 1968. Ceausescu, a relatively unknown Communist Party aparatchik, assumed power in 1964. The 1968 Penal Code revision can be viewed as an opportunity taken to reinforce what would be—by any comparison—a totalitarian regime of surveillance and intense regulation achieved through an invasive state and the annihilation of the private sphere (Human Rights Watch, 1998: 11–12). Thus, the 1968 Penal Code saw the enactment of articles 200–202:

- article 200: sexual relations between persons of the same sex are punishable by imprisonment of one to five years;
- article 201: 'acts of sexual perversion which cause public scandal' are punishable with one to five years' imprisonment;
- article 202: dealt with 'sexual corruption' of a minor.

Sexual perversion was defined as 'any unnatural act in connection with sexual life, other than those provided in Article 200' (Human Rights Watch, 1998: 11).

Thus, by virtue of article 200, homosexuality was made illegal with no requirement of public scandal, and with increased penalties. This legal invasion of the private sphere must be placed in a wider context of sex/gender regulation in Romania, particularly the brutal invasiveness and surveillance of women's bodies through harsh anti-abortion laws enforced in large measure through routine gynecological examinations, in combination with severe prison sentences for performing or obtaining an abortion (see generally Kligman, 1998). Under the Ceausescu regime, there was no realm beyond the interest of the state.

Article 200 served two purposes. First, extensive testimonial evidence establishes that it was regularly and rigorously enforced against those accused of same sex sexual relations, 'amid virtual indifference abroad' (Human Rights Watch, 1998: 13). Secondly, particularly in the final years of the Ceausescu era, article 200 could usefully be used 'against ideological nonconformists' (13). In the 1980s, when Western attention began to focus on human rights abuses in Romania, 'the dubious and disloyal could be charged under Article 200 without attracting international attention—allowing Ceausescu's human-rights record to remain cosmetically clear' (12).

The (arguably inaccurately described) 'fall of Communism' in Romania in December 1989, is engrained on most Western memories with one image: the execution of Nicolae and Elena Ceausescu. Less widely known is the extent to which the National Salvation Front which assumed power, later to win election, represented a high degree of continuity with the Communist regime, both in terms of who governed, and in terms of policy. The absence of civil society in Ceausescu's Romania (surveillance was routinely carried out by citizens on each other, leading to the distrust of any group) left a gap for a post-1989 state apparatus devoid of the ideological anchor of Ceausescu's brand of Communism. The vacuum was filled by a reliance on ethnic national politics; a discourse which had also served Ceausescu very well (see generally Gallagher, 1995).

Thus, although the 'new' government repealed the laws prohibiting abortion, and did so very quickly, it showed no similar desire to repeal article 200. Indeed, the early years of the Iliescu government were not characterised by a 'progressive' approach in this or other areas, nor was there a particular concern with Romania's image in the West (Phinnemore, 2001: 252). With time, this intransigence dissipated, as it became increasingly clear that Romania's future lay westward (Gallagher, 2001: 108). It also became apparent that any invitations to join the institutions of the west would come with both political and economic conditions attached (Phinnemore, 2001). With respect to homosexuality, this was true as early as 1993, when *rapporteurs* from the Council of Europe, visiting Romania following its application for admission, began raising the issue of article 200 (Human Rights Watch, 1998: 30). The response from then Minister of Justice, Petre Ninosu, was far from accommodating: 'if we let homosexuals do as they please, it would mean entering Europe from behind' (31–32).[2] Little did Ninosu realise the conditions that would be demanded by other institutions—the European Union, NATO, IMF, World Bank—throughout the 1990s. It would also become clear that pressure from the European Union, rather than the Council of Europe, would prove to be the effective force for legal change.[3]

The brand of social conservatism exemplified by Ninosu's statement characterised the attitude of many Romanian politicians, and this made it extremely

[2] Ninosu is now a member of the Constitutional Court.

[3] Also of much importance was the work of the International Gay and Lesbian Human Rights Commission, and particularly Scott Long, whose research on human rights abuses in Romania resulted in the *Public Scandals* report: Human Rights Watch (1998).

difficult even for those governments prepared to repeal article 200 to achieve the political backing for such a measure. It was also an attitude strongly fostered by the Romanian Orthodox Church, a central player in politics and society, which seized upon the issue in the name of the defence of a Romanian (Orthodox-Christian) way of life (Human Rights Watch, 1998: 33).

In September 1993, the assembly of the Council of Europe called on Romania to repeal article 200, despite also admitting Romania to the Council. Additional pressure for reform came from a decision of the Romanian Constitutional Court in July 1994, which found that article 200 violated privacy rights guaranteed by Romania's Constitution, to the extent that it criminalised acts committed in private (Human Rights Watch, 1998: 32). However, the Court also (highly problematically) reintroduced the concept of 'public scandal' into the law. In response to these developments, the Romanian Government and Parliament, in November 1996, brought into force a 'new' article 200, which echoed the earlier formulation of criminal regulation found in the 1936 Penal Code. The new article 200 relied again on the public/private distinction to criminalise 'sexual relations between persons of the same sex, if producing public scandal' (para 1) with a penalty of one to five years' imprisonment. Paragraph 5 of article 200 punished 'inciting or encouraging a person, in public, to commit the acts', again with a penalty of one to five years (Human Rights Watch, 1998: 2). In fact, paragraph 5 amounted to a ban on any form of homosexual association. A reliance on public scandal was deployed in order to claim compliance with human rights jurisprudence, which itself has relied heavily on protecting a private sphere, but which historically has done little to protect the expression of sexuality in public life.

The legal change, part of an omnibus penal law reform package, despite providing only a limited decriminalisation of homosexuality, took two years and two defeats in Parliament to enact. This can be explained by the opposition of many nationalist Members of Parliament (upon whom the government relied), as well as a hostile press, and an Orthodox Church asserting its role in the political life of Romania. For all of these forces, resistance to change would be characterised consistently in terms of the protection of a religious-cultural way of life, against outside influences and conspiracies seeking to undermine traditional Romanian values. These tropes have a long history in Romania, and have been consistently deployed in the name of ethnic nationalism. As well, for the Church, the issue of homosexuality provided a device through which it could reassert its authority in public, political life (and other issues, such as abortion, were not politically 'saleable,' given the association of abortion regulation with Communism). The Church, in this way, could assert an independent role, which also enabled it, to some extent, to draw attention away from its own dubious past associations with the Ceausescu regime (Gallagher, 1996).

The 'reform' of 1996—brought in shortly before a general election the ruling party would lose—was a far from satisfactory solution from a human rights perspective. In a country in which the private sphere had little history as a zone free from state intrusion, and in which civil society in the public sphere remained extremely weak to non-existent, there was little 'freedom' either for sexual acts in 'private' (which might well be found to cause public scandal), or for sexual expression of an identity in 'public' through lesbian and gay civil society or commercialised actors (which *definitely* would be interpreted as causing public scandal). The effect has been to close down virtually all homosexual expression (including, for example, information on the spread of HIV: Macovei and Coman, 1999). Add to this legislative double bind an extremely homophobic police force, and the results are predictable. Human rights organisations have documented extensive use of the law, resulting in arrests and convictions, as well as police and prison brutality (Human Rights Watch, 1998: 47). Perhaps most famously, Amnesty International took up the case of the only woman convicted under article 200, in a culture where lesbian women's sexuality has been largely erased. It was within this environment that ACCEPT was formed.

Any analysis of the impact of European integration and other transnational and international forces on the decriminalisation of homosexuality in Romania must place the Bucharest-based human rights NGO, ACCEPT, at the centre.[4] The history of ACCEPT can be traced to 1994, when a group of Romanians and members of the expatriate community formed the 'Bucharest Acceptance Group,' a small collection of volunteers also associated with the Romanian Helsinki Committee. Their major success was the organisation of a symposium entitled 'Homosexuality—A Human Right?' in Sinaia, Romania in May 1995. From that conference, a permanent organisation and important civil society actor, ACCEPT, was born, which was officially registered as a human rights NGO on 25 October 1996. Because of the presence of article 200, ACCEPT activists chose to register as a human rights organisation rather than as a gay and lesbian rights organisation. The latter certainly would have been refused registration by the state, pursuant to the explicit wording of paragraph 5 of article 200, which bans association.

Of importance to note in this period was that the founding of ACCEPT cannot be separated from the securing of funding to set up and develop the organisation and its infrastructure. At the outset, funding was made available, first, by the Embassy of the Netherlands (for the Sinaia Conference), and then by the Dutch Ministry of Foreign Affairs, as part of a programme (called MATRA) designed to strengthen institutions in the target countries of Central and Eastern Europe through their 'twinning' with institutions in the Netherlands. The Romanian activists were twinned with the COC—'the federation of Dutch associations for the integration of homosexualities'—and this partnership would continue, formally and informally, into the future. The COC-ACCEPT project funding and expertise were crucial in the setting up of an organisational infrastructure, the opening of office space, developing programmes and activ-

[4] The following history of ACCEPT is drawn from interviews with Adrian Coman, former Executive Director of ACCEPT, held in Romania in the summer of 2001: Coman (2001).

ities, etc. ACCEPT now provides a community centre in Bucharest for cultural, social and recreational activities; a medical and psychological counselling office; library and reading room; and administrative office.

Despite a limited role as a service provider, however, ACCEPT's primary mission from the outset was as a human rights NGO centred upon the repeal of article 200, and more generally, on the advancement of the human rights of sexual minorities. Importantly, ACCEPT was not established with the *primary* intent of providing social, recreational and cultural support (despite its obvious importance to lesbians and gays in Romania). Rather, as a relatively small group of activists, its main agenda has been as a law reform project, which was to be advanced, not through grass roots mobilisation (an unlikely strategy for success in Romania), but through carefully planned strategic lobbying by a small and dedicated group of activists with an array of supporters from abroad.[5] At the same time, ACCEPT located itself domestically within the human rights NGO community, often working to develop links between human rights struggles (aided by the fact that many who worked for ACCEPT had long credentials in the human rights field). Following its official registration, ACCEPT embarked upon a sustained human rights campaign domestically through lobbying, media exposure, swaying public opinion and challenging stereotypes through more positive images at every opportunity. ACCEPT has sought to develop, throughout its lifetime, 'a different and new discourse that was based on fundamental values, appealing to anyone irrespective of sexual orientation' (Coman, 2001).

In terms of the development of pressure from abroad, this had several tracks. First, the twinning with the COC Netherlands, which included a Dutch project coordinator based for a time in Bucharest, not only assisted with the development of infrastructure, but also provided a link back to a (liberal) EU Member State (and one that had invested money in an NGO challenging state law in Romania).[6] This aspect of the history of the decriminalisation campaign has involved significant pressure from EU institutions (particularly the EU Parliament, but also the Commission), as well as the Council of Europe, national governments from within and outside the European Union, interested individual politicians, NGOs, and the general public (including demonstrations against Romanian politicians when they travelled abroad, which forced them to respond publically). Without question, pressure from abroad—but particularly from EU institutions—has forced legal change, and activists will readily admit

[5] With its legal victories now achieved, the future role of ACCEPT will be an interesting issue. As former Executive Director Adrian Coman (2001) predicted to me: 'in five years, ACCEPT will have specialised services for lesbian and gay people; it will be a resource for any initiative targeted at lesbian, gay, bisexual and transgendered people in Romania, and that would include, for example, strategies of the Ministry for Labour and Social Protection.'

[6] The COC continues to collaborate with ACCEPT with the support of the MATRA programme. The current focus is on reaching out to local lesbian and gay organisations in Romania, and to assist with the development of the Bulgarian lesbian and gay movement (by drawing upon the experience and expertise of ACCEPT).

that without that pressure, the chances of achieving reform would have been remote (Coman, 2001).

Thus, ACCEPT, from its inception, worked tirelessly to raise the issue of article 200 on the agenda of the European Union and to keep it on the agenda of the Council of Europe, which was continuing to monitor the Romanian human rights record in this period (and which included the treatment of the Roma and the Hungarian ethnic minority). Although it did play an early role in law reform, it is fair to say that the influence of the Council of Europe declined during the mid-late 1990s, and the influence of the institutions of the European Union increased in that same period. Any pressure that was exerted by the Council of Europe was resisted successfully by the state. And it would be to the institutions of the European Union that ACCEPT would turn its attention in the drive for the elimination of article 200. Although other avenues were also pursued, such as encouraging pressure from national governments (particularly the Netherlands and Sweden), and lobbying individual politicians and other NGOs, Adrian Coman (2001), then executive director of ACCEPT concludes, 'I think the repeal of Article 200 is strictly the result of EU pressure.' This pressure would last over several years, and represents a key moment in the move towards EU accession in Romania.

The time which the struggle would take, and the ferocity of feelings amongst actors within the state, church, and large sections of the general public which the issue aroused, points to a second dynamic that fervently resisted the movement towards decriminalisation as a form of Europeanisation. This dynamic was summed up by the view of Archbishop Bartolomeu Anania, that 'we want to join Europe, not Sodom' (Dascalu, 2000). In other words, it is the dynamic of ethnic nationalism in which outside challenges to a vision of community are resisted and repelled.[7] The article 200 controversy, I want to argue, can be located on this wider terrain on which the forces of modernisation and tradition are engaged in social struggle.[8] But before examining how modernity appears to triumph over tradition in this particular battle, I want to place both dynamics within a wider historical context.

[7] To give another example, one Romanian politician is reported to have said that 'of course the EU Parliament wants us to abolish Article 200—they are all gay' (Coman, 2001).

[8] See Haddock and Caraiani (1999: 258): 'Modernizers have sought to adopt (something like) the western conception of civil society, with a stress on human rights, the rule of law, economic liberalism and association with pan-European institutions. They have found themselves confronted not only by hard-line nationalists, for whom cosmopolitan language is a betrayal of Romanian national identity, but by traditionalists intent upon reconciling a distinctive Romanian inheritance with a wider *Europe des patries*.'

PEASANTS AND PROLETARIAT: SEX, GENDER AND NATION IN THE ROMANIAN NATIONAL IMAGINARY

As I have already described, from the outset, the intervention of international bodies in the repeal campaign for article 200 was resisted within Romania by politicians, the media and particularly the Orthodox Church. Within opposition discourse, both homosexuality and the pressure to repeal article 200 were identified as 'a corrupt incursion alien to indigenous values' (Human Rights Watch, 1998: 35). This trope, and related ones, would be endlessly repeated in the 1990s. Various explanations can be advanced as to why the article 200 issue assumed such a powerful symbolic position within the Romanian national consciousness (or at least amongst elites).

With respect to the Orthodox Church, article 200 was a useful point through which it could exert its 'moral' authority and its role in political life. Relatedly, the Orthodox Church itself had an ignoble history of collaboration with the Ceausescu regime, and the head of the Orthodox Church, Patriarch Teoctist, was appointed by Ceausescu. Again, article 200 allowed the Church to direct attention away from itself and on to homosexuality (except when allegations of homosexual activity amongst priests came to light) (Coman, 2001; Gallagher, 1996; Human Rights Watch, 1998: 33).

More generally, resistance to the repeal of article 200, and to the role of the European Union and other 'outsiders' in pressuring Romania, can be located on a wide historical plane, which demands consideration of Romanian national identity itself. Romania as an ethnic nation and people antedated the Romanian state, and throughout its history both nation and state have been quite obviously 'constructed identities' and, moreover, 'the Romanian state never enjoyed a clear identity or settled boundaries' (Haddock and Caraiani, 1999: 260). Romania as state emerged from the collapse of the Hapsburg Empire, and the history of the national movement in the nineteenth century is replete with examples in which Romanian identity was manipulated in the service of a political strategy (Verdery, 1991: 34). Those constructions of identity were themselves derived from disparate claims as to the origins of the Romanian people:

> One, the "Latinist" camp, argues that Romanians are the lineal descendants of the legions of Roman Emperor Trajan and of colonists he brought from Rome, after he conquered the area (105–106 A.D.) and incorporated it into his empire as the province of Dacia. A second, the "Dacianist" camp, holds in its most extreme version that Romanians are the descendants of the original inhabitants (known as the Dacians), who adopted the Latin language and some elements of Roman civilization but otherwise transmitted their own customs and bloodline down in to the present. The third, the "Daco-Roman" view—the one most widely held in the twentieth century—regards Romanians as the descendants of intermingled Roman colonists and survivors of the Dacian indigenes (Verdery, 1991: 31).

This quest for national identity in origins—'situated, as is clear, between pro-westernism and indigenism' (Verdery, 1991: 31)—has framed politics throughout the history of Romania, in which 'foreignness' has often proved the ultimate disqualification for a political claim. Thus, for example, groups within the Romanian national movement who identified with Hapsburg institutions claimed a Roman (Western) identity; those associated with Orthodoxy, a mixed or indigenous (but not Eastern) national character (33). This bifurcation between 'European' and 'indigenous' foundations to a Romanian identity continues to have relevance in the present day. Romanian history contains numerous disputes amongst elites over the 'truth' of a Romanian essence, and these arguments are often framed in terms of modernisation versus tradition; Western versus indigenous identities; and national versus foreign values (35).

Moreover, this fixation on essence and origins is connected to a thoroughgoing ethnic imagining of nationhood, by which national outsiders are defined and constituted on an ethnic, rather than territorial, basis. Hungarians, Jews, and Roma have been the most intensively and pervasively constructed in this way. Furthermore, the defence of minority rights itself has been constituted as foreign-inspired. For example, 'pressure from the great powers at the 1878 Congress of Berlin which compelled her rulers to grant its Jewish population equal citizenship' (Gallagher, 1995: 19), was interpreted as outside interference in domestic politics; which also underscores how legal citizenship alone could not end anti-Semitism in Romania.

In fact, much of the intellectual defence of Romanian nationalism (including anti-Semitism and anti-Hungarianism), was provided by the philosopher Nichifor Crainic (1889–1972), whose influence would be felt by both the radical right-wing in the earlier part of the twentieth century, and by the Communists in the second half (Gallagher, 1995: 34). Within Crainic's nationalist ideology, the Romanian village and peasant were central to the nation because of their faithfulness to tradition, their resistance to outside influence, their adherence to orthodoxy, and their ability to remain uncontaminated by 'Western values' and 'Western bourgeois civilisation' (34). This ideological model remained relevant to the post-Communist era, underscoring 'the centrality of collectivist assumptions within Romanian culture' (Haddock and Caraiani, 1999: 264), in which 'western influence was alien to the soul of the Romanian nation as represented by the peasant' (Bowd, 2000: 115). This trope also provided a mode of resisting the cosmopolitanism of the French influenced intellectuals and aristocrats in an earlier period (113).

The Ceausescu regime itself drew heavily upon this same set of ideological nationalist cards, despite the internationalism (and rationalism) associated with Communist ideology (see Verdery, 1991). From his assumption of power, Ceausescu's ideological firmament represented a continuity with the nationalist ideology of the past, rather than a clear break from it. Although, initially, the post-Second World War Communist regime embarked upon a process of 'de-nationalisation' which, in fact, emphasised the Slavic (as opposed to Latin) origins of Romanians (Gallagher, 1995: 52), Ceausescu's regime would be characterised by continuity with those earlier nationalist tropes, and a break from Russian influence. 'Nation' remained, then, 'a symbolic-ideological mode of control' (Verdery, 1991: 100), most graphically illustrated by Ceausescu's public statement of April 1964, 'that announced the Party's refusal to subordinate national needs to a supranational planning body in which others would dictate the form of the country's economy. The declaration insisted that interaction among states within the socialist camp must be based on respect for the sovereignty and integrity of each' (Verdery, 1991: 105). Through the break with Moscow, Ceausescu was able to reimagine his own brand of Communist totalitarianism in national, rather than proletarian, terms. In a continuation of the past, foreign influences again became dangerous, and processes of modernisation, industrialisation and urbanisation (and the individual sacrifices that they demanded), became essential for the good of the nation state itself (Gallagher, 1995: 52; Verdery, 1991: 129). This provided the means of reconciling Ceausescu's bizarre vision of modernity—which often entailed the literal destruction of village life through centralised planning—with the valorisation of the 'tradition' of which village life was emblematic (Verdery, 1991: 44).

As well as providing continuity with the past in terms of the deployment of nation, continuity is also seen in terms of the centrality of collectivism to identity, whether expressed in terms of the village as a microcosm of Romanian identity, or in terms of the nation as an organic identity warding off outside, barbaric influences (see Haddock and Caraiani, 1999). In this respect, Romanian pre- Communist tradition, the Ceausescu era and, I would argue, the post-Communist period have shared a distrust of 'the values of liberal individualism,' of cosmopolitanism, internationalism, and a rights-based conception of the individual (261). Yet, it was a collectivist ideology which, during the Ceausescu years, was statist to such a totalitarian extent that civil society was virtually eliminated, even compared to other dictatorships in the region.[9] This provides one of the many problems faced in attempts to build a Western-style democracy in the post-1989 era. Instead, in this period, political support again would be mobilised in terms of ethnic nationalism and 'citizenship in the new Republic would be defined along ethnic, and not civic lines' (Weiner, 1997: 9).

But the sustainability of nationalist ideology for Ceausescu also, in the end, would contribute to his downfall. His drive to repay international debt in order to ensure the independence of the nation state in the 1980s in turn would lead to economic crisis and sacrifice of such magnitude, combined (in the same period) with Romania's abandonment by the West, so as to create a new dependency on the Soviet Bloc (Verdery, 1991: 30). This undermined claims of national independence, and of Romania's image of itself as a European—and as a *civilised*—country. Within Romanian racist discourse, it was argued that Ceausescu's

[9] On the reasons for the relative weakness of Romanian civil society, see Craiutu (2000: 171); Weiner (1997).

policies were turning a European people into an African one (133). In this moment, Romania becomes reimagined in European (Latinist) terms, and it needed to be protected from Ceausescu's brand of barbarism.[10]

Furthermore, the discourse of civilisation is closely linked to the manipulation of gender and sexuality in the service of nationalist ideology, which, I have argued elsewhere, is true in many national contexts (see generally Stychin, 1998). As was the case more generally with the deployment of nation and the construction of an organic community, the political use of gender and sexuality underscores the continuities more than the ruptures between pre- and post-Communist Romania (see Roman, 2001; Mezei, 1994). In pre-Communist ideology, the idealisation of 'woman' could be found in peasant life, and the idealised peasant woman was 'submissive, dedicated to her household, reserved, and brought up in a culture of self-sacrifice to her man, family, and, occasionally, to her country' (Roman, 2001: 55). During the Ceausescu years, despite the official ideology of sexual equality—and the symbolic (and, again, bizarre) constructed role of Elena Ceausescu as equal partner, scientist, humanitarian and symbol of gender equality—the discursive use of woman and woman's sexuality in the service of nationhood continued to be felt, particularly in terms of woman's role as reproducer (while also carrying the burden of paid employment and unpaid role of care in an economy frequently in a state of severe austerity and lack of basic goods) (Kligman, 1998: 26).

The legacy of the regulation of women's reproductive bodies in Romania is well known.[11] The criminalisation of abortion in the 1960s marked the beginning of a long period of repressive state measures aimed at the total policing of women's bodies, which included compulsory gynecological examinations in the workplace and at police stations, the role of the medical profession in the service of the state, show trials, and imprisonment of women convicted under the law, as well as the criminalisation of contraception (Gallagher, 1995: 61). The inexorable logic of this expropriation of the body in the service of the nation was apparent in 1986, when Ceausescu 'proclaimed the foetus the socialist property of the whole society. Giving birth is a patriotic duty . . . those who refuse to have children are deserters, escaping the law of national continuity' (61).

Here the language of nation is combined with that of militarism, which raises an important point about the use of women's sexuality in the service of the nation. This was a deployment in the context, not of a withering away of the post-colonial state under the pressures of economic globalisation, but rather, in the context of a totalitarian state in which the state and its servants would enforce the codes of gender *directly* in the service of the nation (Kligman, 1998). Consequently, unlike some other national contexts, women's bodies were not policed solely through the force of men qua husbands and fathers (although

[10] This trope evokes an enormous literature on the construction of European 'civilisation' through a savage other; for an excellent introduction to this vast topic, see Fitzpatrick (2001).

[11] That history is comprehensively and incisively documented by Kligman (1998).

certainly this happened through widespread domestic violence), but through the paternalistic gaze of the state—a state which infantilised *both* women and men (28). Thus, the 'family' may have been reified by the Ceausescu state (and its centrality in political discourse grew steadily over the years), but the idea of the family as an autonomous social unit, even as one existing within a larger organic family of the Romanian village, was gone, and replaced by the state as paternalistic to *all* of its children (31). In this way, the public/private dichotomy was obliterated, and men's traditional paternal role within the private sphere was undermined. After all, 'the state also expropriated male rights to the reproductive labor of women' (31), since it was up to the state itself to 'socialize families' (28). As Gail Kligman (1998: 124) has argued, the Romanian public sphere was overwhelmed with familial discourse under Ceausescu, but it was state social organisation itself which bore ultimate familial responsibility which demanded obedience, no matter what the degree of reification of the peasant family. This further underscores the void found in the absence of any notion of civil society.

In this context, the criminalisation of homosexuality seems hardly surprising, representing a threat to reproduction, family, nation and state, an act of individual perverse pleasure in which duty is deserted, and which demands policing for its subversiveness. Homosexuality becomes inspired by outside influences and is corrosive of the national family. In my view, article 200 must be located within this wider ideological context. This also helps to explain the politics of gender and sexuality in post-Communist Romania. For example, reform of abortion law should not be read as suggesting a post-Communist politics of substantive gender equality. Nor does the recent decriminalisation of homosexuality and introduction of anti-discrimination law provide evidence of a radical ideological shift.

IN A WEAKENED STATE: DISCIPLINING ROMANIA

> As qualities of European civilization, the universal and legal, the ordered, the dynamic and progressive are all set against characters projected from the European onto its other—the particular and lawless, the chaotic, static and backward. These projected characters remain in the site of their generation, within European identity, where they are recognized as having been suppressed but as still dangerous (Fitzpatrick, 2001: 125).

The legacy of Communism post-1989 has been the continuation of a highly conservative gender/sex discourse, grounded in the close nexus between church and post-Communist state, and accentuated by the weakness of civil society actors, as well as by the ongoing use of conspiracy theories as a 'pseudo-reasoning method' (Roman, 2001: 59). Only by understanding that socio-political context can the dynamics of transnationalism and globalisation in Romania be fully comprehended.

The history of post-Communist Romania underscores a profound tension around the meaning of Romanian identity, which plays itself out on the terrain of homosexuality, representing not so much a break with the past, as continuity with it. The economic catastrophe that befell Romania in the 1980s was largely a product of Ceausescu's obsession with clearing the foreign debt load at any social cost, as a means of ensuring Romanian political sovereignty. And throughout the history of Romania, examples can be found of constructions of foreigners and outsider powers as trying to undermine Romanian sovereignty. This historical trajectory, combined with the relative lack of any meaningful civil society in the transition to post-Communism, not surprisingly has produced a highly nationalist discourse, laced with expressions of antipathy towards, amongst others, Hungarians, Jews, and homosexuals. As Denise Roman (2001: 59) describes:

> [O]ne should not forget that Romanian post-Communist society lacks the basis of a modern well-defined ethic. Rather, it stands suspended in corruption, a tendency towards an inflammatory Orthodoxy (a form of religious fundamentalism that, when everything else fails, can produce a rudimentary form of morals), egocentric individualism, *a*morality and *im*morality, paternalism, and an education for cynical disdain towards those perceived as inferior or alien: women, Roma, Jews, Hungarians, homosexuals, the poor, the disabled, immigrants (recently from countries such as Somalia, Bangladesh), and the environment.

Roman adds feminism to that list which, like the campaign for homosexual rights, is seen to be foreign-inspired. Such constructions have often emanated from political parties and the state:

> The central place of nationalism in political life means that from 1881 to the present day, rulers have shared a number of reflexes even if they adhere to contrasting ideologies. First, the state must govern in the name of the ethnic majority . . . Second, state laws must not be subject to external interference or regulation as this will encroach upon Romanian sovereignty in unacceptable ways . . . Third, freedom from foreign rule is more important than upholding of freedom against domestic tyranny . . . Fourth, native traditions are the best ones to shape Romanian government (Gallagher, 2001: 105–6).

Thus, we find 'the replacement of a totalitarian state which monopolised expressions of chauvinism by a relatively weak state prepared to exploit nationalism in order to boost its credibility but unable or unwilling to prevent others going to even more extreme lengths to exploit nationalism for their own ends' (Gallagher, 1995: 93). Robert Weiner (1997: 5) argues that this state of affairs results from the absence of 'a civic community or a sense of civic engagement or involvement in public life.' As a consequence, he claims that 'the post-Communist regime in Romania could only mobilize support for itself on the basis of nationalism and ethnicity' manifested most strongly in prejudice against minorities (9; see also Craiutu, 2000).

As a consequence of this mobilisation, it has been far from easy for the post-Communist state and nation to come to terms with international pressures that have been exerted on Romania from numerous quarters since 1989 (see

Phinnemore, 2001). These pressures frequently have stemmed from international concerns over minority issues. Although certainly not the most corrosive pressure on national sovereignty, minority rights lobbying from abroad has often been perceived by the state and the media as the clearest example of foreign interference, which must be resisted at all costs (see Creteanu and Coman, 1998).[12] Yet it is here that the quandary for Romania has arisen, since it was not long after the fall of Ceausescu that it became clear that isolation from the outside world—or, alternatively, an alignment with Russia—was not a desirable option, particularly in terms of economic development (Phinnemore, 2001). This has manifested itself most strongly in the desire to join the European Union, a consensus widely shared by the population; spurred on by both the perception of economic self-interest, as well as by the historical identity as 'European' (again, as standing in for 'civilisation'), which had to be rebuilt following 1989 (Batt, 2001).[13] What was also apparent, however, is that 'when Romania formally applied to join the EU in 1995, there was probably little awareness that it was embracing a political project hostile to many of the core values of Romanian nationalism' (Gallagher, 2001: 115).

For example, Romania found first that progress towards full membership of the Council of Europe was made subject to periodic human rights review, and it accepted that associate status with the European Union required 'respect for the democratic principles and human rights established by the Helsinki Final Act and the [1991] Charter of Paris for a New Europe' (Gallagher, 2001: 108). Moreover, the European Union was given a 'right of regard' over human rights in Romania by the Iliescu regime. Yet, at the same time, for many Romanians (as elsewhere), the treatment of national minorities is the quintessential issue of national sovereignty.

Human rights are only a small part of this difficult transition to a transnational and globalised world order. Post-Communist Romania is best characterised by the degree to which transition has been far from easy, and in terms of how pressure from outside and above becomes the most effective counter to a state that has strongly ethnic nationalist and inward-looking impulses. As a consequence, the attitude 'propagated by mass media leads to blaming the minority groups for the reluctance and the slow pace of the integration into the European Union and NATO' (Createanu and Coman, 1998). But this popular perception is far from an accurate description of Romania's slow and difficult path into multilateral and transnational bodies, particularly the European Union, NATO

[12] In this respect, I (like others) would argue that minority rights issues suggest the contrary to the argument advanced by Stan (2000: 154), that '[i]t is now the rule rather than the exception to witness reactions from a Western government to internal political developments in a country of the region, followed by the positive response from the government concerned, which does not consider foreign "pressure" as interference in its internal affairs.'

[13] See Batt (2001: 250–51): 'Recovering a "lost" European identity for the peoples of central and eastern Europe meant recovering national self-esteem as a member of the family of free, independent and above all *modern* European states.'

and the Council of Europe, as well as its often strained relations with the IMF and World Bank. The 1990s have been described as a 'decade of frustration' with respect to the difficulty of integration (Phinnemore, 2001). Council of Europe membership was delayed because of concerns over Romania's human rights record (Gallagher, 1995: 130).

In terms of European Union membership, however, Romania has benefited from the decision of the European Council at the Luxembourg Summit in December 1997 to adopt an 'all-inclusive' accession process, even though Romania—by all accounts—lagged far behind other accession countries in meeting the EU accession criteria (the Copenhagen criteria adopted by the 1993 Copenhagen European Council) of political and economic reforms (Phinnemore, 2001).[14] The first report of the European Commission, published in July 1997, set the tone for future annual reports on Romania's readiness for membership, pointing out both progress in meeting the Copenhagen political criteria for membership, while also recognising that Romania 'would face serious difficulties to cope with the competitive pressure and market forces within the Union in the medium-term' (Commission of the European Communities, 1997).[15] Subsequent annual reports have echoed those concerns, and the EU perception has been that Romania has been extremely slow in delivering the political, market, and institutional reforms demanded by the European Union, and agreed in the accession negotiations (Quinn, 2002).[16]

One can see, in this moment, the manifestation of Romania's paradoxical identity. The official government position, taken by governments of both the right and centre, has been in favour of EU membership (Chiriac, 2001). But, in practice, despite agreements and promises, Romania has often been unable to meet the standards of discipline imposed upon it by the European Union, leaving it in the slow track towards membership, now with a target date (set by Romania) of 2007 (Quinn, 2002). Much press and popular attention has

[14] The Copenhagen citeria require that a candidate country for accession to the European Union meet the following criteria:

> 'stability of institutions guaranteeing democracy, the rule of law, human rights and respect for and protection of minorities'; the existence of a functioning market economy as well as the capacity to cope with competitive pressures and market forces within the Union; 'the ability to take on the obligations of membership including adherence to the aims of political, economic and monetary union'. In addition, the candidate state must also have created 'the conditions for its integration through the adjustment of its administrative structures, so that European Community legislation transposed into national legislation is implemented effectively through appropriate administrative and judicial structures' (Bell, 2001: 83, citing Bulletin-EC, 6-1993).

[15] It is worth bearing in mind that the Commission reports on Romania are the only Commission reports on the accession countries to mention homosexuality as an accession issue.

[16] As an example, see Council of the European Union (2001: 6):

> The Union notes with concern that Romania has made relatively little progress in meeting the Copenhagen economic criteria. There is a need to accelerate and deepen reforms if Romania is not to fall behind in its preparations for accession. Priority areas are: privatising/liquidating the large loss-making enterprises; stabilising macro-economic conditions (reducing inflation, setting a prudent fiscal deficit); improving the business environment, reforming the banking sector, notably by reducing state ownership and improving supervision.

focused on EU demands—emanating from the European Parliament especially—concerning institutionalised children, the Roma, the Hungarian minority, and article 200. But, in fact, the most serious challenges to membership come, not from the political criteria, but from the Copenhagen economic criteria, underlined by Romania's slowness in achieving market reforms, privatisation, and fiscal and monetary stability (on privatisation, see Stan, 1997). And it has been the failure of governments to achieve these standards of economic and political discipline—to implement them—which in turn has undermined the goal of integration, which can then fuel an inward-looking ethnic nationalism, resistant to a more cosmopolitan, civic notion of citizenship.[17] Combined with the presence of fascist political parties with a substantial following throughout the post-Communist period, particularly the Greater Romania Party, the tension between acceptance of international demands and resistance to them, is acute. As well, it must be remembered that past and present post-1989 Romanian governments include many ex-Communists with little commitment to a reform agenda, and that Romania has had to deal with an economy and bureaucracy in a far worse state than was the case in many neighbouring countries (Stan, 1997). The result was expressed in the November 2000 European Commission report that 'Romania cannot be regarded as a functioning market economy and is not able to cope with competitive pressure and market forces within the European Union.' Romania has remained at the bottom of the list of countries being considered for EU entry (Commission of the European Communities, 2000).[18]

For that matter, similar patterns of discipline and resistance can be seen in the relationship between Romania and the IMF and World Bank throughout the post-1989 period. The conditions for financial support have included privatisation and industrial restructuring; the creation of a climate conducive to foreign investment; the elimination of government price controls and industrial subsidies; and the liberalising of the foreign exchange market (Jones, C, 1997: 41). Loans from both the IMF and World Bank (as well as from the G24 countries, the International Finance Corporation, the European Bank for Reconstruction and Development, and others) have been conditioned upon a range of neoliberal economic reforms such as these, following frustration at the slow pace at which Romania has carried out promised reforms in the past. The making of future loans conditional upon reform provides a strongly neoliberal disciplinary force, particularly given Romania's considerable foreign debt reservice payments, its downgrading by the nine international credit rating agencies in the late

[17] Gallagher (2001: 114) suggests, in this regard, that 'perhaps . . . mainstream parties and indeed much of public opinion in Romania are in the process of acquiring dual identities based on pro-Europeanism and nationalism—the dominant element depending on the degree of national security or insecurity felt at a given moment.'

[18] A similar analysis can be made with respect to Romania's application for membership in NATO: see Phinnemore (2001).

1990s, and the relative paucity of foreign direct investment since 1989 (see Jones, 1999: 48).[19]

My purpose in raising the range of pressures for reform is not to document a scoresheet by which to blame the Romanian state for its failure to achieve an economic agenda set by the institutions of the European Union, NATO, World Bank and IMF. Others routinely construct such scoresheets, which are then deployed as ammunition to further discipline the state. Nor should the historical role of the West in manipulating Romania and supporting the Ceausescu state be forgotten. In the post-Communist era, one can argue that the way in which, for example, the European Union has demanded an extensive reform agenda covering all areas of Romania's economy, bureaucracy and legal system—which Romania has responded to by creating a Ministry of European Integration which does nothing except attempt to meet the criteria for accession—with no promise or guarantees of membership, helps to fuel ethnic nationalism and anti-Western interventionist sentiment; thereby reinforcing Romania's 'victim complex' (Gallagher, 1995: 53).[20] As Tom Gallagher (2001: 115–16) points out, the West:

> makes obtaining a visa to travel to EU states extremely difficult for most Romanians, often entailing waits for days outside foreign embassies [while EU citizens require no visa to enter Romania]. Many Romanians contrast the fact that tariff barriers have been lowered (in line with Romania's Europe Agreement with the EU), allowing west European goods to flood the country, thus jeopardizing local agriculture and industry, while Romanian citizens are effectively blockaded from travelling westwards.[21]

So too, IMF and World Bank conditions often exacerbate already austere living conditions through the lifting of price controls on staple items and the privatisation of industries which survived only under an extremely disjointed centrally planned economy, protected from market forces. My point here is to underscore how the state has been weakened, battered by international pressure from above, as well as pressure from below, from the forces of ethnic nationalism (or fascism), orthodoxy, rampant consumerism by those with resources

[19] A review of the past decade of volumes of *The Banker* and *Euromoney* magazines provides a useful introduction to this history. See eg *Euromoney* (1997: 128):

> [T]he new government is motivated not only by reformist zeal, but by the fact that success will be rewarded with much needed cash from the International Monetary Fund and the World Bank. This is not so much a second chance as a fifth. Romania has had four standby programmes with the IMF since 1990, all of which had to be suspended early because the government failed to carry out agreed reforms. Last year World Bank loans were frozen too. Other conditions for the restoration of money include the sale of two state-owned banks before the end of 1997.

[20] Although, at the same time, 'between 1990 and 1999 the European Union provided assistance to Romania under the PHARE programme totalling 1203 million [Euros] and . . . as part of the pre-accession strategy Romania will receive some 630 million per year from 2000 to 2002': European Parliament (2000: 11).

[21] As of 1 January 2002, the EU travel visa requirement has been lifted for Romanians; however, proof of health insurance and adequate funds is still required (and prevents many Romanians from travelling easily).

(achieved through 'a system based on corruption and patronage networks' (Craiutu, 2000: 182)), and with relatively little sense of civic engagement. It is this context which makes the struggle for the repeal of article 200 unique and noteworthy for what it suggests about transnational European activism and the institutions of the European Union and beyond. And it is to that story that I now return.

DISCIPLINE AND NORMALISATION: ACCEPT-ING ACCESSION

One of the successes of ACCEPT has been its ability to mobilise internationally around the repeal of article 200. The explanations for this success are multifaceted. ACCEPT has been, first and foremost, a human rights NGO and not a grassroots organisation. Its executive possesses a high degree of political sophistication and experience in the human rights sector. Moreover, the lack of a history and experience of strong civil society actors has meant a relative absence of involvement by most lesbian and gay Romanians in the organisation, combined with a Romanian fear and scepticism of 'community.'[22] This, in turn, left space for professionalised human rights activists who were not always themselves lesbian or gay to assume leadership positions. As a consequence, discourses of professionalism and managerialism have come to predominate, as has an agenda of international lobbying, rather than one of social services or cultural development (although there has been some space—and increasingly so—for both).[23]

Moreover, the link with the Netherlands Government was a fortuitous development, as it opened the way to successful funding applications to other international and transnational bodies, including the European Commission.[24] That funding has allowed for the development and support of an infrastructure that could carry on sophisticated international lobbying, and which could follow up with constant pressure on the state, as well as media campaigns aimed at changing perceptions at home. As well, the link with the Netherlands Government provided a political acknowledgment that lesbian and gay issues were on the

[22] Relatedly, in this cultural context, there is often a wide divergence between those who have same sex sexual relations (however that may be defined), and those who may identify as lesbian, gay, or bisexual.

[23] Not surprisingly, there has been a fair amount of dissent amongst some segments of the Romanian gay population around issues of representation ('can ACCEPT speak for gays?'), as well as over the relative roles and merits of grassroots activism and professionalism. The professionalism of ACCEPT is confirmed by those with whom the organisation has dealt; see eg, the comments of Martijn Quinn, Romania Desk Officer at the European Commission (2002): 'they were the best organised lobby I've come across . . . ACCEPT knew the system; were able to use more institutions to put pressure on. . . . If I had to give advice to any NGO in any areas, I would say that that would be a model of how to get your case across. To present your arguments and present your case successfully.'

[24] ACCEPT also has received funding from, amongst others, the Open Society Institute, ILGA Europe, the United Nations, and the Canadian Embassy (all in 2001).

political agenda generally, and on the EU accession agenda specifically (van der Veur, 2001).

But despite the pressure which ACCEPT has exerted on the state internally (and it managed to achieve a considerable degree of access to a number of government ministries), and the savvy way in which it has used the media, it is clear that it was EU institutional pressure—rather than pressure from the Council of Europe, the United Nations, Amnesty International, Human Rights Watch, international human rights NGOs, or foreign governments such as the Netherlands or Sweden—which forced decriminalisation, as well as the inclusion of sexual orientation in anti-discrimination legislation. The European Parliament for some years had passed continuous resolutions calling for an end to article 200. Furthermore, an informal group of sympathetic Members of the European Parliament (MEPs) (called the 'Intergroup on Gay and Lesbian Rights'),[25] as well as other MEPs interested in Romanian accession (such as Baroness Emma Nicholson), pushed this issue forward with lobbying from ACCEPT and, more broadly, with backing from the International Lesbian and Gay Association Europe (of which ACCEPT is a member organisation) (ILGA Europe), and from the International Gay and Lesbian Human Rights Commission (Coman, 2001).[26]

However, it was when the conditions of accession, in the form of the Copenhagen political and economic criteria, were announced, that the potential for using accession as a lever with which to push for gay rights became clear to ACCEPT. As Adrian Coman (2001), former Executive Director of ACCEPT, described to me, 'when the Commission started to put the issue on the agenda with Romanian officials, at the same time ACCEPT succeeded in meeting basically with all the important people, including the Minister of European Integration, the Minister of Justice, the Romanian mission in Brussels.' At this point, one finds in the Reports of the European Parliament on Romania's application for EU membership, and in the Council of the European Union recommendations, as well as in the views of the Commission and in other EU documents, a continual reference to the repeal of Article 200 as a condition for accesssion, along with, of course, numerous other demands.

Article 200 would be raised by the Commission, as well as by EU Parliamentarians, on innumerable occasions: for example, in a letter of 29 May 2001, from eight MEPs to Prime Minister Nastase concerning article 200: 'we look forward to welcoming Romania into the European Union, but an essential prerequisite is that *we must share the same values*. Discrimination on whatever

[25] For example, on 28 June 2001, the Intergroup on Gay and Lesbian Rights held a public hearing on lesbian and gay rights in the EU accession countries, entitled 'EU Enlargement: A Gay Perspective' (2001), which was held in the European Parliament.

[26] In fact, ACCEPT organised the 22nd Annual Conference of ILGA Europe, entitled 'Accepting Diversity', which was held in Bucharest on 4–8 October 2000. Participants included EU politicians, embassy representatives, and included an impromptu speech by the then US Ambassador to Romania. A more detailed discussion of ILGA Europe can be found in chapter 1.

ground may never be permitted' (van der Laan et al, 2001, emphasis added); similarly, another protest from Parliamentarians states, 'Romania's commitments within the EU accession process imply both observing the EU values and principles, as well as passing legislation in accordance with EU standards' (European Parliament, 2001);[27] or, to take a further example, in answer to a parliamentary question, Mr Verheugen (2001) on behalf of the Commission states:

> [T]he criteria for accession to the European Union, as set out at the 1993 Copenhagen meeting of the European Council, make explicit reference to the need for stability of institutions guaranteeing democracy, the rule of law, human rights and respect for and protection of minorities. The Commission is fully committed to ensuring that this condition for accession is respected and will take up cases of human rights abuse in its regular reports on candidate countries' progress towards accession and in its bilateral relations with them.

The two central lesbian and gay law reform issues in Romania—decriminalisation and anti-discrimination legislation—have quite different bases in European law, and Mark Bell (2001) has incisively explained how EU law can provide a source of rights for citizens in the accession countries. As the International Lesbian and Gay Association Europe (2001: 7) explains in its report on the accession countries:

> A precondition for accession, as set out in the Copenhagen criteria, is the establishment of respect for human rights, including the protection of minorities. Moreover, Article 6(2) EU provides that: 'the Union shall respect fundamental rights, as guaranteed by the European Convention for the Protection of Human Rights and Fundamental Freedoms'. It is clear that, as a minimum, the accession countries must bring their laws and practices into line with the jurisprudence of the European Convention.

Yet, interestingly, the Romania desk officer at the Commission describes how, despite pressure that might be exerted by the European Union, from the Commission perspective, 'you are playing a little bit of a bluff game on all human rights issues' in the accession process, particularly given that so-called 'European values' may not always appear to be shared by all *existing* member states (Quinn, 2002).[28] The anti-discrimination law issue has a much more explicit legal basis than decriminalisation, given the Council Framework Directive establishing a general framework for equal treatment in employment,

[27] Such statements, with their emphasis on common values, can also be interpreted as an attempt by EU institutions and politicians to prevent Romanian politicians from turning the European Union into a scapegoat for legal change. Thanks to Adrian Coman for this point.

[28] Although, as Bell (2001: 86) points out, in the context of decriminalisation (and given the findings of the European Court of Human Rights against those signatory states who have criminalised same sex relationships in private), 'all applicant states, like all existing EU states, are signatories of the ECHR [European Convention on Human Rights]. Therefore, requiring new EU Member States to respect the rights set out in the Convention goes no further than the obligations the applicant states have already assumed towards the Council of Europe.'

which Romania is keen to show that it has enacted (although not implemented) in an attempt to meet this element of the *acquis communitaire* (and the anti-discrimination law appeared on the official political agenda before full decriminalisation) (Bell, 2001: 83).[29] This is typical of the Romanian approach, which is to focus on the enactment of legislation, even when there is no mechanism for implementation (an approach which Commission officials find problematic and dismaying) (Quinn, 2002).[30]

In 2002, Romania (and the European Union) finally witnessed the repeal of article 200 and the inclusion of sexual orientation in national anti-discrimination legislation (after its earlier exclusion by a Parliamentary committee, which was followed by informal pressure from the European Commission to include it). In the end, these successes were somewhat anti-climactic, achieved without much official fanfare, and after so much struggle. As the Commission of the European Communities (2001) (earlier) described the significance of this legal move: 'this represents a major and positive development in human rights legislation that brings Romania into line with European standards.' How should this culmination of years of lobbying and struggle be understood? My answer in this chapter is to suggest that it should be read as a cautionary, indeterminate, yet fascinating genealogical tale of law reform. As I have tried to emphasise, law reform in Romania has not been a 'bottom up' social movement process. Rather, it has been 'top down,' and driven by external pressure, although with a strong sense of 'ownership' of the agenda domestically by ACCEPT. In such a context, the relationship between legal and social change may be even more tenuous than in other national contexts, but ACCEPT would be the first to admit this. However, neither should the significance of legal change be underestimated. Criminal law concerning homosexuality was not merely of symbolic importance in Romanian society. It had a brutally material impact. But it is unlikely that most Romanians will feel any sense of 'ownership' of law reform. Instead, for some, it may reinforce their scepticism and bewilderment at 'European values' and reinforce Romania's historically paradoxical relationship with 'Europe,' in terms of its own national identity.

[29] The term *acquis communitaire* refers to the existing body of EU law which an accession country needs to incorporate into domestic legislation as a condition for accession. For example, as Bell (2001: 83–84) explains, 'wherever EU law already imposes anti-discrimination requirements, then applicant states' domestic law must be brought into line with these obligations. Second, any state wishing to accede must establish respect for human rights and fundamental freedoms, including protection of minorities.' The *acquis* has been divided into 31 chapters. The Romanian Ministry of European Integration has responsibility for ensuring—chapter by chapter—that Romanian law is in compliance. Not surprisingly, it is a mammoth task.

[30] It is surely no coincidence, nor is it surprising, that considerable pressure for reform from within the Romanian state has come from the Ministry of European Integration.

CONCLUSIONS

In conclusion, the analysis of a law reform campaign raised in this chapter—with the relationship between pressure exerted from above, and the politics of social change within Romania domestically—raises wider questions for future study concerning this new and rapidly developing vista of European sexual citizenship. These questions go to the heart of the themes advanced throughout *Governing Sexuality*. First, to what extent are we witnessing the emergence of Romanians who embrace a different conception of citizenship—who may identify as lesbian or gay—and who, as a result, express a more cosmopolitan, European sense of identity, based on plural allegiances (Gallagher, 2001: 121)? Could this law reform campaign be seen to contribute to this end? That would potentially represent an enormous shift, which might include the creation of a 'rights based conception of civil society' (Haddock and Caraiani, 1999: 274), rather than the traditionally highly collectivist and communitarian notion of identity through which, as Roman (2001: 55) argues, 'a "minimalist citizen" mentality is created, with low self-esteem, distrust for institutions and the law, fear of public servants, and a tendency to suffer from a persecution complex regarding hierarchical inferiority'. Perhaps, alternatively, we may see emerging some hybrid notion of communitarian and cosmopolitan identities, leaving us to consider what such an identity might actually *look like*. How might the European Union contribute to that process, while mindful of the dangers of imposing a vision of citizenship from above (and bearing in mind the ignoble role which the West has played in Romania in the past)? Can the idea/l of 'civilisation,' which many Romanians (including many ACCEPT members) embrace through the language of human rights, be reclaimed, so as to bypass the historical resonances identified by critics of the European Union, such as Fitzpatrick (2001) and others? Can law reform actually contribute to the development of civil society, and how will lesbian and gay identities emerge in this context, in which law reform around homosexuality has been so transnationally driven? And is 'civil society' the panacea that European institutions assume it to be? Is the discourse of human rights cynically deployed by EU actors so as to mask an underlying neoliberal agenda imposed unquestioningly on the accession countries? To what extent will an emerging gay identity be cosmopolitan and globalised, or will it retain some communitarian roots?[31] To what extent can European actors avoid the colonial impulse? COC Netherlands is now working

[31] Adrian Coman (2001) incisively develops this point in an interview: 'On the one hand, we import elements of lesbian, gay, bisexual and transgender culture. We import symbols, the rainbow flag, celebrating June 28th. On the other hand, there are Romanian elements in this forming culture. For example, having support from straight people, which I haven't seen abroad. Also, by counteracting some of the fears of the population. For example, we say it is not in our culture to march in the streets unless we ask for more money from our employers.' On globalisation and gay identities, see generally Altman (2001).

actively on a lesbian and gay empowerment project in the Republic of Moldova. Will this be a force for 'liberation,' or should it be seen as an example of the colonisation of sexuality by the West?

Finally, in the Romanian context, legal recognition issues are starkly inseparable from the economic, a central theme of this book. Issues of recognition and redistribution can be seen to merge. To what extent can a cosmopolitan, or globalised, identity be meaningful, given the standard of living of the majority in Romania today? For many, a westernised identity can be little more than a dream; one which is linked to migration and a relationship with a westerner who might act as an immigration sponsor. Yet, as I suggested in chapter 5, those relationships can (but need not necessarily) replicate the relationship of inequality between East and West which this chapter has sought to document. It does clearly suggest that an analysis of sexual identities and social change must be linked to existing economic inequalities, a point which I have also tried to suggest throughout this chapter and, indeed, throughout all of the case studies.

In closing, an anecdote perhaps best encapsulates the paradox of Romanian gay politics. In the autumn of 2001, the new American ambassador to Romania, Michael Guest, arrived. A Bush appointment, and NATO expert, the openly gay ambassador arrived with his partner in Bucharest to much press attention, and was duly received by the government (Gall, 2001).[32] Should this event be read as a capitulation of the weakened state to international pressure; underscoring the inequality in the relationship between West and East? Alternatively, does it provide evidence of a movement of social change, which marks a historical shift? My answer in this chapter has been to suggest that both readings provide partial truths about the emerging politics of sexuality and citizenship in a European legal and political order; and it is in the years ahead, as the drive for European accession intensifies, that the implications of sexual citizenship in this dynamic region will become increasingly apparent.

[32] On the other side of the Atlantic, the appointment was sharply criticised by the American religious right!

Conclusions

I FINISH *GOVERNING SEXUALITY* by mentioning a few of the many possible future lines of inquiry regarding European sexual citizenship that may be worth pursuing, and by providing some final thoughts on the project.

Within the European Union, we have witnessed a remarkably rapid development of a range of ways in which same sex identities and relationships have come to be recognised by Member States and EU institutions. These reforms have occurred much more quickly than I would have expected 10 years ago, which perhaps underscores why predicting legal change is a perilous endeavour. Nevertheless, it seems to me that some developments are worth 'flagging' for the future. What I find interesting, first, is the variation in the forms and modes of legal recognition that have occurred in different states. The Danish model differs markedly from the French, for example (on developments in Denmark, see Bech, 1997: ch 6). With pressure beginning to be felt for a harmonised family law in the European Union (see McGlynn, 2000), it will be fascinating to see whether and how these culturally distinct modes of governing sexuality through national law come to be harmonised and disciplined into a particular 'European' form of legal recognition in the future. Given that, historically, the model of the family that has emerged in EU law and politics has been highly conservative in many respects, I would urge that close watch be kept on what a 'European homosexual family' might actually *look like* as it develops in EU law and politics in the years ahead.

Secondly, I have argued in *Governing Sexuality* that we can see forms of transnational social movement activism around same sex sexualities emerging within and across the European Union. Whether and how such activism grows in the future will be worth observing. The extent to which it can embrace national and regional cultural variation (and, relatedly, how well it can recognise and include the vast differences between and amongst lesbian and gay Europeans), will be a fascinating example of social movement development across borders. Also of interest will be the extent to which transnational movements are 'top down' operations (thanks to EU financial support), or genuine 'grassroots' social struggles (and the focus of struggle will itself be an important issue).

Thirdly, within a UK context, the role of rights discourse—and the *lawyerisation* of social movement activism—in the wake of the Human Rights Act 1998, warrants close observation, and not only for lesbian and gay social struggles. Whether we should describe such a development (if, indeed, it is occurring) as a form of the Americanisation of politics, or (given that we are dealing with the semi-incorporation of the European Convention on Human Rights) the Europeanisation of politics, is of little relevance. But it does strike me that what we do see is a form of politics increasingly *far removed* from the days of the Gay Liberation Front of the 1970s, or indeed, even from the anti-section 28 struggles of the 1980s (whether for better or worse). Whether that shift will exacerbate (or be resisted!) in the years to come will be an important issue for the future of lesbian and gay politics in the United Kingdom.

Fourthly, in the years to come, it will be worth testing the validity of Bech's (1997: 194) thesis that with the gaining of equality we will witness 'the disappearance of the modern homosexual', as same sex sexualities become nothing more than minor deviations which lose much of their political and cultural significance (198). This would amount to a depoliticisation of sexuality, and whether legal equality might contribute to such a (potentially sad and problematic) end to identity also will be of importance. Yet, while lesbian and gay sexualities might be disappearing in the 'North' and 'West,' they are only just beginning to make an appearance in Central and Eastern Europe in a non-pathologised form, and law may well continue to have an important role to play in this regard in the future.

Although I have described *Governing Sexuality* as sounding a cautionary note about the use of citizenship discourse in the domain of European sexualities, I do not think that I have written a pessimistic book. In 1998, I alluded to the ambiguities of sexual citizenship discourse (see Stychin, 1998: 199–201)—its potential as well as its constraints; its enabling and disciplinary functions—and, having written this book, I am more convinced than ever that rights and citizenship are politically complex and indeterminate. Perhaps as a result, not of greater study but of age, I have come to believe that living with this indeterminacy is not necessarily politically problematic nor hypocritical. The (increasingly clichéd) binaries of 'assimilation' and 'transgression,' which I have referred to periodically in *Governing Sexuality*, so popular in much queer theory of the late 1980s and 1990s, seem to me to be blunt intellectual tools for capturing the complexity of human existence. I have yet to meet anyone who is a politically 'pure' form of either, and I am increasingly aware that *things are not always as they seem* when it comes to how people construct their ways of living. Nevertheless, that is not a justification for a withdrawal from political struggle, and I have tried to be upfront throughout this book as to the politics which underpin it.

Finally, on a personal note, as I finish writing *Governing Sexuality*, I celebrate my tenth anniversary as an academic, with the completion of the third of a trilogy of books that explore the themes and questions raised here (see also Stychin, 1995b; 1998). I hope that readers who have followed the course of my work will see both change and continuities in my thinking. I suspect that the publication of *Governing Sexuality* marks the end of my intellectual journey on these particular themes. I am confident, however, not only that the dynamic and unpredictable destiny of legal struggles around same sex sexualities will continue in the years to come, but also that a multiplicity of critical, progressive voices will continue to be heard, in order to question, probe, and challenge the ways in which law governs us, and in which we govern ourselves.

References

ACKERS, HL and STALFORD, H (1999) 'Children, Migration and Citizenship in the European Union: Intra-Community Mobility and the Status of Children in EC Law' 21 *Children and Youth Services Review* 699.

ACKERS, L (1996) 'Citizenship, Gender and Dependency in the European Union: Women and Internal Migration' in T Hervey and D O'Keeffe (eds), *Sex Equality Law in the European Union* (Wiley, Chichester) 221.

ADAM, BD, DUYVENDAK, JW and KROUWEL, A (1999) 'Gay and Lesbian Movements Beyond Borders?' in BD Adam, JW Duyvendak and A Krouwel (eds), *The Global Emergence of Gay and Lesbian Politics: National Imprints of a Worldwide Movement* (Temple University Press, Philadelphia) 344.

ALEJANDRO, R (1993) *Hermeneutics, Citizenship, and the Public Sphere* (State University of New York Press, Albany).

ALTMAN, D (2001) *Global Sex* (University of Chicago Press, Chicago).

ARENDT, H (1958) *The Human Condition* (University of Chicago Press, Chicago).

ARMSTRONG, KA (1998a) 'Legal Integration: Theorizing the Legal Dimension of European Integration' 36 *Journal of Common Market Studies* 154.

—— (1998b) 'Tales of the Community: Sexual Orientation Discrimination and EC Law' 20 *Journal of Social Welfare and Family Law* 455.

BACH-IGNASSE, G and ROUSSEL,Y (2000) *Le Pacs: juridique et pratique* (Denoël, Paris).

BACKER, LC (1997) 'Harmonization, Subsidiarity and Cultural Difference: An Essay on the Dynamics of Opposition Within Federative and International Legal Systems' 4 *Tulsa Journal of Comparative and International Law* 185.

BAKAN, J (1997) *Just Words: Constitutional Rights and Social Wrongs* (University of Toronto Press, Toronto).

BALL, CA (1996) 'The Making of a Transnational Capitalist Society: the Court of Justice, Social Policy, and Individual Rights under the European Community's Legal Order' 37 *Harvard International Law Journal* 307.

—— (2000) 'Communitarianism and Gay Rights' 85 *Cornell Law Review* 443.

BAŃKOWSKI, Z and CHRISTODOULIDIS, E (1999) 'Citizenship Bound and Citizenship Unbound' in K Hutchings and R Dannreuther (eds), *Cosmopolitan Citizenship* (Macmillan, Basingstoke) 83.

BARLOW, A and DUNCAN, S (2000a) 'Supporting Families?: New Labour's Communitarianism and the "Rationality Mistake": Part I' 22 *Journal of Social Welfare and Family Law* 23.

—— (2000b) 'Supporting Families?: New Labour's Communitarianism and the "Rationality Mistake": Part II' 22 *Journal of Social Welfare and Family Law* 129.

BARLOW, A and PROBERT, R (1999) 'Reforming the Rights of Cohabitants: Lessons from Across the Channel' *Family Law* 477.

BARNARD, C (1996) 'The Economic Objectives of Article 119' in T Hervey and D O'Keeffe (eds), *Sex Equality Law in the European Union* (Wiley, Chichester) 321.

Batt, J (2001) 'European Identity and National Identity in Central and Eastern Europe' in H Wallace (ed), *Interlocking Dimensions of European Integration* (Palgrave, Basingstoke) 247.

Beaman, LG (1999) 'Sexual Orientation and Legal Discourse: Legal Constructions of the "Normal Family"' 14 *Canadian Journal of Law and Society* 173.

Bech, H (1997) *When Men Meet: Homosexuality and Modernity* (T Mesquit and T Davies (trans), Polity Press, Cambridge).

Beck, U (2000) 'The Cosmopolitan Perspective: Sociology of the Second Age of Modernity' 51 *British Journal of Sociology* 79.

Beger, NJ (2000) 'Queer Readings of Europe: Gender Identity, Sexual Orientation and the (Im)Potency of Rights Politics at the European Court of Justice' 9 *Social & Legal Studies* 250.

——(2001) *Que(e)rying Political Practices in Europe* (University of Amsterdam, Amsterdam).

Bell, D (1995) 'Pleasure and Danger: The Paradoxical Spaces of Sexual Citizenship' 14 *Political Geography* 139.

Bell, D and Binnie, J (2000) *The Sexual Citizen: Queer Politics and Beyond* (Polity Press, Cambridge).

Bell, D and Kennedy, BM (eds) (2000) *The Cybercultures Reader* (Routledge, London and New York).

Bell, M (1998) 'Sexual Orientation and Anti-Discrimination Policy: The European Community' in T Carver and V Mottier (eds), *Politics of Sexuality: Identity, Gender, Citizenship* (Routledge, London and New York) 58.

——(1999) 'Shifting Conceptions of Sexual Discrimination at the Court of Justice: from *P v S* to *Grant v SWT*' 5 *European Law Journal* 63.

——(2001) 'The European Union—a New Source of Rights for Citizens in the Accession Countries?' in International Lesbian and Gay Association Europe (ed), *Equality for Lesbians and Gay Men: A Relevant Issue in the EU Accession Process* (International Lesbian and Gay Association Europe, Brussels) 80.

Bell, M and Waddington, L (1996) 'The 1996 Intergovernmental Conference and the Prospects of a Non-Discrimination Treaty Article' 25 *Industrial Law Journal* 320.

Bellamy, R (1995) 'The Constitution of Europe: Rights or Democracy?' in R Bellamy, V Bufacchi and D Castiglione (eds), *Democracy and Constitutional Culture in the Union of Europe* (Lothian Foundation Press, London) 153.

Bellamy, R and Castiglione, D (1996) 'The Communitarian Ghost in the Cosmopolitan Machine: Constitutionalism, Democracy and the Reconfiguration of Politics in the New Europe' in R Bellamy (ed), *Constitutionalism, Democracy and Sovereignty* (Avebury, Aldershot) 111.

Bellamy, R and Greenaway, J (1995) 'The New Right Conception of Citizenship and the Citizen's Charter' 30 *Government and Opposition* 469.

Bellamy, R and Warleigh, A (1998) 'From an Ethics of Integration to an Ethics of Participation: Citizenship and the Future of the European Union' 27 *Millennium: Journal of International Studies* 447.

Benhabib, S (1992) *Situating the Self* (Polity Press, Cambridge).

——(1996) 'Toward a Deliberative Model of Democratic Legitimacy' in S Benhabib (ed), *Democracy and Difference: Contesting the Boundaries of the Political* (Princeton University Press, Princeton) 67.

Benn, M (2000) 'New Labour and Social Exclusion' 71 *Political Quarterly* 309.

BINNIE, J (1995) 'Trading Places: Consumption, Sexuality and the Production of Queer Space' in D Bell and G Valentine (eds), *Mapping Desire: Geographies of Sexualities* (Routledge, London and New York) 182.

—— (1997) 'Invisible Europeans: Sexual Citizenship in the New Europe' 29 *Environment and Planning A* 237.

—— (2000) 'Cosmopolitanism and the Sexed City' in D Bell and A Haddour (eds), *City Visions* (Prentice Hall, Harlow) 166.

BINNIE, J and VALENTINE, G (1999) 'Geographies of Sexuality: A Review of Progress' 23 *Progress in Human Geography* 175.

BOURDIEU, P, DERRIDA, J, ERIBON, D, PERROT, M, VEYNE, P and VIDAL-NAQUET, P (1996) 'Pour une reconnaissance légale du couple homosexuel' *Le Monde*, 1 March.

BOWD, G (2000) 'Orphans and Origins: Romania, France and Problems of Identity' 36 *Forum for Modern Language Studies* 113.

BOYD, SB (1998) 'Family, Law and Sexuality: Feminist Engagements' 8 *Social & Legal Studies* 369.

BRAIDOTTI, R (1994) *Nomadic Subjects: Embodiment and Sexual Difference in Contemporary Feminist Theory* (Columbia University Press, New York).

'Britain Eases Immigration for Gay Partners' (na, nd), <http://religioustolerance.org/hom_0055.htm>.

BROWN, W (1995) *States of Injury: Power and Freedom in Late Modernity* (Princeton University Press, Princeton).

Brown v Rentokil (1998) *European Court Reports*, 1998, I-4185.

BRUBAKER, R (1992) *Citizenship and Nationhood in France and Germany* (Harvard University Press, Cambridge, Mass.).

BURCHELL, D (1995) 'The Attributes of Citizens: Virtue, Manners and the Activity of Citizenship' 24 *Economy and Society* 540.

BUTLER, J (1997) *Excitable Speech: A Politics of the Performative* (Routledge, New York and London).

—— (1998) 'Merely Cultural' 227 *New Left Review* 33.

CABRILLAC, R (1999) 'Libres propos sur le PACS (après l'adoption du texte en première lecture par l'Assemblée nationale)' 7 *Recueil Dalloz* 71.

CANT, B (1997) 'Introduction' in B Cant (ed), *Invented Identities?: Lesbians and Gays Talk About Migration* (Cassell, London and New York) 1.

CARF (1999) 'Exclusion: New Labour Style' <http://www.carf.demon.co.uk/feat24.html>.

CARON, D (1998) '*Liberté, Égalité, Séropositivité*: AIDS, the French Republic and the Question of Community' 9 *French Cultural Studies* 281.

CASTELLS, M (1983) 'Cultural Identity and Urban Structure: The Spatial Organization of San Francisco's Urban Gay Community' in NI Fainstein and SS Fainstein (eds), *Urban Policy under Capitalism* (Sage, London) 237.

—— (1997) *The Power of Identity* (Blackwell, Cambridge).

CHAPIN, J (1998) 'Closing America's "Back Door"?' 4 *GLQ* 403.

CHAUNCEY, G (1994) *Gay New York* (Basic Books, New York).

CHEDGZOY, K, FRANCIS, E and PRATT, M (eds) (2002) *In a Queer Place: Sexuality and Belonging in British and European Context* (Ashgate, Aldershot).

CHIRIAC, M (2001) 'Deadlocked Romania' 100 *Current History* 124.

CHRISTODOULIDIS, EA (ed) (1998) *Communitarianism and Citizenship* (Ashgate, Aldershot).

CLIFT, B (2000) 'Third Way or Réalisme de Gauche?' 101 *Radical Philosophy* (May/June) 2.

Collier, R (2000) 'Straight Families, Queer Lives?: Heterosexual(izing) Family Law' in C Stychin and D Herman (eds), *Sexuality in the Legal Arena* (Athlone Press, London) 164.
Coman, A (2001) Personal interview with author (former Executive Director, ACCEPT), Sinaia, Romania, 7 August.
Commission of the European Communities (1997) *Regular Report on Romania's Progress Towards Accession*, unpublished.
—— (1999) Press Release: 'Proposal for a Directive on the Right to Family Reunification' (IP/99/920) <http://europa.eu.int/rapid>.
—— (2000) *Regular Report on Romania's Progress Towards Accession*, unpublished.
—— (2001) *Regular Report on Romania's Progress Towards Accession*, unpublished.
Cooper, D (1993) 'The Citizen's Charter and Radical Democracy: Empowerment and Exclusion within Citizenship Discourse' 2 *Social & Legal Studies* 149.
—— (1994) *Sexing the City: Lesbian and Gay Politics within the Activist State* (Rivers Oram, London).
Cooper, D and Herman, D (1995) '"Getting the Family Right": Legislating Heterosexuality in Britain, 1986–91' in D Herman and C Stychin (eds), *Legal Inversions: Lesbians, Gay Men, and the Politics of Law* (Temple University Press, Philadelphia) 162.
Council of the European Union (2001) *Working Party on Central Europe Recommendations*, unpublished, 19 March.
Craiutu, A (2000) 'Light at the end of the Tunnel Romania 1989–1998' in G Pridham and T Gallagher (eds), *Experimenting with Democracy: Regime Change in the Balkans* (Routledge, London and New York) 169.
Crawford, A (2000) 'Justice de Proximité: The Growth of "Houses of Justice" and Victim/Offender Mediation in France: A Very UnFrench Legal Response?' 9 *Social & Legal Studies* 29.
Creteanu, A and Coman, A (1998) 'Homosexuality in the Written Media in Romania' in I Popvici and A Newel (trans), *Minorities in the Media* (Center for Independent Journalism, Bucharest).
D v Council (1999) *Reports of European Community Staff Cases (ECR-SC)*, 1999, II–1.
D'Emilio, J (1983a) 'Capitalism and Gay Identity' in A Snitow, C Stansell and S Thompson (eds), *Powers of Desire: The Politics of Sexuality* (Monthly Review Press, New York) 100.
—— (1983b) *Sexual Politics, Sexual Communities* (University of Chicago Press, Chicago).
Daley, S (2000) 'French Couples Take Plunge That Falls Short of Marriage' *New York Times*, 18 April.
Darian-Smith, E (1999) *Bridging Divides: The Channel Tunnel and English Legal Identity in the New Europe* (University of California Press, Berkeley and Los Angeles).
Dascalu, R (2000) 'Romanian Orthodox Church Debates Homosexuality Issue' Reuters News Agency, 12 September.
David, A (1995) 'Certificats de concubinage aux couples homosexuels: oui, cinq fois oui' *Le Monde*, 20 September, 12.
de Burca, G (1995) 'The Language of Rights and European Integration' in J Shaw and G More (eds), *New Legal Dynamics of European Union* (Clarendon Press, Oxford) 29.
—— (1996) 'The Quest for Legitimacy in the European Union' 59 *Modern Law Review* 349.
Décision 99-419 (1999) *Petites affiches*, 239, 6.
Defrenne v Sabena (No 2) (1976) *European Court Reports*, 1976, 455.

DE LANGE, R (1995) 'Paradoxes of European Citizenship' in P Fitzpatrick (ed), *Nationalism, Racism and the Rule of Law* (Dartmouth, Aldershot) 97.

DELANTY, G (2000) *Citizenship in a Global Age* (Open University Press, Buckingham).

DENYS, C (1999) 'Homosexuality: A Non-Issue in Community Law?' 24 *European Law Review* 419.

DIETZ, M (1992) 'Context is all: Feminism and Theories of Citizenship' in C Mouffe (ed), *Dimensions of Radical Democracy* (Verso, London) 63.

DONOVAN, C, HEAPHY, B and WEEKS, J (1999) 'Citizenship and Same Sex Relationships' 28 *Journal of Social Policy* 689.

DRIVER, S and MARTELL, L (1997) 'New Labour's Communitarianisms' 52 *Critical Social Policy* 27.

DURHAM, M (2001) 'The Conservative Party, New Labour and the Politics of the Family' 54 *Parliamentary Affairs* 459.

Economist (na) (1996) 'Nothing to get excited about, bien sûr', 30 March, 34.

EDELMAN, L (1994) *Homographesis* (Routledge, New York).

*Egan v Canada (*1995) *Supreme Court Reports* [Canada], 1995 (2), 513.

ELMAN, RA (2000) 'The Limits of Citizenship: Migration, Sex Discrimination and Same-Sex Partners in EU Law' 38 *Journal of Common Market Studies* 729.

EPSTEIN, D, JOHNSON, R and STEINBERG, DL (2000) 'Twice Told Tales: Transformation, Recuperation and Emergence in the Age of Consent Debates 1998' 3 *Sexualities* 5.

ERIBON, D (2000) *Papiers d'identité* (Fayard, Paris).

ERNST, CE (1997) '*Activisme à l'américaine?* The Case of Act Up-Paris' 15.4 *French Politics & Society* 22.

ESCOFFIER, J (1998) *American Homo: Community and Perversity* (University of California Press, Berkeley and Los Angeles).

ESPIN, OM (1999) *Women Crossing Boundaries: A Psychology of Immigration and Transformations of Sexuality* (Routledge, New York and London).

Euromoney (na) (1997) 'Now for a real privatization', April, 128.

European Parliament (2000) *Report on Romania's Application for Membership of the European Union and the State of the Negotiations*, unpublished.

—— (2001) *Report on Romania's Application for Membership of the European Union and the State of the Negotiations*, unpublished.

EVANS, DT (1993) *Sexual Citizenship* (Routledge, London and New York).

—— (1998) '(*homo*)Sexual Citizenship' in CR Barker, EA Kirk and M Soh (eds), *Gender Perceptions and the Law* (Ashgate, Aldershot) 117.

EVERSON, M (1995) 'The Legacy of the Market Citizen' in J Shaw and G More (eds), *New Legal Dynamics of European Union* (Clarendon Press, Oxford) 73.

FAIRCLOUGH, N (2000) *New Labour, New Language?* (Routledge, London and New York).

FASSIN, E (1998) 'Ouvrir le mariage aux homosexuels' *Le Monde Diplomatique*, June, 22.

FASSIN, E and FEHER, M (1999) 'Parité et PACS: anatomie politique d'un rapport' in D Borrillo, E Fassin and M Iacub (eds), *Au-delà du Pacs* (Presses Universitaires de France, Paris) 13.

FAVELL, A (1998) *Philosophies of Integration: Immigration and the Idea of Citizenship in France and Britain* (Macmillan, Basingstoke).

FILLIEULE, O and DUYVENDAK, JW (1999) 'Gay and Lesbian Activism in France: Between Integration and Community-Oriented Movements' in BD Adam, JW Duyvendak and A Krouwel (eds), *The Global Emergence of Gay and Lesbian Politics: National Imprints of a Worldwide Movement* (Temple University Press, Philadelphia) 184.

FINEMAN, MA (1995) *The Neutered Mother, the Sexual Family and Other Twentieth Century Tragedies* (Routledge, New York and London).

FIONDA, J (1999) 'New Labour, Old Hat: Youth Justice and the Crime and Disorder Act 1998' *Criminal Law Review* 34.

FITZPATRICK, P (1998) 'New Europe and Old Stories: Mythology and Legality in the European Union' in P Fitzpatrick and JH Bergeron (eds), *Europe's Other: European Law Between Modernity and Postmodernity* (Ashgate, Aldershot) 27.

—— (2001) *Modernism and the Grounds of Law* (Cambridge University Press, Cambridge).

FLANAGAN, WF (1995) 'People with HIV/AIDS, Gay Men, and Lesbians: Shifting Identities, Shifting Priorities' in D Herman and C Stychin (eds), *Legal Inversions: Lesbians, Gay Men, and the Politics of Law* (Temple University Press, Philadelphia) 195.

FOSS, RJ (1994) 'The Demise of the Homosexual Exclusion: New Possibilities for Gay and Lesbian Immigration' 29 *Harvard Civil Rights: Civil Liberties Law Review* 439.

FOUCAULT, M (1972) *The Archaeology of Knowledge* (AM Sheridan (trans), Tavistock, London).

—— (1977) *Discipline and Punish* (AM Sheridan (trans), Penguin, London).

—— (1980) *Power/Knowledge: Selected Writings and Interviews* (C Gordon (ed and trans), Harvester Press, Brighton).

—— (1981) *The History of Sexuality Volume One* (R Hurley (trans), Penguin, London).

FRASER, N (1989) *Unruly Practices: Power, Discourse and Gender in Contemporary Social Theory* (Polity Press, Cambridge).

—— (1997a) 'Heterosexism, Misrecognition and Capitalism: A Response to Judith Butler' 15 (52/53) *Social Text* 279.

—— (1997b) *Justice Interruptus* (Routledge, New York).

FRAZER, E (1999) 'Unpicking Political Communitarianism: A Critique of "the Communitarian Family"' in G Jagger and C Wright (eds), *Changing Family Values* (Routledge, London and New York) 150.

FRAZER, E and LACEY, N (1993) *The Politics of Community: A Feminist Critique of the Liberal Communitarian Debate* (Harvester Wheatsheaf, Hemel Hempstead).

FREDMAN, S (1997) *Women and the Law* (Clarendon Press, Oxford).

FREEDEN, M (1999) 'The Ideology of New Labour' 70 *Political Quarterly* 42.

FUDGE, J and GLASBEEK, H (1992) 'The Politics of Rights: A Politics with Little Class' 1 *Social & Legal Studies* 45.

GALL, C (2001) 'It's Still No Breeze for Gays, Even Diplomatic Ones' *New York Times*, 16 October.

GALLAGHER, T (1995) *Romania After Ceausescu: The Politics of Intolerance* (Edinburgh University Press, Edinburgh).

—— (1996) 'Looking for Acceptance', *Gay Community News* (Dublin), February <http://www.raglb.org.uk/archive/gaycom.htm>.

—— (2001) 'Nationalism and Romanian Political Culture in the 1990s' in D Light and D Phinnemore (eds), *Post-Communist Romania: Coming to Terms with Transition* (Palgrave, Basingstoke) 104.

GARAPON, A (1995) 'French Legal Culture and the Shock of "Globalization"' 4 *Social & Legal Studies* 493.

GAUDU, F (1998) 'A propos du "contrat d'union civile": critique d'un profane' 2 *Recueil Dalloz* 19.

Gay and Lesbian Immigration Task Force (1999) 'Gay and Lesbian Partner Migration' <http://www.glitf.org.au>.

GIDDENS, A (1992) *The Transformation of Intimacy* (Polity, Cambridge).

GOLDBERG-HILLER, J (1998) '"Entitled to be Hostile": Narrating the Political Economy of Civil Rights' 7 *Social & Legal Studies* 517.

——(2000) 'Making a Mockery of Marriage' in C Stychin and D Herman (eds), *Sexuality in the Legal Arena* (Athlone Press, London) 113.

Grant v South West Trains (1998) *European Court Reports*, 1998, I-621.

GUNTHER, S (1999) 'The Indifferent Ghetto' 6.1 *Harvard Gay and Lesbian Review* 34.

HABERMAS, J (1996) 'Three Normative Models of Democracy' in S Benhabib (ed), *Democracy and Difference: Contesting the Boundaries of the Political* (Princeton University Press, Princeton) 21.

HADDOCK, B and CARAIANI, O (1999) 'Nationalism and Civil Society in Romania' 47 *Political Studies* 258.

Handels-og Kontorfunktionaerernes Forbund i Danmark (1998) *European Court Reports*, 1998, I-7327.

Handels-og Kontorfunktionaerernes Forbund i Danmark v Dansk Arbejdsgiver forening (1990) *European Court Reports*, 1990, I-3979.

HART, J (1992) 'A Cocktail of Alarm: Same-Sex Couples and Migration to Australia 1985–90' in K Plummer (ed), *Modern Homosexualities: Fragments of Lesbian and Gay Experience* (Routledge, London) 121.

HERDT, G (1997) *Same Sex, Different Cultures: Exploring Gay and Lesbian Lives* (Westview Press, Boulder).

HERMAN, D (1993) 'Beyond the Rights Debate' 2 *Social & Legal Studies* 25.

——(1994a) *Rights of Passage: Struggles for Lesbian and Gay Legal Equality* (University of Toronto Press, Toronto).

——(1994b) 'The Good, the Bad, and the Smugly: Perspectives on the Canadian Charter of Rights and Freedoms' 14 *Oxford Journal of Legal Studies* 589.

——(1997) *The Antigay Agenda: Orthodox Vision and the Christian Right* (University of Chicago Press, Chicago).

HERMAN, D and COOPER, D (1997) 'Anarchic Armadas, Brussels Bureaucrats, and the Valiant Maple Leaf: Sexuality, Governance, and the Construction of British Nationhood through the Canada-Spain Fish War' 17 *Legal Studies* 415.

HERVEY, T (1998) *European Social Law and Policy* (Longman, London).

——(1999) 'Sex Equality as Substantive Justice' 62 *Modern Law Review* 614.

HERVEY, T and SHAW, J (1998) 'Women, Work and Care: Women's Dual Role and Double Burden in EC Sex Equality Law' 8 *Journal of European Social Policy* 43.

HILSON, C and DOWNES, TA (1999) 'Making Sense of Rights: Community Rights in E.C. Law' 24 *European Law Review* 121.

HOCQUENGHEM, G (1993) *Homosexual Desire* (D Dangoor (trans), Duke University Press, Durham).

Home Office (1998) *Supporting Families: A Consultation Document* (HMSO, London).

——(1999) 'Concession Outside the Immigration Rules for Unmarried Partners' <http://www.homeoffice.gov.uk/ind/concess.htm>.

HOSKYNS, C (1996) *Integrating Gender: Women, Law and Politics in the European Union* (Verso, London).

HUGHES, H (1997) 'Holidays and Homosexual Identity' 18 *Tourism Management* 3.

Human Rights Watch and the International Gay and Lesbian Human Rights Commission (1998) *Public Scandals: Sexual Orientation and Criminal Law in Romania* (Human Rights Watch and the International Gay and Lesbian Human Rights Commission, New York).

HUTCHINGS, K and DANNREUTHER, R (eds) (1999) *Cosmopolitan Citizenship* (Macmillan, Basingstoke).

INGRAM, GB (1997) 'Marginality and the Landscape of Erotic Alien(n)nations' in GB Ingram, A-M Bonthillette and Y Retter (eds), *Queers in Space: Communities, Public Places, Sites of Resistance* (Bay Press, Seattle) 27.

Intergroup on Gay and Lesbian Rights (2001) *EU Enlargement: A Gay Perspective* (European Parliament, Brussels).

International Lesbian and Gay Association Europe (1998) *Equality for Lesbians and Gay Men: A Relevant Issue in the Civil and Social Dialogue* (International Lesbian and Gay Association Europe, Brussels).

International Lesbian and Gay Association Europe Executive Board (2001) 'Introduction' in International Lesbian and Gay Association Europe (ed), *Equality for Lesbians and Gay Men: A Relevant Issue in the EU Accession Process* (International Lesbian and Gay Association Europe, Brussels) 7.

ISIN, E and WOOD, P (1999) *Citizenship and Identity* (Sage, London).

JACOBS, MP (1997) 'Do Gay Men have a Stake in Male Privilege?: The Political Economy of Gay Men's Contradictory Relationship to Feminism' in A Gluckman and B Reed (eds), *Homo Economics: Capitalism, Community, and Lesbian and Gay Life* (Routledge, New York and London) 165.

JENNINGS, J (2000) 'Citizenship, Republicanism and Multiculturalism in Contemporary France' 30 *British Journal of Political Science* 575.

JOANNY, S (1998) 'Famille patriarcale: un vavalement de façade' 81 *Cahiers du féminisme* 24.

JONES, C (1997) 'Rumbles Felt in Romania' *The Banker*, June, 41.

—— (1999) 'On the Road to Reform' *The Banker*, June, 47.

JONES, KB (1997) 'Citizenship in Feminism: Identity, Action, and Locale. An Introduction' 12 *Hypatia* 1.

KAPLAN, C (1998) *Questions of Travel* (Duke University Press, Durham).

KAPLAN, MB (1997) *Sexual Justice: Democratic Citizenship and the Politics of Desire* (Routledge, New York and London).

KINGDOM, E (1996) 'Transforming Rights: Feminist Political Heuristics' 2 *Res Publica* 73.

KLIGMAN, G (1998) *The Politics of Duplicity: Controlling Reproduction in Ceausescu's Romania* (University of California Press, Berkeley and Los Angeles).

KNOPP, L (1998) 'Sexuality and Urban Space: Gay Male Identity Politics in the United States, the United Kingdom and Australia' in R Fincher and JM Jacobs (eds), *Cities of Difference* (Guilford Press, New York) 149.

KOFMAN, E (1995) 'Citizenship for Some but not for Others: Spaces of Citizenship in Contemporary Europe' 14 *Political Geography* 121.

KUKATHAS, C (1996) 'Liberalism, Communitarianism, and Political Community' 13 *Social Philosophy and Policy* 80.

KYMLICKA, W and NORMAN, W (1995) 'Return of the Citizen: A Survey of Recent Work on Citizenship Theory' in R Beiner (ed), *Theorizing Citizenship* (State University of New York Press, Albany) 283.

LABORDE, C (2001) 'The Culture(s) of the Republic: Some Contradictions in French Republican Thought' 29 *Political Theory* 716.

LACEY, N (1987) 'Legislation Against Sex Discrimination: Questions from a Feminist Perspective' 14 *Journal of Law and Society* 411.

—— (1998) *Unspeakable Subjects: Feminist Essays in Legal and Social Theory* (Hart Publishing, Oxford).

Les Echos (na) (1999) 'Le nombre de couples non mariés a augmenté de 60% entre 1990 et 1998', 7 January.

LEVITAS, R (1998) *The Inclusive Society?: Social Exclusion and New Labour* (Macmillan, Basingstoke).

LISTER, R (1997) *Citizenship: Feminist Perspectives* (Macmillan, Basingstoke).

LUIBHEID, E (1998) ' "Looking Like a Lesbian": The Organization of Sexual Monitoring at the United States-Mexican Border' 8 *Journal of the History of Sexuality* 477.

Lustig-Prean and Beckett v United Kingdom (1999) *European Human Rights Law Reports*, 29, 548.

LÜTZEN, K (1998) 'Gay and Lesbian Politics: Assimilation or Subversion: A Danish Perspective' 35 *Journal of Homosexuality* 233.

M v H (1999) *Supreme Court Reports* [Canada], 1999 (2), 3.

MACOVEI, M and COMAN, A (1999) 'Implications for HIV/AIDS of Laws Affecting Men Who Have Sex With Men in Romania' 18 *Medicine and Law* 335.

MANALANSAN, MF (1995) 'In the Shadows of Stonewall: Examining Gay Transnational Politics and the Diasporic Dilemma' 2 *GLQ* 425.

MANCINI, GF and O'Leary, S (1999) 'The New Frontiers of Sex Equality Law in the European Union' 24 *European Law Review* 331.

MARSHALL, B (1997) *Guy Hocquenghem: Beyond Gay Identity* (Duke University Press, Durham).

MARSHALL, TH (1950) *Citizenship and Social Class and Other Essays* (Cambridge University Press, Cambridge).

MARTEL, F (1999) *The Pink and the Black: Homosexuals in France since 1968* (JM Todd (trans), Stanford University Press, Stanford).

Martinez Sala v Freistaat Bayern (1998) *European Court Reports*, 1998, I-2708.

MCCOLGAN, A (1997) *Just Wages for Women* (Clarendon Press, Oxford).

MCGHEE, D (2001) *Homosexuality, Law and Resistance* (Routledge, London and New York).

MCGLYNN, C (1996) 'EC Sex Equality Law: Towards a Human Rights Foundation' in T Hervey and D O'Keeffe (eds), *Sex Equality Law in the European Union* (Wiley, Chichester) 239.

—— (2000) 'A Family Law for the European Union?' in J Shaw (ed), *Social Law and Policy in an Evolving European Union* (Hart Publishing, Oxford) 223.

MCROBBIE, A (2000) 'Feminism and the Third Way' 64 *Feminist Review* 97.

MEZEI, S (1994) 'Gendering the Social Body in Postcommunist Romania From "Homogenization" to Diversity: New Discourses, Old Practices' 17 *Women's Studies International Forum* 313.

MONK, D (1998) 'Beyond Section 28: Law, Governance and Sex Education' in LJ Moran, D Monk and S Beresford (eds), *Legal Queeries: Lesbian, Gay and Transgender Legal Studies* (Cassell, London and New York) 96.

MORAN, J (2001) 'Childhood Sexuality and Education: The Case of Section 28' 4 *Sexualities* 73.

MORE, G (1993) ' "Equal Treatment" of the Sexes in European Community Law: What does "Equal" Mean?' 1 *Feminist Legal Studies* 45.

—— (1996) 'Equality of Treatment in European Community Law: The Limits of Market Equality' in A Bottomley (ed), *Feminist Perspectives on the Foundational Subjects of Law* (Cavendish, London) 261.

MORGAN, P (1998) 'Class Divisions in the Gay Community' 78 *International Socialism* 77.

MORRIS, A and GELSTHORPE, L (2000) 'Something Old, Something Borrowed, Something Blue, but Something New? A Comment on the Prospects for Restorative Justice under the Crime and Disorder Act 1998' *Criminal Law Review* 18.

MORUZZI, NC (1994) 'A Problem with Headscarves: Contemporary Complexities of Political and Social Identity' 22 *Political Theory* 653.

MOYNAGH, P (1997) 'A Politics of Enlarged Mentality: Hannah Arendt, Citizenship Responsibility, and Feminism' 12 *Hypatia* 27.

NARDI, P (1998) 'The Globalization of the Gay and Lesbian Socio-Political Movement: Some Observations about Europe with a Focus on Italy' 41 *Sociological Perspectives* 567.

National Coalition for Gay and Lesbian Equality v Minister of Home Affairs (1999) *Butterworths Constitutional Law Reports* [South Africa], 2000 (1), 39.

NOIRIEL, G (1996) *The French Melting Pot: Immigration, Citizenship, and National Identity* (G de Laforcade (trans), University of Minnesota Press, Minneapolis).

O'DONOVAN, K (1993) 'Marriage: A Sacred or Profane Love Machine?' 1 *Feminist Legal Studies* 75.

P v S and Cornwall County Council (1996) *European Court Reports*, 1996, I-2143.

PASCALL, G (1999) 'UK Family Policy in the 1990s: The Case of New Labour and Lone Parents' 13 *International Journal of Law, Policy and the Family* 258.

PERRIGO, S (1999) 'Women, Gender and New Labour' in GR Taylor (ed), *The Impact of New Labour* (Macmillan, Basingstoke) 162.

PHELAN, S (1995) 'The Space of Justice: Lesbians and Democratic Politics' in L Nicholson and S Seidman (eds), *Social Postmodernism* (Cambridge University Press, Cambridge) 332.

—— (2001) *Sexual Strangers: Gays, Lesbians and Dilemmas of Citizenship* (Temple University Press, Philadelphia).

PHINNEMORE, D (2001) 'Romania and Euro-Atlantic Integration Since 1989: A Decade of Frustration?' in D Light and D Phinnemore (eds), *Post-Communist Romania: Coming to Terms with Transition* (Palgrave, Basingstoke) 245.

PILLEBOUT, J-F (1987) 'Pauvres concubines' *Le Journal des Finances*, 13 June, 755.

Pink Paper (na) (2000) 'Nightmare for Immigration Pair', 622, 2.

PISIER, E (1998) 'PACS et Parité: du même et de l'autre' *Le Monde*, 20 October, 18.

PLUMMER, K (1995) *Telling Sexual Stories* (Routledge, London and New York).

POULIQUEN, J-P (1999) 'Pacs et république font bon ménage' *Libération*, 9 July.

POWELL, M (2000) 'New Labour and the Third Way in the British Welfare State: A New and Distinctive Approach?' 62 *Critical Social Policy* 39.

PRATT, M (1998) 'The Defence of the Straight State: Heteronormativity, AIDS in France, and the Space of the Nation' 9 *French Cultural Studies* 263.

QUINN, M (2002) Personal interview with author (Romania Desk Officer, Commission of the European Communities), Brussels, 11 February.

RAHMAN, M (1998) 'Sexuality and Rights: Problematising Lesbian and Gay Politics' in T Carver and V Mottier (eds), *Politics of Sexuality: Identity, Gender, Citizenship* (Routledge, London and New York) 79.

—— (2000) *Sexuality and Democracy: Identities and Strategies in Lesbian and Gay Politics* (Edinburgh University Press, Edinburgh).

RICHARDSON, D (2000) *Rethinking Sexuality* (Sage, London).

RIESENBERG, P (1992) *Citizenship in the Western Tradition* (University of North Carolina Press, Chapel Hill).

ROBSON, R (1998) *Sappho Goes to Law School* (Columbia University Press, New York).

ROCHE, M (1992) *Rethinking Citizenship* (Polity Press, Cambridge).

ROLLET, B and WILLIAMS, JS (1998) 'Visions of Excess: Filming/Writing the Gay Self in Collard's *Savage Nights*' in O Heathcote, A Hughes and JS Williams (eds), *Gay Signatures: Gay and Lesbian Theory, Fiction and Film in France, 1945–1995* (Berg, Oxford) 193.

ROMAN, D (2001) 'Gendering Eastern Europe: Pre-Feminism, Prejudice and East-West Dialogues in Post-Communist Romania' 24 *Women's Studies International Forum* 53.

ROSE, N (2000) 'Community, Citizenship, and the Third Way' 43 *American Behavioral Scientist* 1395.

SCOTT, J (1998) 'Changing Attitudes to Sexual Morality: A Cross-National Comparison' 32 *Sociology* 815.

SCOTT, JW (1997) ' "La Querelle des Femmes" in the Late Twentieth Century' 226 *New Left Review* 3.

Sénat Avis présenté au nom de la commission des finances, du contrôle budgétaire et des comptes économiques de la Nation sur la proposition de loi, adoptée par l'Assemblée Nationale, relative au pacte civil de solidarité No 261 (1999) (Librairies-Imprimeries Réunies, Paris).

Sénat Rapport fait au nom de la commission des Lois constitutionelles, de législation, du suffrage universel, du Règlement et d'administration générale sur la proposition de loi, adoptée par l'Assemblée Nationale, relative au pacte civil de solidarité No 258 (1999) (Librairies-Imprimeries Réunies, Paris).

SEVENHUIJSEN, S (2000) 'Caring in the Third Way: The Relation Between Obligation, Responsibility and Care in *Third Way* Discourse' 20 *Critical Social Policy* 5.

SHAW, J (1996) 'Law, Gender and the Internal Market', in T Hervey and D O'Keeffe (eds), *Sex Equality Law in the European Union* (Wiley, Chichester) 283.

—— (1997) 'European Union Citizenship: the IGC and Beyond' 3 *European Public Law* 413.

—— (1998) 'The Interpretation of European Union Citizenship' 61 *Modern Law Review* 293.

SHKLAR, JN (1991) *American Citizenship: The Quest for Inclusion* (Harvard University Press, Cambridge, Mass).

SINFIELD, A (1996) 'Diaspora and Hybridity: Queer Identities and the Ethnicity Model' 10 *Textual Practice* 271.

SMART, C (1989) *Feminism and the Power of Law* (Routledge, London and New York).

Smith and Grady v United Kingdom (1999) *European Human Rights Law Reports*, 29, 493.

SMITH, AM (1994) *New Right Discourses on Race & Sexuality* (Cambridge University Press, Cambridge, Mass).

SOLOWAY, LS (nd) 'Challenging Discrimination Against Gays and Lesbians in U.S. Immigration Law: The Lesbian and Gay Immigration Rights Taskforce' <http://www.girtf.org/html/about.html>.

SOYSAL, Y (1994) *Limits of Citizenship: Migrants and Postnational Membership in Europe* (University of Chicago Press, Chicago).

STAN, L (1997) 'Romanian Privatization Program: Catching up with the East' in L Stan (ed), *Romania in Transition* (Dartmouth, Aldershot) 127.

STAN, V (2000) 'Influencing Regime Change in the Balkans: The Role of External Forces in Transition' in G Pridham and T Gallagher (eds), *Experimenting with Democracy: Regime Change in the Balkans* (Routledge, London and New York) 152.

STEINER, E (2000) 'The Spirit of the New French Registered Partnership Law: Promoting Autonomy and Pluralism or Weakening Marriage?' 12 *Child and Family Law Quarterly* 1.

Stonewall News (na) (1998) 17 February <http://www.stonewall.org.uk/stonewall/cgi-bin/news.cgi?equalpaylost>.

STYCHIN, CF (1995a) 'Essential Rights and Contested Identities: Sexual Orientation and Equality Rights Jurisprudence in Canada' 8 *Canadian Journal of Law and Jurisprudence* 49.

—— (1995b) *Law's Desire: Sexuality and the Limits of Justice* (Routledge, London and New York).

—— (1997) 'Troubling Genders: A Comment on *P. v S. and Cornwall County Council*' 2 *International Journal of Discrimination and the Law* 217.

—— (1998) *A Nation by Rights: National Cultures, Sexual Identity Politics, and the Discourse of Rights* (Temple University Press, Philadelphia).

—— (1999) 'New Labour, New "Britain"? Constitutionalism, Sovereignty and Nation/State in Transition' 19 *Studies in Law, Politics, and Society* 139.

*Sutherland v United Kingdom (*1998) *European Human Rights Law Reports*, 24, 117.

TAMAGNE, F (2000) *Histoire de l'homosexualité en Europe: Berlin, Londres, Paris 1919–1939* (Seuil, Paris).

TASCA, C (1998) 'Un nouveau cadre, un nouveau regard' *Le Monde*, 10 October, 7.

TERRETT, S (1998) 'A Bridge too Far? Non-Discrimination and Homosexuality in European Community Law' *European Public Law* 487.

Toonen v Australia (1994) Communication No 488/1992, 31 March.

TURNER, BS (1990) 'Outline of a Theory of Citizenship' 24 *Sociology* 189.

Ulrich Hofmann v Barmer Ersatzkasse (1984) *European Court Reports*, 1984, 3047.

VALENTINE, G (1996) 'An Equal Place to Work? Anti-Lesbian Discrimination and Sexual Citizenship in the European Union' in MD García-Ramon and J Monk (eds), *Women of the European Union: The Politics of Work and Daily Life* (Routledge, London and New York) 111.

VALOCCHI, S (1999) 'The Class-Inflected Nature of Gay Identity' 46 *Social Problems* 207.

VALVERDE, M (1999) ' "The Lifestyle that Fits the Doctrine of Sexual Orientation": The Disappearing Homosexual of Human Rights Law' unpublished paper presented to the American Law and Society Association Annual Conference, Chicago, May (on file with author).

VAN DER LAAN, L *et al* (2001) Unpublished letter by eight Members of the European Parliament to Prime Minister Nastase, 29 May.

VAN DER VEUR, D (2001) Personal interview with author (former project coordinator for the COC-Accept Project and currently Senior Consultant to COC Netherlands), Amsterdam, 19 December.

VAUGHAN, B (2000) 'The Government of Youth: Disorder *and* Dependence?' 9 *Social & Legal Studies* 347.

VERDERY, K (1991) *National Ideology Under Socialism: Identity and Cultural Politics in Ceausescu's Romania* (University of California Press, Berkeley and Los Angeles).

VERHEUGEN, G (2001) Answer by Commission of the EC official to parliamentary question, unpublished.

Vilela v Mme Weil (1997) *Recueil Dalloz*, 1998, J 111.

WAITES, M (2000) 'Homosexuality and the New Right: The Legacy of the 1980s for New Delineations of Homophobia' *Sociological Research Online* 5 <http://www.socresonline.org.uk/5/1/waites.html>.

WALBY, S (1994) ' Is Citizenship Gendered?' 28 *Sociology* 379.

WALKER, K (2001) 'Moving Gaily Forward? Lesbian, Gay and Transgender Human Rights in Europe' 2 *Melbourne Journal of International Law* 122.

WALKER, RBJ (1999) 'Citizenship After the Modern Subject' in K Hutchings and R Dannreuther (eds), *Cosmopolitan Citizenship* (Macmillan, Basingstoke) 171.

WALLACE, C (1999) 'European Integration and Legal Culture: Indirect Sex Discrimination in the French Legal System' 19 *Legal Studies* 397.

WARLEIGH, A (1998) 'Frozen: Citizenship and European Unification' 1 *Critical Review of International Social and Political Philosophy* 113.

WARNER, M (1999) *The Trouble with Normal: Sex, Politics, and the Ethics of Queer Life* (Free Press, New York).

WATNEY, S (1990) 'Practices of Freedom: "Citizenship" and the Politics of Identity in the Age of Aids' in J Rutherford (ed), *Identity, Community, Culture, Difference* (Lawrence & Wishart, London) 157.

WEEKS, J (1995) *Invented Moralities* (Polity Press, Cambridge).

WEINER, R (1997) 'Democratization in Romania' in L Stan (ed), *Romania in Transition* (Dartmouth, Aldershot) 3.

WEINRICH, JD (1997) 'Strange Bedfellows: Homosexuality, Gay Liberation, and the Internet' 22 *Journal of Sex Education and Therapy* 58.

WESTON, K (1995) 'Get Thee To a Big City: Sexual Imaginary and the Great Gay Migration' 2 *GLQ* 253.

WHEELER, S (2002) *Corporations & The Third Way* (Hart Publishing, Oxford).

WILKINSON, A (1999) 'New Labour and Christian Socialism' in GR Taylor (ed), *The Impact of New Labour* (Macmillan, Basingstoke) 37.

WILLIAMS, P (1987) 'Alchemical Notes: Reconstructed Ideals from Deconstructed Rights 22 *Harvard Civil Rights: Civil Liberties Law Review* 401.

WINTEMUTE, R (2000) 'Lesbian and Gay Inequality 2000: The Potential of the Human Rights Act 1998 and the Need for an Equality Act 2002' *European Human Rights Law Review* 603.

WINTEMUTE, R and ANDENAES, M (eds) (2001) *Legal Recognition of Same-Sex Partnerships: A Study of National, European and International Law* (Hart Publishing, Oxford).

WISE, S (2000) ' "New Right" or "Backlash"? Section 28, Moral Panic and "Promoting" Homosexuality' *Sociological Research Online* 5 <http://www.socresonline.org.uk/5/1/wise.html>.

WOODHULL, W (1993) *Transfigurations of the Maghreb: Feminism, Decolonization and Literatures* (University of Minnesota Press, Minneapolis).

X v Air France; Mme X v Caisse primaire d'assurance maladie de Nantes (1989) *Recueil Dalloz*, 1990, J 582.

YOUNG, CFL (2000) ' "Aging and Retirement are not Unique to Heterosexuals": *Rosenberg v Canada*' in C Stychin and D Herman (eds), *Sexuality in the Legal Arena* (Athlone Press, London) 151.

YOUNG, IM (1995) 'Polity and Group Difference: A Critique of the Ideal of Universal Citizenship' in R Beiner (ed), *Theorizing Citizenship* (State University of New York Press, Albany) 175.

YOUNG, IM (1997) 'Unruly Categories: A Critique of Nancy Fraser's Dual Systems Theory' 222 *New Left Review* 147.

ZAPPI, S (2000) 'Daniel Villant, le couple gay et la loi sur l'immigration' *Le Monde*, 13 September.

Index

Page references for notes are followed by n